The Early History of a Mining Town

Ishpeming, Michigan 1852-1920

By Robert D. Dobson

Published by
Dobson Publications
224 Shoreline Drive
Negaunee, Michigan 49866

THE
EARLY
HISTORY
OF A
MINING TOWN

ISHPEMING, MICHIGAN   1852-1920

BY
ROBERT D. DOBSON

FIRST EDITION.
THIRD PRINTING. 2021

10-Digit ISBN 0-9747708-4-1
13-Digit ISBN 978-0-9747708-4-0

Originally Published September, 2005
by
Dobson Publications
224 Shoreline Drive
Negaunee, Michigan 49866

PRINTED IN THE UNITED STATES OF AMERICA

The Table of Contents:

First Ten Pages: An Introduction of Details, Maps and Photos

Abbreviations:

MAJOR MINING COMPANIES
M. A. Hanna
C&H: Calumet and Hecla Copper Company
CCI: The Cleveland Cliffs' Iron Company.
Oliver: The Oliver Mining Company of Minnesota.
J&L: Jones and Laughlin Mining Company.
Lake Angeline: The Pittsburgh and Lake Angeline Mining Company.
The Superior: The Lake Superior Mining Company.

RAILROADS
C&NW: The Chicago and Northwestern Railroad.
CM&St.P: The Chicago, Milwaukee, and St. Paul Railroad.
DM&M: The Detroit, Marquette, and Mackinaw.
DSS&A: The Duluth, South Shore, and Atlantic Railroad.
E&LS: Escanaba and Lake Superior.
IR&HB: The Iron Range and Huron Bay Railroad.
LS&I: The Lake Superior and Ishpeming Railroad.
M&O: the Marquette and Ontonagon Railroad.
MH&O: The Marquette, Houghton, and Ontonagon Railroad.
M&W: Marquette and Western Railroad.
MS&A: The Minneapolis, Soo, and Atlantic Railroad.

Bibliography:

Adair, Cornelia. My Diary. Austin: University of Texas Press, 1965.
Boyum, Burton H. The Saga of Iron Mining in Michgan's Upper Peninsula. Marquette: Longyear Research Library, 1977.
Cascade Historical Society. Richmond Township, 1872-1972, Centennial Booklet, 1972.
Casey, R. J., and Douglas, W. A. S. Pioneer Railroad (Story of the Chicago and North Western). New York: Whittlesey House, 1948.
Cooley, Kathleen. White Deer Lake (The McCormick Camp) Ishpeming: Globe Printing, 2004.
Cummings, William John. Iron Mountain's Cornish Pumping Engine. Iron Mountain, 1984.
Fountain, Daniel. Michigan Gold. Duluth: Lake Superior Port Cities, 1992.
Friggens, Thomas G. No Tears in Heaven (Barnes-Hecker 1926 Mine Disaster) Lansing: Michigan Historical Center, 1988.
Hatcher, Harlan. A Century of Iron and Men. Indianapolis: Bobbs, Merrill Company, 1950.
Hoffman, Bernard. Reflections from Old Crystal Falls. 1990.
Ishepeming Carnegie Library Calendars. Ishpeming, Globe Printing, 1982-2002.
Ishpeming Rock and Mineral Club. Field Trip and U. P. Gem and Mineral Show. Ishpeming: Globe Printing, 1972.
Ishpeming Historical Society. A Visit to the Past. Vol. I. 2000.
Ishpeming Historical Society. Ishpeming Sesquicentennial. Ishpeming: Globe Printing, 2004.
Jenkins, Thurston Smith. The Days of Mines (Ishpeming Holmes Mine). Naperville: Bradley Printing Co., 1987.
LaFayette, Kenneth D.. Flaming Brands. Marquette: Northern Michigan University Press, 1977.
Lambert, B. J. (Ed.). Baraga County Historical Pageant. Ishpeming: Globe Printing, 1970.
Lankton, L. D. & Hyde, C. K. Old Reliable (Quincy Mining Co.). Hancock: Book Concern Printers, 1982.
Lyman, Barbara. The Mirrored Wall. (Story of Iron Ore in Negaunee-Ishpeming) Ishpeming: Globe Printing, 1973
Michigamme Area Centennial Booklet, 1872-1972. (Ed.) Ishpeming: Globe Printing. 1972.
Newett, Iron Ore (Ishpeming Weekly Paper). Microfilms 1-15: 1879 – 1920.
Pyle, Susan N. (ed.). A Most Superior Land. Lansing: Michigan Natural Resources, 1983.
Stakel, Charles J. Memoirs of Charles J. Stakel. Marquette: Longyear Research Library, 1994.
Stone, Frank, B. Philo Marshall Everett. Baltimore: Gateway Press, 1997.

2021 Foreword, With Acknowledgments—

This book first appeared in print after nine years of very enjoyable research of several Marquette County newspapers, including the <u>Mining Journal</u> from 1-27-1869 to 1-25-1879, The Marquette <u>Weekly Plain Dealer</u> from 6-25-1867 to 4-30-1868, the Negaunee <u>Mining News</u> from 3-9-1868 to 7-15-1868, and the Negaunee <u>Mining Review</u> from 7-28-1870 to 10-21-1871. The largest part of the research, however, was completed by taking notes of 15 microfilms of the weekly Ishpeming <u>Iron Ore</u> newspaper from October 11, 1879, through July 7, 1920. Of course, there were also many other printed items used in this project. When Mr. Newett, the <u>Iron Ore</u> editor and owner is mentioned, it is his paper we are referring to. If we simply use the word "paper" or "newspaper", we are also referring to Mr. Newett's paper.

For the sake of the reader, I have often put the dates, as well as the name of the sources used, in with the text. This will save me hours of work of citing my works, normally at the back of the book. The footnotes would be innumerable. I hope, by publishing the source names, and the dates, in the book itself, that the reader may easily locate the source for further self-study of particular areas.

The microfilm reels of the <u>Iron Ore</u> and the <u>Mining Journal</u> are found at both the Ishpeming Carnegie Public Library, and the Peter White Library in Marquette. If you have something to add, please also write me. I may have missed some information in that there are copies of the <u>Iron Ore</u> missing from the microfilms from time to time.

I wish to thank the above libraries, and the J. M. Longyear Research Library in Marquette. A special thanks goes to the Library of Michigan in Lansing for their help in securing the 15 reels of the <u>Iron Ore</u> so that I was able to conduct my research in the Menominee Spies Library for several years. My thanks also to the Negaunee Historical Museum for the use of many of their rich resources, and to Mr Steve Schmeck of Cooks, Michigan.

I also wish to thank my wife, Ethel, for her proofreading these many pages. We know that there may still be some errors and we welcome corrections. The name of Mr. Braastad is easy to misspell, and as I accidentally okayed an incorrect spelling, as well as the correct one on spell-check, it may appear misspelled in places. You will also see how spellings have changed through the last 140 years. Ski is Skee for jumping, Clarksburg was Clarksburgh, and Street is never capitalized, even when named with a certain street, such as Pine street. You will note some others, as well. Both spellings will appear in this book.

There will be one other problem you will encounter as you read the sections covering week by week news of separate years. A writer knows that each new thought or subject should have its own paragraph. As I did not want this book to be longer than it is, I have placed numerous news items in single paragraphs. I often tried to group subject matter, but often I had to mix subject material that was like "night and day." The mixing is correct in that all the news happened in the chronological order as printed. After reading a few pages, your mind will adjust to this pattern. At least, I hope so.

There is also a new continuation of this book, from the year 1920 to the 1954 Ishpeming Centennial." It is blue-covered and titled: "The Second History of Ishpeming, Michigan. It was published in 2015.

Thank you,
Robert D. Dobson

HERE IS A PARTIAL "ART NOUVEAU" WORK OF ISHPEMING'S WILL BRADLEY WHEN HE WAS THE HEAD OF THE ART DEPARTMENT OF COLLIER'S MAGAZINE. THE ORIGINAL IS IN COLOR.

THIS IS FROM THE MARCH 30, 1907 ISSUE. "COVER DESIGN BY WILL BRADLEY." TITLE IS "MUSIC HATH CHARMS."

PREVIOUS TO LEAVING ISHPEMING, HE WORKED AT THE IRON ORE NEWSPAPER UNTIL 1886.

Mining Terms:

Cage: An open elevator with gates, used for taking men, timbers, and other items in and out of the mine through a shaft.

Caps and Legs: Legs and caps were notched to fit together in cross-ways in mine crosscuts, drifts and levels to keep the rock roof from falling on miners. Boards were then laid on top of them, the length of the tunnels. Caps and legs were mostly made of wood, but could also be metal in later years. Hard ore mines often did not require caps and legs.

Diamond Drill: This invention allowed miners to go deeper from surface or underground in search of pockets or veins of iron ore. It was a round bit with black diamonds imbedded in it and could cut a round hole from an inch to up to 16 inches in size and formed a core which was removed for study.

Drift: a slightly up-hill tunnel built off of a level to get to the ore. More drifts, called crosscuts are often added from drifts in the ore area.

Dry: This is the change-house for miners to use and hang up their clean clothes when putting on their mine clothes, and to keep their mine clothes after showering and going home.

Hoist: A large barrel from four to twelve feet in diameter which coils the steel cable on and off of one or two skips. A hoist is also required for the cage.

Hoist House: The Hoist house contains the hoist and often steam making equipment to drive the hoists, drills, and pumps before the days of electricity.

Level: The levels are the main drifts from the shafts and are sunk often in fifty to one-hundred feet intervals down in the shaft to begin the process of going to beds of ore. Running a bit up-hill, they drain all the water from the mine into the shaft where it is often pumped up to surface from the bottom.

Motor-man: When electricity replaced mules and horses in the mines, the motor-man ran the low, flat, electric engine, to pull ore from the drifts and levels to the shaft and the skips.

Pig Iron: made in the Upper Peninsula furnaces using a flux. Iron ore was melted to about 3200 degrees with charcoal and impurities separated out, allowing a higher percentage of iron to be sent to open hearth furnaces, and for the separated remains, called "slag" to be left in the Upper Peninsula.

Raise: tunneling upward in the mine, to get to a level above, or to an ore body higher up, or to remove ore.

Shaft: This is a vertical or inclined hole put down in the ground from a small 8 x 8 foot pattern to 9 x 22 foot, or larger. The shaft could have one or two skips, a cage, a ladder, and place for all wires and piping.

Shaft House: This building usually was over the shaft and might contain a crusher to make ore smaller when it came to surface, and some partitions in which to separate and hold different kinds of ore for future mixing, loading into railroad cars, or placing on stockpiles in the non-shipping winter months. At lease one shaft house at the Salisbury Mine was not directly over the shaft. Shafts could also be built simply to get more air into a mine.

Skip: This often was a series of buckets welded together to hold several tons of ore on each trip to surface. When in the shaft-house, it was self dumping. In the early days, men rode in and out of the mine in the skip. Skips could have large buckets hung below them to help unwater mines when needed. They often traveled at 1,500 feet a minute or faster.

Stope: A stope is a hole being made when removing iron ore. It can be very, very large in a hard ore mine, some say as big as a city block. In a soft ore, or hematite iron mine, pillars must be left periodically to hold up the roof over the miners. Stopes could later be filled with mine rock from another section of the mine and then the pillars with their iron ore, mined and shipped with other iron ore.

Trammer: Trammers pushed cars to the shafts in the early days, and then back up into the mine workings to be loaded with more ore. They also pushed ore in cars out from the shafts on trestles to dump on piles for winter storage. They were replaced with horses and mules, and then electric locomotives.

Winze: These were openings made between levels some distance from a shaft. They could be used for air circulation, getting to stope ore from above, or for efficiency. They did not go to the mine surface as did a shaft.

Below is a view of empty Lake Angeline. We are looking west. On the far left are Lake Angeline homes on Terrace Hill at the end of Angeline Street. Other homes are down the street going westerly. The trestle is where the pumping station was that emptied the lake. As the bottom of the lake was further north (to the right), an extra pipe was laid down to the deepest section. Behind the trestle on the hillside is the Excelsior Peat Furnace with the smokestack. The smokestack in the front, near center is the hoist and shafthouse of the Lake Angeline East End Mine. The small shaft house (arrow) is a shaft of the Cleveland Lake Mine. The shaft on the far side of the old Lakebed is a Superior Hematite Mine Shaft. The railroad along the shore to the left is now gone and under water from early caving ground, and the new railroad grade is part of a hiking-biking trail further up on the hill-side.   Tom Dobson Photo

The French Church at Lake and Johnson Steets and a decorated Steam Locomotive of the LS&I Railway, heading east. Many homes at the far right are still present. Year unknown. Friends of the Ishpeming Carnegie Library, June, 1981, Calendar.

Above is the second location of the Lyric Theater. Here, it is at the corner of Cleveland and Main. See the other location on page 79. The Theater seems to be a lot fancier now, with a lighted sign, but the lights still look like city gas ones. Picture credit to the Friends of the Ishpeming Carnegie Library, January, 1983, Calendar.

Below is a photo taken from the area of Mr. Mather's Cottage in the Cleveland Location, and looking north-west. The field, center right was where the Ishpeming Hospital was built. In the foreground are the two shafts of the Moro Mine and Bluff Street. The foundations can still be seen. On the far right, one can see the CCI Brownstone building on Division, which is still present. Tom Dobson photo.

It has occurred to me that the reader may like to know what the Ishpeming Street Cars looked like in 1900. Here is a photo of one, with a good number of passengers, in front of the Episcopal Church, going towards town on First Street, and owned by the Marquette County Gas & Electric Co. Friends of the Ishpeming Carnegie Library, June, 1982 Calendar.

Mr. Braastad's store had a nice steam engine float in this 1900 parade. It almost looks to be driving on the Steet Car tracks. Credit to Friends of the Ishpeming Carnegie Library, June, 1982 Calendar,

Left: Mine Shaft. On right:: Lowering Mule; both photos courtesy of the Negaunee Historical Museum

On the left is the 1895 Ishpeming City Hall. It does not look the same today in at least one respect. The public demanded a bathroom facility down town, and it was built in the front corner of the building, where it can be seen today, although unused. Photo is the courtesy of the Friends of the Ishpeming Carnegie Library, April, 1982, Calendar.

This photo on the left appears to be Mr. Hendrickson as he begins his somersault from the Ishpeming Ski Hill in 1912. He was good, and so was the fellow who took the picture. Both did a nice job. We note that skiers are also watching. Credit to the Friends of the Ishpeming Carnegie Library, February, 1982, Calendar.

10

Chapter 1:
Moving Down To the Swamp

The first two mines in town were the Cleveland (1852) and the Lake Superior (1857). The town had no name. In fact, there was no town, but two mining locations, each with some houses and commercial buildings. All the land was company owned and the companies built most of the buildings. Others who built at the two locations leased or rented some land.. That was, however, until the Iron Cliffs Company, owner of the Cleveland Mine, decided to sell as real estate the swamp just north of the Lake Superior Mine. Thus it came to be that there would be a down-town location on privately owned real estate. The moving down-town involved mostly a group of buildings on South Pine Street by the still standing Burt Office, now the ECI building. That was the Lake Superior Mine office.

Mr. G. D. Johnston came to the Lake Superior Mine and took charge of opening up the Lake Superior Mine in 1857 and stayed on as the superintendent of the mine until 1875. He built one of the first buildings in the area, it being a large boarding house, in which he slept himself, and had a chance to see wolves outside in the moonlight on at least one occasion. This building was one moved down to the swamp. In fact, Captain Johnston was one of the pioneers of the new "down-town". Note was made by the Iron Ore in the July 28, 1891, issue when Mr. Johnston's death was announced, that "Captain Johnston, together with Mr. Robert Nelson, bought the land (almost 120 acres) and laid out the city of Ishpeming, theirs being the original plat." Mr. Johnston's death was in Cripple Creek, Colorado. The date of the purchase of the land for the new town was 1868, and it was soon divided into lots for sale.

On June 25, 1870, according to the Marquette Weekly Plain Dealer, Captain Nelson moved his meat market to the lower part of the cedar swamp. The United Methodist Church built its first church on Division Street near the present high school where it was located until the 1960's. At Cleveland and First, a large furniture store went up. On July 28, 1870 a note in the paper said that Main Street had a school house and a drug store, and a bank would also be added. Close by Mr. Nelson's store would be the first Chicago and North Western Depot.

The Negaunee Mining Review on July 28, 1870, printed a very nice article on the moving of Ishpeming. The microfilm is not very clear and I have to fill in some words, but this is basically what it says: "....every available spot of ground presents a new frame in a state of erection." Those who formerly had situated near the depot (I believe it was on Bluff St. near the Cleveland Mine) are rapidly moving to the swamp until there are but few uptown stores left and they are making arrangements to move down where the railroad (The Chicago and North Western) is. The new Catholic Church has been placed upon its new site and will now be speedily finished. For so ponderous a building it has been moved rapidly and with remarkable ease. It now is on Main Street, just south of the new schoolhouse." (The church was built in 1867 at the Superior Mine with the mine supplying the wood.)

The Mining Journal Weekly paper in the January 12, 1870, issue noted that a new restaurant just opened in "lower Ishpeming." That was a much nicer name for the swamp.

Note that all the first buildings probably were constructed of wood. The reason that those standing today are made of stone is that the down-town Ishpeming had a great fire in 1874. The great Chicago and Peshtigo fires had occurred in 1871.

Here is part of the report soon printed in the Ishpeming newspaper, the Iron Home, soon after the occurrence of the fire on April 19, 1874:

At 8 o'clock the alarm of fire was sounded throughout the city. The whole populace rushed upon the streets. A flood of smoke was traced to a hardware store, on the northeast corner of Main and Pearl streets. Soon the flames burst through the sheathing of the frail and cheap-made building and formed a bond-fire of a most formidable character.

People to the number of fifteen hundred, or more, anxious, good workers, were on the ground in prompt response to the whistle calls, the churches and every house yielding a quota proportionate with its strength.

The fire spread with a rapidity and intensity which is seldom known. Fire plugs were frozen up, and the fire-fighting apparatus generally, like the working firemen, seemed to have been taken by surprise. Meanwhile the conflagration was extending up and down Main street, on both sides, and a light breeze springing up from the east carried large brands of fire over the western portion of the city.

Thus it was but about two hours before one entire square---between Division and Pine streets— was a mass of flames. Fears were entertained that most of the city would be burned. The neighboring city of Negaunee was telegraphed to(o) and asked to lend assistance. She promptly responded by sounding her steam fire engine, but a fire which broke out in that place and is noticed further along, called back that force. We were in dire distress, but the elements in fire and water favored us. Snow and water had not quite left roofs, and back and side premises. The fight was not easy, especially where direct hand-to-hand work was demanded. The profusion of cinders, hot ashes, and brands of fire which arose in the air from the conflagration fell to the earth in great showers.

The fire communicated rapidly from the building where it originated to the neighboring tenements, and at about 11 o'clock---having three hours' run---there seemed to be a hope of conquering it. Some buildings in the path which it took were torn down and the water works were gotten into effective operation;

whilst a good proportion of the populace seemed determined to conquer or die.

But it was a weird, wild scene of destruction and devastation. The streets were filled with household goods and articles of merchandise, all thrown together promiscuously as if by volcanic action---mud, red ore slough, snow, ice, and debris forming a combination of the strangest and most conglomerate character---men, women, and children, running frantic---fear, predominating and many citizens having their goods packed preparatory to move on a moment's notice.

The fire department proved its great efficiency, but found itself sadly crippled for want of water, through the stupidity of some one who left a cap off a plug. But finally, persistent exertion prevailed, and by tearing down buildings and keeping those in advance of the fire well wet down, the east course of the conflagration was stopped, midway between Main and First street and on the west on the line of Pine street.

The entire block of buildings bounded by Division street, on the south, Main street on the east, Pine street on the west, and Pearl street on the north was destroyed. Also one-half of the block between Division street and Pearl, on the east side of Main, was burned. The fire also carried away a portion of the improvements on the north side of Pearl street, between Main and Pine, and the burned district comprises near about, if not quite, two squares, of the principal business portion of the city.

The article continued to tell of all the businesses and people affected by the fire. The entire article reprint can be found in the Iron Ore in the August 12, 1911 issue. On August 19, 1911, the Iron Ore printed this follow-up Iron Home article about thievery after the fire:

Thieving was carried on to a large extent. Any article which could be carried by one person was sure to be taken if not left under guard. Thus dry goods, clothing, boots, shoes, head clothing, mirrors, ornaments, bureau drawers, etc., which were known to have been saved, could not be found after the fire. Many of these goods "turned up" quite a distance from the scene of action, within two days after the fire, as if they hade been dropped accidentally in the course of transmission. The police have also found quite a quantity of them, ranging from cooking utensils to sewing machines.

Note is also made in an article of the very first issue of Mr. Newett's Iron Ore paper on October 11, 1879, that within a few short months of the 1874 fire, "the city had arisen triumphant from its ashes, having been built up in a much more solid and substantial manner than before the fire." Mr. Newett also notes that the population of the town numbers "some 7,000 inhabitants."

We should also note that many businessmen wanted to open businesses that the mining companies themselves did not want on their property. Thus anyone could now buy a lot and open up just about any kind of business. By 1886, 38 bars were listed in the "swamp".

There were other fires from time to time, as well, and in 1878 the city's finest hotel for visiting guests, the Barnum House, burned down. However, following the fire of 1874, the town had formed a volunteer fire department and bought a most up-to-date "rotary steam engine". It was called, "without doubt, the best machine of the kind in this section of the country." It did not save the hotel, but may have saved others from burning. Although other hotels existed, the need was great, and within a few months there was a new grand Barnum House. It is also interesting to note that when there was a large fire in Negaunee in 1880, the fire equipment of Ishpeming was quickly loaded on railroad cars and taken by a locomotive to the fire.

The town in the swamp started as a township, and then became a village, and in 1873 became a city. By 1879, the average attendance in school was up to 840 children, placed in 12 rooms with 12 teachers. It was only a grade school.

The most interesting item of the new town is the map of its layout. If you look inside the cover, you will see that there is a peculiar street or passageway that leads on an angle from the South side of the town by Third Street and runs N. N. W. up to Canda. There is no street there today; in fact it probably wasn't a street as it doesn't have a street name. Yet it doesn't have any other name either. The author believes that it may be an early railroad grade and the Marquette & Ontonagon Railroad, that became the Duluth, South Shore and Atlantic on the south side of town, may have had a branch going to the north side of town when the town was laid out. .

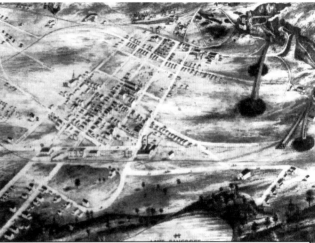

THIS IS A SKETCH OF ISHPEMING IN THE "SWAMP" AS DRAWN IN 1871. USED BY PERMISSION OF JACK DEO, SUPERIOR VIEW GALLERY OF MARQUETTE.

HERE IS AN EARLY PHOTO OF ISHPEMING LOOKING OVER LAKE BANCROFT TO THE NORTH-EAST. NOTE AREA OF THE PRESENT PLAY-GROUND SEEMS TO BE A AREA OF MINING EXPLORATION. ONE OF THE LARGE HOMES IN THE CENTER OF THE PHOTO ON LAKE BANCROFT IS THAT OF MR. NEWETT OF THE IRON ORE NEWSPAPER. ISHPEMING FRIENDS OF THE CARNEGIE LIBRARY CALENDAR PHOTO.

Chapter 2:
The City Mines
Before 1879

The mines of the very early years were open pits because the ore was seen on surface and black powder was not the best for blasting open tunnels, and drilling was all by hand. One person held a rod with an "X" punch on the end and turned it while a second person hit the other end with a sledge hammer until a deep hole was formed, and into which, the black powder was placed.

Following the Civil War, however, in 1867, and during the building of the Union Pacific Railroad to California, nitro-glycerin came into use. This was also known as dynamite. Steam engine power was also being developed with machinery to compress air, and drilling was soon done through the use of hoses and piped air to drills that could more quickly build drifts or tunnels, as well as the shafts themselves. For many years the shafts were put down right into the ore bodies, but the softness of much of the ore caused the shafts to go out of line and new ones had to be constantly built. With longer drifts now possible, shafts could more easily be put down in rock, and the tunnels could go a longer distance to the ore.

By 1879, Mr. Newett tells us that the six mines in the City of Ishpeming are the LAKE SUPERIOR, CLEVELAND, NEW YORK, BARNUM, PITTSBURG & LAKE ANGELINE, AND THE SALISBURY. We are printing a map of these and other later mine locations inside the back cover of the book. These six mines paid a monthly average of $61,000. a month for labor, or $732,000 per year for the

1879 period. Mr. Newett notes also that most of the money stayed in the area. Note is made of several other mines just outside the city limits and names the Nelson, Saginaw, Winthrop, Lowthian, National and Mitchell. These, of course, added even more money into the hands of people who came to Ishpeming to shop.

As earth moving equipment was practically non-existent at this time, it was noted in one 1867 local paper that "Tunneling is much easier than removing tons of surface to reach the good ore". The first "steam shovel" would not arrive for some years. The Mining Journal notes on January 1, 1870 that Nitroglycerin is in use at the Washington Mine and one other. So well did it work at the Washington Mine in Humboldt, that the paper notes that this mine is almost "all tunnel openings."

Other mines are continuously opening up outside of the city of Ishpeming. In 1869 there is the Schoolhouse, The Ogden, the Cascade (The original name of Palmer), the Spur, the Smith and several Negaunee Mines such as the Pioneer, the Collins, the Pendill, the Mary Charbeneau, Maas, and Grand Central. Just outside the north city limits was the Detroit Mine. By 1872, even more mines were opening, too numerous to mention. A list of mines in existence in 1891 in Marquette County is found printed later in this book.

There was for many years, a great need for housing, as the population was always outgrowing current housing. In May of 1872, 800 miners arrived from Sweden. Often the trains had extra cars for the extra immigrants. Wives often came later, and often with children in tow. On one train, there were several cars of Swedish women who were on their way out west to marry husbands under "contract." By the same token, miners moved on if things got slow and there were lay-offs, with single men usually laid off first. There was no government help, and for unemployed with no savings, there was only the poor-house in Marquette, near the quarry. In 1872, however, the Journal states that there is a "Scarcity of Laborers" and that "2000 could be used". It also notes that wages are averaging at $2.25 a day. (Surface work paid less than did underground mining).

Steam pumps were able to keep water out of mines and shafts, except for maybe a very wet spring when run-off water would pour into pits and shafts and the run-off would be greater than the pumps could handle.

In early mines, miners had to go up and down on wet, mud-soaked ladders, and the only items used to remove mined ore were large buckets on cables. Gradually, skips were invented with one or two holding buckets, and they rode into the mines on rails, and men could also ride in them. Then, cages were invented, not only for men to ride in, but to help carry the thousands of feet of timber down into the mine, and up again when it was broken from the great underground pressures of the earth. The pressure always wanted to close up many of the holes and tunnels that were made. At first, in small shafts, when the skip was in use, the cage was disconnected, and when the cage was in use, the skip was disconnected. This must have caused a great deal of extra work, as all the miners were brought to surface for lunch.

By the 1880's and 90's, shafts were quite large, about 9 x 22 feet, and there were often three or four compartments in a shaft, for a skip, for a cage, for steam pipes and electric lines, and for the escape ladder and ventilation.

The mines operated on a "Boom and Bust" system often. By 1877, it was a bust time. The Journal reported that at Michigamme, "A large number of miners are to leave next month for

the West". Even in 1868, 25 miners were leaving for the Sweetwater Gold Mines, probably in the Wind River area of Wyoming. (There is no Wyoming yet, until 1890.)

As there was no electricity in the early years, miners had to push the car loads of ore in the drifts to the shaft in order to be put into the skips. It was said that the limits of the push distance was about 300 feet. It was slightly downhill, luckily, so that water coming into the mine would drain down to the shaft, also, to be pumped up to surface from the bottom. Without electricity, miners wore large candles that mounted on their hard hats, and as they also had a metal spike attached, they could be removed and stuck in a nearby crevice or timber while they worked. Later, about 1905, carbide lamps such as the X-Ray brand, dropped water onto a powder of carbide. Acetylene gas would be produced and as the gas came out of a small hole a flint lighter would be used to light it into a steady flame. The size of the flame was adjusted by a water regulator. Eventually, about 1915, batteries that could light a lamp for a full eight hours were invented, and recharged between shifts and were worn on one's belt. The light was still located on the mine's cap. Several years passed, however, before they came into general use.

Mines consisted of several buildings. There was a shaft house, usually built over the shaft itself, and a hoisting house, or engine house, from which the cables wound from drums and went to the top of the Shaft House to raise the buckets, skips, and cages. There was a steam plant with a furnace and large boilers to make steam and steam pressure to run pumps and drills and the hoists. There was a blacksmith shop for completing mine repairs. There was also a timber yard and building for cutting caps and legs. Caps on legs held up the roofs of the drifts.. And for the miners, there was always a Dry. The dry was heated by steam and often so warm that they were always catching on fire at one mine or another. Miners had a storage area for their clothes they wore to work while putting on their work clothes. When they went home, their work clothes were at the dry. Often the storage area was made up of baskets hung on chains where clothes could dry out between shifts. Mines were very wet. Men sometimes wore rubber boots and rubber suits. There were also large shower rooms in the drys. Work clothes were so red in color that women in modern times often used a separate washing machine for mine clothes. Miner wore home-made "skull caps" to keep their hair cleaner under their hard hats.

Production increased steadily, and the six mines in the city limits were producing 400,000 tons of ore a year by 1879.

HERE IS A SMALL VERSION OF A DRILL BIT USED BY MINERS BEFORE STEAM-DRILLS. THE X SECTION WOULD BE PLACED ON THE ROCK AND TURNED AS IT WAS HIT ON THE END BY ANOTHER MINER. GRADUALLY A HOLE WOULD BE FORMED IN WHICH BLACK POWDER WAS PLACED FOR BLASTING.

HERE IS A PHOTO OF EARLY MINERS AT THE MORO MINE ON BLUFF STREET IN ISHPEMING. WE PUT IT HERE SO THAT YOU MIGHT SEE THE LARGE CANDLES THAT WERE USED IN THE MINES IN THE EARLY DAYS. CANDLES COULD BE REMOVED FROM THE MINE HATS AND STUCK IN CREVACES AND INTO WOOD WHEN WORKING. . THE CARBIDE LAMPS REPLACED THEM IN THE EARLY 1900'S. THOSE IN THE PHOTO ARE STANDING ON THE PRESENT BLUFF STREET CLOSE TO JASPER STREET. THE REMAINS OF THESE TWO SHAFTS ARE STILL THERE. COURTESY OF THE ISHPEMING FRIENDS OF THE CARNEGIE LIBRARY, AND BETTY JARVIS, FOR THE USE OF THIS MARCH 2000 CALENDAR PHOTO.

Chapter 3:
Life in General Before 1879

About 1850, the road to Marquette was just passable for wagons pulled by six horses each, and filled with iron from the Jackson Forge at the current Michigan Mining Museum location.

We note that wagons had to be used all winter as Mr. Philo Marshall Everett noted that the sleigh runners of the heavily loaded sleighs would dig right through the snow to bare ground.

In 1855, the famous "Plank Road" was built for a very short period, through a Michigan Legislative Enactment. It was 16 feet wide, with eight-foot planks at least three inches thick placed side by side on the grade. Iron straps were fastened on to guide the 50 teams of mules pulling the cars of ore, as the ore cars often wanted to come off the timber road. As it was downhill to Marquette, there was often great expense when imported horse teams were run over by their ore cars, at $1,400 a team. Hay and feed were also imported and expensive. If there was an accident on the road, other mule trains could not get by. The spring after its first year, a steam locomotive was delivered to the Marquette harbor, by a Mr. Ely, and a regular railroad built up to the Jackson Mine, following close to the plank road in most places. Mr. Stone's map in his book, Philo Marshall Everett, shows that the Ely Railroad actually went all the way to the Cleveland, Lake Superior, and National Mines. The original plank road then seemed to become part of the first public road to Marquette, especially from Negaunee to Eagle Mills. This information largely comes from the Marquette Township Sesquicentennial Book of

1998. In actuality, people tried using the plank road as a public road even as it was a commercial venture. Gates were put up here and there, but as a useless cause. Nor did the metal straps work. Mr. Frank Stone, in his book, suggests that they could have moved the ore better with wagons on the plank road if they had left the metal straps off. They didn't guide the wheels well at all.

There was little steel in use at this time in America, but the iron ore from the Ishpeming area made a very strong iron, and thus was in demand. Iron rails often broke, as well as wheels of train cars, and other iron castings, causing delays and accidents throughout the country..

In 1868, although there was a railroad to Marquette to haul ore and passengers, there was no railroad yet from the south to Ishpeming. It was noted in the Mining and Manufacturing News in the January 23, 1868, issue that the only way out of the Upper Peninsula in winter was a stage route to Green Bay and that it was two days away from Ishpeming. The Great Lakes were closed in the winter, so mail went and came by dog-sled for several early years.

The Chicago and Northwestern reached Lake Angeline, Michigan (Remember, no Ishpeming yet) in 1870. Soon after the C&NW arrived, it is noted in the paper quite often that people began to travel to Chicago, California, and to Europe. For those interested in the railroads, we might add that the C&NW by 1888 also went to Republic, Champion, Clowry, to Michigamme, and even to the Copper Country using the rails of the Duluth, South Shore and Atlantic from Michigamme on. This comes from the book, Pioneer Railroad by Casey and Douglas.

Crime was quite rampant in the early years. Ishpeming was first called "Lake Superior," and "Hell Town" was commonly used. Newspaper crime notes read as follows:

"A number of "Chicago Professionals" are hanging around town."

"Bank Robbery."

"Fight on Ishpeming street results in four disfigured faces."

"Two attempts of rape last week. One man arrested."

"Arrest of Local Counterfeiters."

There were at least two traveling circuses to come to town before 1879. The first was "Dan Costello's Great Circus Egyptian Caravan" that came in 1870. The second was the "Great Forpaugh Show." A large two-column ad appeared in the paper on July 20, 1878. They came by rail mostly, and often came when ore production was at low ebb in sales, and the railroad tracks were available. On several occasions, the editor of the Iron Ore, Mr. George Newett commented that he was surprised at the fine attendance at the circuses even though many men had been laid off.

Progress was made in many areas in these early years. Tom Edison, in 1870, was busy working on his X-Ray machine, and would lose his close friend to the rays which amazingly made the "human body transparent," and were then found to be deadly as well. We will find that Tom came to Marquette County on several occasions.

Steam Locomotives were gaining in size and the rails as well. A train was seen going through town in 1867, pulling 59 ore cars carrying nine tons of ore each. Steam Locomotives were also being tried for Road Travel and work in the woods, using tracks like a bull-dozer today..

Area newspapers also reported that the first permanent bridge had been built for a railroad to cross the Mississippi River (1868), that Queen Victoria was thought to be "not quite right"

(1867), and closer to home, that gold had been found in 1872 on the North Shore of Lake Superior in Canada.

Other local news tells us that 200 children are enrolled in the Ishpeming School District in 1867 from the Lake Superior, Cleveland, New York, and Lake Angeline Locations. An interesting anomaly appeared in 1867 that an empty hole, about 12 feet by 6 feet by 4 feet was found inside a local underground solid ore body.

A lot more was happening, during these years on a larger scale, such as the building of Iron Furnaces. That deserves its own chapter. Much iron ore had some rock in many of the chunks, and it was desired to leave the rock in Marquette County and ship only iron ingots—or pig iron. The first Sault Ste. Marie lock on the St. Mary's River had been built in 1855, and boats could now progress right to steel mills.

HERE IS A PHOTO OF THE CHICAGO AND NORTHWESTERN RAILROAD AFTER IT REACHED THE ISHPEMING AREA IN 1879. IT WENT TO MICHIGAMME AND REPUBLIC AT THIS TIME, AND FOR SEVERAL YEARS, WENT ALL THE WAY TO THE COPPER COUNTRY VIA THE DULUTH, SOUTH SHORE AND ATLANTIC RAILWAY TRACKS. LATER, IT ONLY WENT AS FAR AS CLOWRY, WITH THE LARGE TURN-AROUND NEAR THE HURON BAY GRADE. LATER, IT ENDED ITS ROUTE IN ISHPEMING. FROM A 1917 C&NW ADVERTISEMENT. NOTE: THERE SEEMS TO BE TWO MAIN ROUTES TO ISHPEMING, ONE GOING THROUGH NATIONAL MINE.

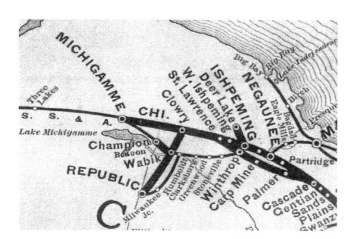

HERE IS A VERY OLD SHAFT HOUSE ON THE FORMER NEW YORK MINE PROPERTY AT DIVISION AND SEVENTH STREETS. IT HAD TWO HOISTS, ONE OPERATING OUT OF EACH SIDE OF THE BUILDING, AND GOING TO TWO SHAFTS, ONE F WHICH IS JUST TO THE RIGHT OF THE PHOTO AND IS FENCED IN. THE OTHER WENT DOWN INTO A PIT.

ON THE OPPOSITE SIDE OF THE ABOVE HOISTING HOUSE IS THIS OPENING WHERE THE CABLE CAME OUT AND WENT THE THE SHAFT HOUSE. IT IS A LONG OPENING AS THE CABLE WOUND UP ON A HOISTING DRUM, HIGHER AND HIGHER AS IT RAISED UP A SKIP WITH ORE IN IT FROM EITHER UNDERGROUND OR FROM THE BOTTOM OF AN OPEN PIT

FROM THE 1912 SHOW. (IRON ORE)

WILLIAM F. "BUFFALO BILL" CODY FIRST CAME TO THE ISHPEMING AREA IN 1880 AND HIS NAME IS RECORDED IN THE OLD NEGAUNEE BREITUNG HOTEL BOOK IN OCTOBER 31 OF THAT YEAR. THE BOOK IS NOW AT THE NEGAUNEE HISTORY MUSEUM. HE RETURNED WITH SHOWS IN 1902 AND IN 1912. THE POSTER HERE IS

Chapter 4:
The Town, 1879 to 1882

In 1879, Mr. Newett, and Mr. McCarthy, began the <u>Weekly Agitator</u>. On January 7, 1882, Mr. McCarthy retired, and the newspaper became the <u>Iron Agitator</u>, and finally, on September 18, 1886, the <u>Iron Ore</u>. I will refer to these papers as "the newspaper," "paper," or the <u>Iron Ore</u>. Other newspapers will be titled when used.

The meaning of the town name was one of the first items that Mr. Newett mentions. Here is what he says: "The word Ishpeming is a Chippewa word signifying 'on the summit.' It was chosen because within the city limits are a natural divide, from one side of which flows the Carp River into Lake Superior and upon the other the Escanaba into Lake Michigan."

At this time yet, the city has no water system, and certainly, no sewer system. Partridge Creek ran through town, and the main railroads followed it, along its bank. Of course, that is where Bank Street is. It was an open sewer and eventually went into the Carp River. However, because the Carp would flood sometimes and had very little downhill grade on its way to Deer Lake, the sewer would back up into town. What was a mess turned into a real mess. Not only was sewer all over, but Mr. Newett's paper stated that wood sidewalks "are carried out into the streets." We will cover the sewer development eventually, but first there was the drinking water problem.

The Cliffs Shafts were being built to replace the Barnum Mine. The Barnum had an open pit, and was on the south side of Division Street. It was the pit into which the garbage was placed and burned for many years. The Cliffs Shafts

were two shafts, and they will be in a separate mine chapter.. Here, what is important is that, as one shaft was being built on Strawberry Hill's west end, the more it went down, the more area wells were going dry. There was worry that even Lake Bancroft would be drained. And, in wintertime, the city water hand pump often froze up. In the second issue of his newspaper, Mr. Newett notes that when shafts drain the Ishpeming swamp and wells go dry, water will have to be obtained from Lake Angeline. And it soon it was. . In the meantime, before a new water supply was accomplished, the smart people of Ishpeming got their water from where theirs had gone, at the "A" Shaft of the new Barnum, or Cliffs Shafts Mine.

The water supply from Lake Angeline will not be in use very long. Three area mines had property to the shores of Lake Angeline, and had discovered ore under the lake. But being a sandy bottom, it did not look good for mining the ore with water in the Lake, and so plans were quite quickly made to have the Lake removed.

One new mining item every week is the mention of Diamond Drills. The diamonds were imbedded into the bits and could drill far down into the earth and even drill down while in the bottom drifts of the mines. The drills always didn't go down straight, and sometimes curved so much that they broke off. On one occasion, miners found a drill rod appearing in their drift after blasting out some rock. .

In the third issue of the newspaper of 1779, there is mention of an item that is startling.......electricity. We have mentioned that Tom Edison was working with X-rays. For this he needed electricity. Batteries worked for his x-rays, and light bulb invention, but he needed a way to make electricity and so he invented the dynamo which made direct-current and anyone who had a dynamo could produce electricity. Tom originally was against alternating current as too dangerous.

The October 25, 1879, issue of the newspaper noted that an electric arc light was being tested at the Lake Superior Mine and might be also used at the Cleveland and Champion Mines. By the next spring an article appeared saying that the Escanaba Iron Port newspaper will be printed by an electric press. In May of 1880, a new Brush Generator would be in the No. 1 engine house at the Cleveland mine and would supply electricity for arc lights. Details were that eight lights were now in use and eight more would soon be put on line. Soon the lighting went underground, using incandescent bulbs as we know them today, and miners were able to do much more work at a faster pace than was possible with only the lighting from their hats. Note, however, that lights on hats remained until the end of underground mining about 1970.

To allow people to get across the Partridge Creek where it crossed Main Street, a 110-foot wood bridge was spanned across the creek. The City of Ishpeming also soon was talking about a large arc light down-town, on a tower. Publicity told of how electric lights gave off far more light than gas lights. However, direct current didn't travel very far before losing its power, and no decision was made about installing a Cleveland Ohio Brush lighting system. Arc lights were not a bulb, but two carbon rods where the electricity jumped between them and much smoke as well as light was given off. Note was also made in the paper, however, that Tom Edison was working on a system "to divide light", and then it could be used in stores and they could stay open at night and use his light-bulbs. In a sense, what Tom was working on was a "piping system" for

electricity. It resulted in the invention of transformers to use high voltage for traveling down the streets, and then to lower voltage for each building's use.

On January 22, 1881, the City is communicating with Mr. Edison about his electric light including his bulbs. In November of the same year, the Lake Superior Mine bought the Brush Electric Arc light using a #7 Brush 20 hp. Machine. We also note that in a few years, as electricity goes underground, that it will be very useful for little electric engines (called "motors") to be used to replace men in getting the cars of ore from the "stopes," down the drifts, to the skips in the shaft, and back again up the slight drift grades. What a labor saver!

In this period from 1879 to 1882, other things are happening, too. Ishpeming, being the largest city in Marquette County, tries to get the county courthouse to be located here, saying that Marquette is only a summer town when the ice is off Lake Superior. Even the Chicago and Northwestern Railway came to Ishpeming from Chicago, and not to Marquette. To change the subject, I don't think I have missed many important items in the Iron Ore. However, in the Negaunee Historical Museum is the old Breitung Hotel registration book, and registered for October 31, 1880, is the name of William "Buffalo Bill" Cody. He stayed in 1-B, and paid $7.00. He must have been here with his Wild West show, but I had nothing in my notes for that October. I thought we might also find the name of Annie Oakley or Chief Sitting Bull, but they were not listed.

The city provided its first library at this time, but made a charge of $2.00 if you wanted to take out books. It was very popular and many came and read the papers daily, and magazines, and took out books. A year after it began, in 1881, the library had 1,200 books. The $2.00 fee stayed on for many years until the library realized it had never given any back, and that it was about impossible to do so, and dropped the charge sometime after 1900.

The city was so large at this time already, that there were several other newspapers in existence, including the Iron Home, which became the Ishpeming Iron Chronicle, which soon moved to Norway, Michigan and became the Norway Current. In 1891, the city even had a daily, the Lake Superior Democrat.

Ishpeming was like the gold mine towns out west at this time. People continued to pour in. Mines were very busy and one individual counted 312 ore cars go by him in one hour in 1880. The newspaper notes on February 14, 1880, that the Winthrop mine is short of men and only half enough are on the night shift. On March 6th, 80 laborers arrived from Chicago, and a note in the March 13 issue notes that "We are besieged with people," and notes that there was an extra car on the C&NW RR. The March 27 issue notes that very few are leaving the area, and men come in daily on every train. April 10 tells us that 40 Scandinavians from Europe arrived. The April 24th issue notes that all seem to be employed presently. New men arriving go to work immediately. The May 22 issue notes that there is an ad for people who want to teach to take the exam that is to be given (Schools were so overfilled in 1881 that schools were working in shifts.) And near the end of 1880, on November 13, it is noted that many Belgian immigrants have arrived All this, of course resulted in the C&NW getting larger locomotives, and some new ones were now burning coal, rather than wood. A sad note regarding a new immigrant involved a Swedish woman with two small children who had just arrived by boat in the Marquette harbor. As she got off on the dock she was run over by train cars backing up. "She leaves a husband who has

been mining in Ishpeming," and she laid in the area for two hours before dying. This occurred in the summer of 1881. Many immigrant people still arrived by boat from the east and in 1880 the "City of Cleveland" passenger ship made a round trip to Marquette every five days.

There might also have been a very serious train accident in 1881 by the C&NW on leaving Ishpeming. The wheel trucks on a car broke and began to tear up the rails and the ties as well. The extreme rocking ride prevented the conductor from pulling the emergency cord, but luckily a teen-age boy did, and the train precariously came to a stop entering Negaunee on the bridge over the large Jackson Mine Tunnel and the cars luckily did not topple into it. Mr. Newett noted that all on the train "have reason to thank their stars for their decidedly narrow escape."

HERE ARE TWO PORTABLE DIAMOND DRILL MACHINES, BOTH RUN BY STEAM. THE TOP ONE IS FROM 1882, AND BELOW, FROM 1913. MINING JOURNALS OF 5/13/82, AND 1913 IRON MINING AND AGRICULTURE SOUVENIR EDITION.

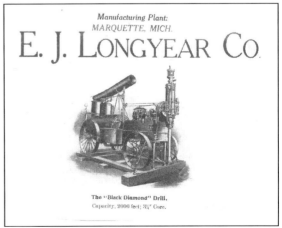

Chapter 5:
People of Interest

Among the many immigrants came many interesting people. Here is some of the news for around the 1880's,

The Broad's family in Humboldt had seven girls and no boys. Three sets of triplets were born in one week in Ishpeming according to the issue of July 16, 1881. One traveling fellow made money with a telescope. He charged a fee at night to look at the stars, planets, moon and a comet through it. Another fellow had a beautiful "Strasburg Clock" which people could come and see for ten cents. One man did balloon ascensions and acrobatics from it. Magicians at Austin's Hall were popular. One magician, Zera, gave away 50 free presents at every performance. His wife became ill while in town, and died here three weeks later, while he was on his tour, fulfilling his schedule. Three other men tried to make money by musical entertaining in bars and then passing the hat. They left town broke, and Mr. Newett notes that they did their business in the wrong order.

Theater was big in Ishpeming, with drama groups coming regularly to the Opera House. One was the Forbes Dramatic Company of 16 professional actors. The Whites' Theatre Company soon came and had such success that, after leaving and going to Republic where drama was also popular, they returned to Ishpeming again. The most popular play by far was "Uncle Tom's Cabin." It came every year, if not more often, and was performed by several groups. Some had real animals, and it seemed that everyone went just to see how differently each play compared to the other "Uncle Tom's Cabin" shows. Often they had a street parade in the morning, like the circuses. These plays were not based so much on Harriet Beecher Stowe's book, but on a play partly based on it, with the same name, by a writer called George Aiken. All over town, theatre bills were posted, and lots of stage shows were arriving in the year 1880. Mr. Newett was also constantly encouraging someone to build a nice, new, large opera house in town, and gave very good coverage to the shows with reviews and photos in his paper..

In 1880 Henry Ward Beecher preached in Marquette, and Dr. Chiles, a veterinarian surgeon opened an office in Ishpeming. Two women climbed down a ladder down into the Lake Superior Mine. The 240 foot depth was a first for two women noted the newspaper. In the same year, some other ladies made the news by being arrested for prostitution at the Milwaukee House on Pearl Street. Six "scamps" were arrested for busting Mr. Allen King's picket fence on Bluff Street. "They are now in jail" said the newspaper, on October 9, 1880.

In town, the most interesting local people were those who hooked up dogs to pull sleighs of groceries, children, and so on. We don't know if they also pulled wagons in the summer, but we do know that some paperboys used them to pull their papers along their routes.

The following was in the Ishpeming paper, but had to do with some interesting Indian visitors to L'Anse from Lake Beanesay (Minnesota?) They were four "genuine Chippewa Indians" and were an attraction because of "the length they wear their hair and numerous strings of bright ornaments around their necks and wrists."

By far the most interesting person to visit town in this three year period was "Kit Carson" of Texas, who registered at the Nelson House on Thursday, August 19, 1880. Mr. Newett described him as having long hair and beard, and a sombrero, but no buckskin clothes, and said that he claimed to be a cousin of the original Kit Carson. Every night he would entertain the public with lectures in front of the Rock Store, and was said by the listeners to be very instructive. In early September he went to Negaunee from where he "was suddenly called away" about the middle of the month. How he made his money, or afforded to travel, we do not know. He seemed to be an honest entertainer.

Sitting Bull and his followers were sadly arrested in 1881. It marked the last of the free Indians on the open plains. President Garfield died in September from being assassinated.

One important town leader during the period of this book was Mr. Frederick Braastad. He came to the U.S. in 1868 and came to this area, working in the New York Mine, and then becoming part of the work-force of an Ishpeming New York Location store. He moved to Kansas for a year, then returned to Negaunee where he was a clerk. Back in Ishpeming, for five years he became the manager of the Nora Store Company, and then opened his first store at Second and Cleveland Avenue. He was also owned an interest in the Winthrop Mine in National, south of Ishpeming. In 1888 he built a two story store in Ishpeming, and in 1904 he made it into the large building still there today. His son, Arvid, also became part of the business. Fred Braastad was also a director of the Peninsula Bank, the Electric Street Railway, was elected to the office of city alderman, and was also the Mayor. He even found time to go to Lansing and become the State Treasurer for two years.

There is come confusion regarding his later life. In a Mining Journal article for the Ishpeming Centennial in 1954, it was stated that in 1906, he made an abrupt change in his career when he sold all of his interests in Ishpeming and

moved to Canada. It also added that his selling included 300 acres in the Carp River Valley where he farmed, and 60 acres in the Dead River area. The Journal further reported that a Chicago firm bought the store and ran it until 1919 when it was sold to the Gossard Company. In the Iron Ore, however, we find a much different story. If you turn to the year in this book of 1914, you will find Fred alive and well in town, and then just planning to sell his building and planning to retire---and to stay in town. He died of cancer in 1917. He is buried in the Ishpeming Cemetery, as well as many of his family members.

Another leading early leader was Mr. P. John Outhwaite. His father had come here and taken possession of the Jasper Bluff behind where the old Cleveland School is still located. Finding the ore not that worth mining, he returned to Cleveland. A few years later, John Outhwaite came to the area and began to work at the Cleveland Mine, eventually becoming a bookkeeper. He helped to found the Cleveland Iron Company and was a vice-president. He eventually became the agent for all of the companies U. P. lands. He married the daughter of Robert Nelson, "the Father of Ishpeming," and eventually became associated with the Nelson House. He was involved in politics, and from 1876 on was elected as Mayor on several occasions.

In 1890, he became Ishpeming's first Fire Chief. The town had largely burned down in 1876, so the city bought its first steam pumping engine and after the Barnum House burned down, the city purchased a new improved pumper. Ishpeming's second steam fire pumper was named after Mr. Outhwaite. He was so popular, that his picture was painted on the side of the first motorized fire truck, purchased in 1923. He is buried by Olive Street in the Ishpeming Cemetery.

Graves of Four Leading Citizens.

THIS IS THE GRAVE OF MR. ANDREW AUGUST ANDERSON, BORN 1842 AND DIED IN 1887. THIS MAY BE THE FATHER OF THE A. A. ANDERSON, JR. WHO BUILT THE FINE THREE STORY JEWELRY STORE AT MAIN AND PEARL STREETS. HIS NAME IS ALSO HERE, AND WAS BORN 1N 1870 AND DIED ON OCTOBER 4, 1910. ON MOUNTAIN ASH. NOTE THE BRAASTAD GRAVES JUST TO THE WEST .

THE GRAVE OF JOHN P. OUTHWAITE, BORN IN 1844 AND DIED IN 1919. HIS WIFE MARY IS ALSO BURIED HERE AND SHE DIED IN 1936.

ALSO BURIED HERE IS THEIR SON JOHN N. OUTHWAITE, BORN IN 1871 AND DIED IN 1922. HIS WIFE, MARY M. IS BURIED HERE ALSO, HAVING DIED IN 1965.

THE GRAVE IS NOT IN GOOD CONDITION AND NEEDS SOME UPKEEP. THE LOCATION IS ON THE NORTH SIDE OF OLIVE AND HICKORY.

THIS IS THE SIMPLE AND SINGLE GRAVE OF JULIUS ROPES. HE WAS BORN IN 1835, AND DIED ON 4/16/1904. THERE ARE NO OTHER GRAVES TO BE NOTED. HIS SON, A GRADUATE OF WHAT IS NOW MICHIGAN TECHNOLOGICAL UNIVERSITY MOVED AWAY TO MONTANA, AND IT MAY BE THAT HIS MOTHER MOVED THERE ALSO AND IS BURIED THERE.

THE GRAVE IS ON THE SOUTH SIDE OF ELM STREET, JUST AS BIRCH STREET VEERS OFF TO THE SOUTH. HE IS ON SECTION 35.

HERE IS THE GRAVE OF FREDERICK BRAASTAD. HIS DEATH WAS ON JUNE 9, 1917. HE DIED OF CANCER. HIS WIFE LIVED UNTIL 1942. THE DOUBLE-GRAVE-SITE IS FILLED WITH FAMILY, INCLUDING A SON, DR. FRED AND HIS WIFE WHO DIED IN 1996 AND 1998, SON ARVID WHO DIED IN 1956, DAUGHTERS LILLIAN WHO DIED IN 1952, AND INGEBORG WHO DIED IN 1965, AND SON JULIUS WHO DIED IN 1966. THEY LOST THREE CHILDREN, JOHN (1880-1880), FORENCE AMELIA (1885, AGE TWO), INGEBORG (1888, AGE 1).

NOTE THAT AFTER INGEBORG DIED, THE NEXT DAUGHTER WAS GIVEN THE SAME NAME. THE GRAVESITE IS ON THE NORTH SIDE OF MOUNTAIN ASH ON SECTION THREE.

Chapter 6:
The Six Original City Mines

Each of the mines we mention could use a book of its own, and might get one if my retirement is long enough. Some of the material in the early years comes from <u>History of Upper Peninsula of Michigan</u>, by Western History Company, published in 1883. Most material is from Mr. Newett's paper.

Here are details about the six original Mines within the city of Ishpeming. One item relating to them is that by 1882 they were the first businesses to be connected by telephones. And by 1891, electricity was being used to explode the dynamite in the mines and also for lights and electric power.

The mines in 1883 are paying 6/7ths of the city and school taxes as printed in the May 26, 1883, paper. There are deaths recorded every week or so, and the statistics for 1889 show that 34 men died in local mines for the year. Hard times by August of 1896 caused men to be let go. The news of the many layoffs occurring at the Ishpeming area mines led the companies in Leadville, Colorado to come to town to hire miners as "scabs". It was not a good situation as the miners in Leadville at the time were on strike.

We remind the reader that the location of all of these mines is inside the back cover of this book.

After 1900, much of the history of each mine is listed along with the daily history of town and area events and not in this chapter.. The mines by 1900 are far too numerous to be given separate columns in this history book..

THE CLEVELAND MINE

The Cleveland Mine owned 2,200 acres total, and the principal mine was between the New York and the Lake Superior Mines. It also developed two other mines, the Cleveland Lake, and the Cleveland Hematite, both also included in this history.

A Dr. Cassels came from Cleveland to the area in 1846, looking for copper and silver. Mr. Everett, who had obtained the Jackson Mine property, directed him to the Ishpeming locality. Cassels received a "permit" from the U.S. War Department the same year. Nothing happened until 1853 when the Cleveland Iron Company was organized. In 1855, 1,449 tons of iron ore were shipped out to furnaces "down the lakes." According to records, this was the first large amount of ore to be shipped from the Marquette Iron Range, beating the Jackson first major shipment by one year. Eventually in the 1880's it was shipping 200,000 tons annually, and after 30 years of shipping, it had a total amount shipped of over two million tons. 550 men were employed at the mine by 1883. Being the first Ishpeming mine, it was natural also that the Cleveland Location would have the first area public school, and the first railroad station when trains arrived.

In 1879 a disaster occurred at the Cleveland Mine when 500,000 tons of rock fell inside the mine and partly into the New York as well. The main entrance into the mine was plugged up. In an effort to get to the ore by clearing out the rock, a year was spent putting in a double and a single inclined shaft through the rubble, using over a million board feet of timber to shore up the ground. The incline was 25%, quite steep for walking, but walkable. Mr. Newett noted in October of 1879 that "the amount of timber that is daily disappearing is astonishing." The ore from the incline pit was so good that the Cleveland was soon drilling east and west of the incline pit; with one diamond drill located down-town, south of the Catholic Church to search how far the ore body went.

In 1880 work was begun on a large new engine house and a sketch of the plan was put in the paper. The size of it would be 80 x 44 feet, and the steel cable would be wound on six-foot drums hoists.. At this time, four-foot drums were common, but could not carry as much cable for deeper shafts. This engine house would have four drums for four hoists in one room and the air compressors and two engines for the four hoists will be in another room. As an engine ran two hoists, one would be unspooling and going down while the other was raising a cage or skip and winding on cable. It hoists from the incline and saw-mill pits. Ore is being raised also from shaft "I", and a shaft "K" is being put down 215 feet to reach 55 feet of iron ore discovered with a Diamond Drill. Attached to the engine house, forming an "L" was a 44 x 40 foot Boiler room. Both rooms were made only of iron and stone, excepting window and door areas and "are quite fire-proof" noted the newspaper.

The Cleveland mine at this time was paying its men "entirely in Gold and Silver" reported the newspaper on March 20, 1880. Many others were paying with coin also at this time, including the C&NW railway. It was noted once that the men were complaining about the coin and would rather be paid in greenbacks. The newspaper announced weekly which mines were paying that week, and where the pay car (railroad) would be on what days. Of course, it was filled with thousands and thousands of dollars as the men were paid only once a month.

Many of the mines had Cornish pumps for pumping water out of the mines. They were often very large. There is one currently preserved in Iron Mountain, at the old "D" shaft of the large Chapin Mine, and can be toured. The Cleveland Mine Corning Pump had a 15 inch cylinder for plunging water, with a seven-foot stroke. By comparison, the Chapin plunger was 28 inches in diameter with a ten-foot stroke.

In 1895 we find that a portion of the surface over the original Cleveland Mine incline shaft caved in. Three years later the old trestle burned down at the incline shaft. That was okay, as it wasn't in use anymore.

The Cleveland Mine itself was located just north of present M-28 (Division Street) and east of Seventh Street. Mine buildings are still in that area.

THE CLEVELAND LAKE MINE

Another Cleveland Mine was located on the property extending south of the Cleveland Location at the Lake Angeline north shoreline at the east end. This was also a very lucrative mine and was one of three mines that desired the Lake Angeline to be eventually drained, the others being the Lake Angeline East End Mine and the Lake Superior Hematite. It was the Cleveland Lake Mine that made the "Cleveland-Cliffs Iron Co. a prosperous concern," according to a CCI general manager in later years. A Mining Journal article on September 22, 1960, noted that the ore of the Cleveland Lake mine "was blue ore, in iron content, the richest type found on the range."

In 1886, with water still in Lake Angeline, the Cleveland Iron Company began the Cleveland Lake Mine on the north east shore of the Lake. They put several shafts below the lake level along the lake and no water seeped into them. By 1890 one shaft was down 215 feet at a 65 degree angle under the lake but was not operating yet. The road to the mine evidently was from the Hill Street area of Cleveland Location, as it was not until fall of 1890 that it was thought to put a road in from South Pine Street along the north shore of Lake Angeline. A Railroad went in about that time also in the same direction. In April of 1892, new skips were installed at the mine, with the ability to hold three tons. Mr. Newett used the word, "large." During 1892 Lake Angeline was being drained, and by the end of the year it was gone, allowing full mining of the Cleveland Lake Mine to move ahead. There were two shafts eventually, an inclined to the eastern end of the lake, and a vertical one toward the west end of the old Lake bed, both on the old north shore. Some remains of the inclined shaft can be seen today from S. Pine Street, and the vertical shaft engine house remained until 1960 when it was torn down.

In 1893, in the June 10 edition of the newspaper, note was made that a brand-new system had been invented for the hoisting engineer to know where the skip was at all times, and to make costly mistakes avoidable. The Lake Mine was the first to try it out and after several months, it proved its worth by preventing two human errors. A large dial went around and showed each level as the skip or cage came to it, for accurate stops underground. The cable at this time moved at 1,500 feet a minute and only came to a stop on the last revolution of the hoisting drum. The new system also prevented the skip from going in the wrong direction, and if the brakeman failed to stop the skip as it came up into the shaft house, the skip would stop before going up through the top of the shaft house, and over the large hoisting wheel. This invention became universal, and a similar large wheel can be seen today in the Quincy #2 Mine Nordberg hoist house in Hancock.

In early 1896 the Cleveland Lake Mine was removing pillars and planned to cave in the old lake bottom surface in an orderly manner, without any of the surface mud from the old lake bottom coming into the mine. It was successful, at least until September 5. On September 5, there was an unplanned cave-in at a Lake Shaft of the Cleveland Mine. Mud from the surface entered the mine into the first level. Luckily there were no deaths. On March 20, 1897, another unplanned cave-in took place and it left a surface hole 60 feet deep and 140 feet in diameter. The Cleveland Lake mine at this time decided to mine using an open pit. Still, in 1899, we find a news item that mud again broke through the old Lake Angeline lake bed and into the mine. Evidently both shaft and pit work were taking place.

The Cleveland Lake Mine continued in operation to 1927, having shipped one of the largest amounts of ore of any mine, a total of over 15,500,000 tons. This was not the end of the story, however. It was decided in 1950 to remove 21,000 tons of a former "mine rock" pile at the Lake Mine by Euclid trucks to a railroad loading dock where it was transported for processing and sale. Pumping out of the workings of all of the old Lake Angeline mines continued through 1946 when the near-by Holmes Mine closed, allowing all mines south of Ishpeming to be flooded. The pump house was located at the Lake Angeline Mine. The many drifts of all the mines, and the Lake itself were full of water by 1951.

THE CLEVELAND HEMATITE MINE

The other Cleveland Mine was the Cleveland Hematite which was on the north-west side of town in an area called the Teal Lake group of mines. Many of these mines were Negaunee mines. It was started by the Cleveland Iron Mining Company, and then sold to Robert

Nelson, who mined it as the Nelson Mine in 1876. After removing a great deal of iron ore, he then sold it back to the Cleveland Iron Mining Company in 1881 for $30,000. The Cleveland Iron Company began extensive diamond drilling, and discovered much ore from 215 feet to 308 feet down with the ore being about 50 feet in thickness, much of it being "first class ore."

In 1895, The Cleveland Hematite mine was working three shifts of eight hours each, but noted that ore was running out. After being abandoned for over 40 years, it eventually became the Mather "A" Mine in the 1940's. Remnants of the rock piles of the original mine can be seen just to the north east in aerial photos of the Mather "A" shaft. (These might also be the remains of an "Ames Mine" that operated briefly in 1893 and 1894.) The book, Historic Resources of the Iron Range in Marquette County tells us that there were four Cleveland Hematite Mine shafts just behind the present National Guard Armory on U.S.-41. It looks to the author that one was right in the south-east corner of the lawn of the Armory itself. All work was underground.

THE NEW YORK

The New York Mine owned 40 acres, and was right next to the Cleveland on the north side. Its pit is still very visible from Seventh Street. It began just a year later than the Cleveland, in 1864, and up to 1880, had mined almost half of what the Cleveland had mined, 866,413 gross tons, versus 1,942,000 gross tons from the Cleveland. It was owned by Mr. A. R. Harlow of Marquette. The mine consisted of four inclined pits and followed the ore bodies, which tilted from about 32 to 57 degrees downward.

1883 was a large shipping year for the New York, also called the "York" mine. By 1888, there was another mine just east of the New York Mine, and it had two shafts, the second which is down 100 feet with a second drift started in it. It is called the East New York Mine. A note in the newspaper on 12/30/1893 stated that the York Mine is "nearly worked out," and it stopped shipping for 5 years. However, with the "ups and downs" in the sale of ore, the mine shipped again in 1899 and 1900 and lastly, in 1919. Its total shipments were 1,124,182 tons, some from underground.

THE LAKE SUPERIOR

The Lake Superior Mine land was awarded to John Burt in 1850 and began as two long and narrow open pits, 105 feet deep,, west of South Pine Street and not too far from the present ECI offices, which is the old "Burt Office Building" of the Mine. If you look down the south side of the building to the west in the 1880's, you would see Shaft House No. 1, just inside the present fence area. We have a photo of it. (You will also see a low flat extension at the rear of the Burt Office and may wonder what that was. It was a bowling alley for the executives.). The shaft today is inconspicuously covered. The reason for two pits was that the ore body seemed to be like a basin, underground in the middle, but at surface on the north and south edges. The ore body ran east and west. This was a hard ore mine.

The mine was organized in 1853, and its first shipments were made in 1858. In 1870, it was the first mine to use a diamond drill for exploring for iron ore on the Marquette Range. The Lake Superior Mine became very large. On April 23, 1881, the paper noted that the Lake Superior mine distributed $70,000 to its workers this week (they are paid monthly).

There was a huge pit in the hard ore mine, built in the South Barnum Mine area, south west of Ishpeming's down-town and the "Burt" Office. It had a hoisting and pumping room of 54 x 92 feet and had two 8-foot drums, holding 1500 feet of 1.5 inch steel cable each. These were the largest drums in use in any iron mine in the Upper Peninsula, but were exceeded by 25 foot drums at the Calumet and Hecla Copper Mine in the Keweenaw Peninsula of the U.P. The pumps were two 14-inch plunger pumps. There was also a boiler room of 40 x 55 feet, and an Air compressor room of 40 x 37 feet. Compressed air ran the drills in the mine. There were seven shafts and they mined ore from 280 to 400 feet down. Shafts could be vertical or inclined. In 1881, 262,235 tons of ore were shipped, and a grand total since opening 24 years before, of 2,666,456 tons. Approximately 500 men were employed in 1881.

It was announced in the spring of 1882 that the hard ore mine will now install 12 foot hoisting drums. The mines are getting deeper and also need thicker steel cable for heavier loads in larger shafts.

In 1886 the men at the mine were reduced from about 500 to 350.. At the same time, in 1886, the Lake Superior Iron Company put down a diamond drill in a quartz vein north of the city to check for gold. It looked good and an 8 x 8 foot shaft went down. They were also working with an exploratory area by Third Street, west of the Detroit Mine, where they had several shafts, one down 400 feet.

In the 1870's and 1880's, the Lake Superior Company opened two other mines called the Lake Superior Hematite and a mine between Main and Pine Streets, by Johnson Street. We will cover those two mines at this time, and then also give the reader some details of the Section 16 Mine before returning to the Lake Superior Iron Company work in total from the 1890's on.

THE LAKE SUPERIOR HEMATITE MINE

By 1868, there was a second mine, called the Lake Superior Hematite, as its ore was different, although it was right next to the L. S. Hard Ore Mine. A written picture of this underground mine was printed in the October 1, 1868 issue of the Marquette Plain Dealer, when the editor was able to go down into the mine. The mine was then only 11 years old. Here is part of his report:

"We donned a miner's suit, and provided with a lighted candle descended the main shaft by ladder. An intelligent miner guided us down and enlightened us on the principles of the pumping, hoisting, and other mining machinery, we found in the shaft. We were surprised at the amount of work that has been done here. Drifts run in every possible direction. The floors are covered with three inch plank, there is a cistern 16 feet in depth and with the pumping machinery combine to keep the drifts free of water......Something novel to us was to find two cart horses that had been underground for two months and seemed in good condition......We forgot to mention that the depth of the main shaft was 100 feet..."

The Hematite Mine began south of the Hard Ore mine, between it and the hill to the south., with the ore body from the Hematite Mine crossing South Pine Street, and going south-east over to the shore of Lake Angeline. Hematite is a soft, very red, ore, often mined with just a pick and shovel. A December, 1880, article in the Mining Journal notes that the ore is "of a fine-grained granular variety", and notes that it runs downhill underground towards the Lake, and is up to 40 and 50 feet thick. This mine had ultimately three shafts. One was the shaft that sits right next to Pine Street, not too far south of the mine office, on the east side of the road.. This was the shaft that the men used to descend into the workings and was called the "Cage Shaft". By 1881, this shaft was not only pumping out the mine, but as Lake Angeline was near, it was also the "Pump House" for sending city water to Ishpeming residents.

Shaft "2" was originally just about 130 feet from the shoreline of the original Lake Angeline. It ran down at a 65 degree angle. It received a large shaft-house in October of 1890. The shaft was down 444 feet and the waste rock was put into Lake Angeline. The shipping of ore began. However, in November, a month later, there was a bad fire in this shaft over a period of two weeks. No sealing up was required. Ironically, after Lake Angeline was pumped out in 1891,, in November of 1892 the shaft closed and 90 men were out of work. We find that in June of 1893 that exploratory work is being carried on at the bottom of the shaft, and the shaft was later used once again for mining..

Today, both shafts are fenced in, and according to a report about 1913, the eastern most one by the lake had settled about 12 feet lower than the land around it while still in use. It may even be a bit lower today, and it is now next to the present shoreline,. The shaft, which is just behind the homes on the east side of S. Pine street is on private property. Back in the 1890's, it was soon discovered that the ore body also ran south along the Lake area to the border of the Lake Angeline Mine. Thus, a third shaft was built behind the homes at the south- west corner of the Lake. The Hematite Mine did a great deal of diamond drilling, with one drill hole going down 960 feet on the "baseball diamond." It was known as the Owls' diamond

already in 1913, because of the Owls' organization in town.

THE LAKE SUPERIOR MINE AT THE SOUTH END OF MAIN STREET

On December 13, 1879, the "Cage" or "A" shaft was sunk by the Lake Superior Mine along South Pine Street. A diamond drill was "put down" 457 feet north of this shaft and took a sample core for 963 feet. It hit 50 feet of ore just 215 feet from the surface., and a drift was made towards the ore body.. As 15 tenement houses of the company were in this place, they were moved down to First Street near Division. (10/23/1880). The drift went through this ore, and mined it from below, but left a roof of 20 feet of iron ore over it to hold up the dirt and sand. To get the ore of this roof, a pit was dug down 200 feet between Pine and Main Streets and south of Johnson Street. The May 22, 1880, issue of the newspaper noted that the Lake Superior Company had built a large derrick to hoist from the pit to a rail line at the head of Main Street. (There was no LS&I railroad in existence there at this time) The deep pit was completed about June 4, 1881.

Many of you remember this large pit that was in front of the present Pioneer Bluff Apartments. After the ore was removed from the pit, a drift was put in at the bottom of the pit, to go west, under S. Pine Street, to get the ore under the road. Mr. Newett tells us that townspeople came every day to watch the miners at work in this open pit. After several years the dirt at the west end of the pit where Pine Street was, began to fall into the pit as the ore body was mined out.. Pine Street was getting narrower and narrower and bending into a hoop around the mine. Mr. Newett thought that they should probably move the street, but the town demanded the Superior Mine repair Pine Street, as Pine Street served many other local mines, as well as the Excelsior Furnace, and National Mine area and beyond.

The railroad brought in much sand to cover a wood tunnel that formed a drift in the sand under the road, and South Pine was restored in 1890. The pit we evidently saw in the 1950's was evidently already partly filled, and the drift, with the wood tunnel entrance, was long covered with water. Many of us remember the same South Pine Street caving in and being closed off on the east lane on many occasions, as caving still occurred from time to time. In fact, if you look at the ground currently, where the pit was, you will see a dip at the west side of the nice lawn, and in the road as well, even though it has only been a few years since the pit was completely filled. The wood tunnel is probably still rotting.

THE SECTION 16 MINE

The Section 16 Mine was located on the south side of the hill from the Lake Superior Hard Ore Mine, and west of the Lake Angeline Mine. The Section 16 mine was another Lake Superior Iron Company Mine in the city of Ishpeming, starting in October of 1887. The ore it mined was mostly "Abbotsford" hard specular, the best grade the company shipped. The Section 16 Mine had a cave-in in the summer of 1890. Luckily the Lake Angeline Mine had a safety drift to the Section 16. This was used to reach the "cave-in" area. There were evidently no deaths. At the end of 1890, the paper tells us that a large shaft house is going up at Section 16 Mine. In June of 1893 the shaft was down 530 feet. In February of 1894 we read a note that again the surface was broken for a new shaft north of the railroad tracks in the west end of the old wood yard. It will be 7 x 8 feet, and on an incline.

A RETURN TO THE LAKE SUPERIOR

MINE GENERAL WORKINGS IN 1890

In 1887, we know that 500 men are working at this time at the Lake Superior Mine, with 90 men laid off for the winter.

At the end of 1889, the Lake Superior total payroll for November was $45,000., and shipped the greatest amount of ore of all Marquette county mines for the year of 276,579 tons of ore. The Cleveland shipped 262,835 tons of ore, and the Lake Angeline was at 226,614 tons.. We note that the Republic mine, although not near Ishpeming, was overall second in tonnage with 263,555 tons That town was growing at this time and even had its own newspaper, the Republic Sun (11/29/1890). The Salisbury was also listed at 57,626 tons. The paper noted that the Detroit Mine does not have an encouraging outlook.

In 1891, the Lake Superior purchased the largest steam shovel in the area, a 60 ton. However, problems were encountered when they found it did not have enough power to lift any ore in its bucket. Not beaten, the Shovel was rebuilt with more power.

The west end of the mine had run out of ore by 1891 and the process began of filling up the underground mined out rooms with rock, starting at the bottom. Then the pillars of ore of each level were removed, the rock now holding up the roof of each level.

In 1893, the Lake Superior Mine began to pay its men with checks, but mines were having a hard time selling their ore. Only 99 men were now working here, with 250 laid off, while the Lake Angeline had 750 working. Only a week or two after this report, however, the Lake Angeline received orders from Pittsburg to also reduce its forces, and to close its "C" shaft.

In the summer of 1894, as pillars were being removed at the Lake Superior hard ore, Mr. Newett tells us that the entire #6 shaft is being filled with rock. Work, however, in October of that year was suspended at the Hematite Mine near Lake Angeline, and that 125,000 tons were sitting on the property, still unsold. The stock of the Lake Superior Mine dropped from an $80.00 a share high to only $20.00 a share in this period according to the newspaper issue of April 14, 1894. In early 1895, Mr. Newett reports that 600 men are still employed, but this may include all of the Lake Superior Mines, including the Section 16.

In February of 1896 the Lake Superior Iron Company found more hematite ore under Lake Angeline and planned to put down its Lake Shaft down to 800 feet to reach it. At the same time, they were now taking hard ore from the old Barnum Mine through their mine. By the spring of 1896, in April, mines again had ore not sold and a total of about 600 miners were planned to be "let out." The Lake Superior in that same month paid $55,000 for a months pay to about 1000 miners, but then layoffs began at most of the mines. The Lake Superior Lake Shaft, now down 816 feet, suspended operations.

By 1897 Mines were again working full speed, and the Lake Superior mine, using results from its diamond drills near the Lake Angeline Mine Office, decided to start mining ore underneath the old west end of the former Angeline Lake bed.

Without any news in 1898, we read two news items on the Lake Superior on February 25, 1899. The first is that the Lake Superior Iron Company may be sold, and secondly that they are shipping ore all winter by rail. This seems to be a first although we don't know where they are shipping, but perhaps to the Gary, Indiana area via Chicago. This is pure speculation, however.

In the newspaper on April 29, 1899, there is a news item that the Oliver Mining Company of Minnesota had purchased the Lake Superior Mine in its entirety. Almost immediately, a mine shaft was started at the Iron Mountain Lake, now Lake Ogden, on the old Cliff Drive. At the time of this writing, in 2005, the large Tilden Open Pit Mine Stock pile is up to the north shore of the Iron Mountain Lake and covers the old railroad track into the Ogden Mine.

Please note that all of the Lake Superior Mine, which was owned by the Oliver Mining Company of Minnesota for many years, is now in private ownership. Some private access is allowed, but the investigator must obey the signs.

THE BARNUM AND THE CLIFFS SHAFTS

The Barnum Mine was owned by the Iron Cliff's Company which eventually became the Cleveland Cliffs Mining Company when it merged with the Cleveland Mining Company in 1891. Previous to the merger, Mr. Barnum often came to visit the mines here as President of the Iron Cliffs Company..

The single original pit was just north of the Lake Superior Mine, and, as the ore went across property boundaries from one mine into the other, and down in both mines, a wall of ore was left on each level to divide the two, like a fence. Today the pit is partially filled, as for many years the garbage of Ishpeming was placed and burned in this pit. One can still drive to near it on west Johnson Street. The first note we see about the Barnum is in an early 1870 Ishpeming area newspaper when there is information on their constructing "receptacles for storing nitro-glycerin, having decided to use this powerful explosive hereafter." It also notes that "the prejudice heretofore existing among the men is rapidly dying out, and the prospect now is that before long it will come into general use."

In an article from an area paper on January 10, 1874, it is noted that the ore is a "clean, beautiful slate" ore. Mr. Sedgwick of the Jackson mine was stated to be in charge of the Barnum. It notes that there is also a second Barnum opening near-by, and it originally was called the Parsons Mine, and at this time was now mined by the Lake Superior Iron Company..

The Barnum Mine seemed to be running out of ore when a diamond drill discovered 50 feet of ore at a depth of 585 feet. The ore body was found to go for 3,800 feet, or about three-quarters of a mile north. This resulted in the moving of the mine from the south side of Division Street to the west end of Strawberry Hill. From 1879 to 1882, an "A" shaft was put down, 10 x 14 feet with two compartments, and lined with twelve-inch square sawed pine timber. As the Barnum knew the ore was there, when "A" shaft was completed, 12,000 tons of ore were removed in just four months.

If you are aware of what is taking place here, is that the "A" shaft is the current eastern pyramid shaft still standing at the end of West Ridge Street. Of course, it was not a concrete pyramid for about twenty years yet, but just a typical Iron and Steel Mine Shaft. If you always wondered why the Cliffs Shafts, were also called "The Barnum", now you know. For many years the Strawberry Hill mine was the Barnum, or the "New Barnum." Here is the rest of the story.

The beginning of the New Barnum and the shafts began with an article in the Weekly Agitator's March 20, 1880, issue about a shaft down on Strawberry Hill, called "A". It was already down 50 feet and pumps were working with the note that working conditions were very wet. Note was also made that there was a western "B" shaft underway. It will be the "B" shaft that is in the news. It notes that the engine house for both shafts will be in the center of the two, and will work both shafts with two four-and-a-half-foot drums for winding cable.

"B" shaft started out quite well......for the first 25 feet. By July 17, 1880, it is noted in the paper that "A" is now down 145 feet, but no word about "B". On August 7, "A" is down 150 feet, and there is a note that "B" shaft work is stopped until the "sand problem" is solved. At the end of December there are more details about "B": "Still having a quick-sand problem..... five or six feet of sand in bottom of shaft in 24 hours......pumps plug and stall.....will be 450 feet deep when completed."

The problem did not improve. The newspaper noted on March 26, of the next spring, that the "sand shaft" at Strawberry Hill's swamp was filled with 20 feet of sand in the bottom of the shaft and sinking the shaft is difficult. At the same time, "A" shaft is down 330 feet and the Engine House and other buildings were being erected. On June 11, 1881, it was announced that "B" shaft was abandoned for now because of the quicksand problem. It was down only 42 feet.

Work on "A" shaft continued and at the end of August it was down 415 feet with only 35 feet to go. At the end of November, the railroad was putting in a branch track for "A" shaft.

In 1882, a new effort was made to control the "B" shaft problem. A heavy iron tube or caisson, ten feet in diameter, was built and allowed to sink as the men built the shaft downward, holding back the sand. Shaft timbering was stopped until the shaft and steel "barrel" slid down and past the bothersome sand. However, it did not work as the quicksand pressure was so great that when the caisson got to within 6 feet or so of the rock ledge it was badly crushed by the pressure. Thus work was stopped once again on "B" shaft. In the meantime, "A" shaft on Strawberry Hill was equipped with a cage to carry miners and timber. For many years the ore was also brought up on the cage. A first level was built from the shaft out to the bottom of the hill near-by the railroad to the south, and materials were carried in to the shaft in that drift. It is noted that this new Cliff Shafts Mine had such hard ore that no timbering was ever needed. By 1887, the "B" shaft problem of quicksand was solved, and the shaft house was built and the new shaft completed.

The Old Barnum was still running, but by 1886, the ore pillars left to hold up the roof of the mine on each level started to be removed and planned caving in was taking place.

In 1893, the New Barnum Mine was forced to shut off its pumps and the mine partially flooded because of poor ore sales. In 1894 the new mine installed a large 28 ton crusher built by Lake Shore Iron Works in Marquette, but because of the hardness of the ore, it broke some of the castings from time to time. It was entirely rebuilt to a weight of 41 tons. Eventually a second crusher was also installed enabling the mine to crush to two different sizes.

In 1894, the Cliffs Shafts had mined for a distance of 2,410 feet by 600 feet wide. The ore was found underground at a depth of 424 feet. The area is not solid ore, but found in pockets which were stoped out. The newspaper noted that the mine is under Lake Bancroft, and to the

east the mine is just 80 feet from Main Street of town. Then, due to poor ore sales, the mine closed down entirely. Even the steam boilers were stopped.

On October 2, 1897, it was announced that the Cliffs Shafts will again be run by the Cleveland Cliffs Iron Company, after being idle since 1894. In spite of the fact that so many mines were "down" for much of 1897, it is surprising to read in the paper in the autumn, that all mines went "full steam." In fact, the mines were so busy by winter that the paper notes that "All men can now find work in the woods or the mines." In fact there was once again, a shortage of miners. Yet in Butte, Montana, 1,200 miners were idle and mines are only working moderately.

By April of 1898, the Cliffs Shafts are pumped out and men enter the shafts to start cleaning up.

We note in 1899 that the Cleveland Cliffs offices moved from the Cleveland Mine area on Division Street to the Cliffs Shafts area on Lake Bancroft. The original road from Strawberry Hill to U.S.-41, north of the city, went behind the south side of this office along the rock wall still present, and right in front of the dry that is now the museum. Lake Bancroft was larger at this time.

The Cliffs Shaft Mine produced a total of almost 29 million long tons of high grade hard iron ore when shipping stopped in 1968 and is the longest living iron ore mine in the entire Lake Superior Region.

THE LAKE ANGELINE

At the time of this writing, the Lake Angeline Mine is a mine still quite accessible to the public, it still being owned by the Cleveland

Cliff's Iron Company, and is full of public trails for biking, hiking, and jogging east from South Pine Street to the former Cliff's Drive road by Suicide Ski Hill, and from Hill Street in the Cleveland Location. There are many shafts, pits, and some caving areas that are fenced in. Please obey the signs. In the old mines, the first levels often started only 50 feet down, and stopes may be even closer to the surface after mining ore out. It may be that some of these early levels and drifts are above the water table and empty, making them more susceptible to caving in when disturbed.

The Mine was officially owned by the Pittsburgh and Lake Angeline Iron Company, but the Pittsburg part was hardly ever used in any newspaper articles. The Mine started in about 1864, and 17 years later, in 1881, it had shipped 525,637 tons of iron ore.

The original mine was 1000 feet long and consisted of two pits, with a pillar of land between. In that pillar was a shaft to pump out water. The pits ran east and west. The western one contained "workings" 1 and 2. . The eastern pit held "workings" 3 and 4. By 1882, the ore had run out of area 4, and work area 3 had rock falling down from the overhanging face, so that it was dangerous for the men to try to remove the ore as an open pit operation. It was decided then, to go under area 3 from the 2 workings, through the pillar, to obtain the ore of workings 3. The ore on this west end (3 & 4) was a softer hematite ore, but that on the east end (1 & 2) was a hard ore

The mine is then working more toward the east and several houses were built on the south side of Lake Angeline in 1882, and Angeline Street was extended to the top of Terrace Hill to the south of the Mine. By 1888 we find that the mine is shipping an average of 60 ore cars a day. In 1890, what might have been a very serious

accident was averted when 12 men that were cut off by an underground landslide in their portion of the mine were rescued 12 hours later.

In 1890, the other Ishpeming Newspaper, The Peninsula Record talked about the Lake Angeline mine, but was so badly written and incorrect as to how things operated underground, that Mr. Newett used his Iron Ore newspaper to set things straight with a large 4 column front-page rebuttal. The key item was how the ore was mined from large deposits many feet high. The old system was to put up pieces of wood and build "squares" upon each other to keep reaching to the top of the ore body, using tons of wood. This was the Record's explanation. "No," said Mr. Newett, and he explained the present system. It might be interesting for the reader to read how it worked.

From the September 20, 1890 issue of the Iron Ore: "The miners of the Lake Angeline, with the shafts into the ore, open levels every fifty feet. Starting at a distance from the shafts that gave the latter solid ground, they begin the opening out of "rooms." These rooms are eighteen feet in width and are carried to a height of four sets.....The room when worked to the top of the last set has a height of 38 feet. There has been a body of ore mined out having dimensions of 18 x 38 feet, and as wide as the lens of ore may be. Above there is still twelve feet of ore which remains untouched. This room mined out to the described extent, the miners then cut a rise (raise) through the roof to the level above, and through this opening dirt is milled down and the place lately occupied by ore is filled with rock and dirt from other portions of the mine which can easily be obtained..........The room filled, the miners then go along the level to open another room. They leave a pillar of ore of about the same size as the room, 18 feet, between the rooms." Mr. Newett goes on to note that when the second room is mined to 38 feet, a hole is also made to the next level and rock dumped in it to fill it up. He then tells us that they take out the 18 feet of pillar left to hold up the roof, and then also the remaining 12 feet of ore at the top of the rooms up to the next level. He admits to the competing newspaper that there are, indeed, some cracks that form underground, but notes that are not in the business of "gardening."

By 1891, the Lake Angeline Mine built a large, new dry for the miners with hardwood floors. The newspaper notes that hardwood floors are now popular. It also joined a drift with a drift of the Cleveland Lake Mine during that summer. In 1892, Lake Angeline was pumped dry at a rate of 24 million gallons a day by using a ditch.(June 12, 1892) Pumping using a pipe began in July as the ditch kept filling itself in by erosion. The pump was expected to remove the last two-thirds of the body of water in one month. On December 24, 1892 the paper noted that the pumping of Lake Angeline was completed but that the pump would run periodically as water reforms in the bottom.

In October of 1892, the Lake Angeline Mine started a three-month trial of an 8-hour day. At the end of the year it was formally adopted. It was, however, only working two shifts as things were slow by 1893. In 1893 it had prepared for hauling ore with electric motors in the mine. In 1893 it also received orders to close, which followed a motion to strike by the miners. By May of 1894, however, many men were hired, including 75 transfers from the Volunteer Pit. The water was being pumped out of the lower levels of the mine. Note was made, however, that no ore had been sold. On the other hand, some mines were doing well. The Winthrop in National was producing 600 tons a day of ore with plans to ship 50,000 tons for the year. What seemed to make the difference is whether the ore was Bessemer or non-Bessemer.

The new steel mills were using the Bessemer process and needed an ore with certain qualities for this oxygen process. Some mines had these and some did not. During this time Mr. Mather himself, from Cleveland, announced a layoff of 150 men from their mines, as "non-bessemer ores are selling slowly."

By 1897 the Lake Angeline had several shafts, and note is made that a new shaft is doing well and three old shafts are being abandoned.

THE LAKE ANGELINE EAST END MINE

The East End Mine of the Lake Angeline today can be seen from South Pine Street as a point of land on the East Side of the Lake, jutting out westerly in the water. The old railroad grade from the Lake Angeline pit and Street area is part of the hiking trail system, and a hoist house foundation of the East End Mine is still in quite good condition. This mine began sometime after the Lake itself was drained in 1892. It was also known as "Old Fifty-Six."

After a large area-wide 1895 strike was over, there occurred on January 11, 1896, a large cave-in at the Lake Angeline East End Mine on the second level. That level was blocked up, and the mine then went down and began a third level from the shaft to come up to the second level and to obtain the ore. It was only three months later when "hard times" befell the mines and the Lake Angeline dismissed 300 men and planned to maybe close the East End mine instead. Men were asking if maybe they could even work half-time. Then they even asked if maybe they could work for three months "for paper" (I.O.U's). But it was announced that the entire mine would close on September 26. It was only about a week's notice. Luckily, the Lake Superior Company would continue to operate its mines, and continued to do exploring with diamond drills. They were even drilling just 300 feet east from the Lake Angeline Mine Office, and on the edge of their own property.

We should also note that it was in these years of the 1895 and 1896 that the brand-new Lake Superior and Ishpeming Railroad began and to get their track to the Lake Angeline and Salisbury Mines. They built their track around the north and west side of the Lake Superior Mine and around the hill south of that mine and through the Junction area and came through what is now the Section 16 Lake (pit) from the west.

As things go in mining, by the end of the year 1896, the mines were again hiring, but those laid off had to contend with many others arriving in town who also wanted to get hired. Mr. Newett asked, "Who is sending them?" Mr. Newett also noted that national news showed that there was still a lot of unsold ore way down in Cleveland, Ohio, sitting on the docks.

We now get to April of 1897, and we find that indeed, a third level has been put into the East End Mine of the Lake Angeline Company. Not only that, but it is using electricity to run motors to take out the ore and they are "doing well." In April of 1899 the East End Mine drifted south into Terrace Hill and removed ore from inside of it. Eventually a fourth level was added that found rich ore, and then a fifth, and by 1913 there was a sixth level with a sub shaft down from that drift. There was not much diamond drilling by this company, Mr. Newett Noted, and tongues of ore are simply followed as they are discovered underground. Mr. Newett also noted in the January 4, 1913, issue of the Iron Ore that the East End Mine was a "wonderfully big one."

THE SALISBURY MINE

This mine was built, going south from the Lake Angeline Mine, on the opposite and south side of the large Terrace Hill. It was a mine formed in 1872 to pick up the ore body from the Angeline as it came through and under the hill, and off of the Lake Angeline Mine property. Like the Barnum, the Salisbury was also a Cliff's Iron Company Mine. It was a small mine, but it had a rich ore that improved the deeper the shafts went down in the earth. Steel Companies contracted for its ore, and the mine ran almost continuously even when other mines were unable to sell their ore. It ran for 52 years until 1924.

It began at the far east portion of the property, where Terrace Hill, and another hill to the right, joined together. Two open pits were dug in the valley between. A band of land was left between the two pits, and eventually a shaft was put into the south-east corner of the eastern-most pit. This shaft, built in 1877, went under the second pit and then, when a third pit was dug some distance away to the west, the tunnels, or drifts, from shaft one also went under pit three. It followed along the base of Terrace Hill and an 1883 article noted that there was 70 feet of ore above the length of the drift. The hoisting drum from the sole shaft was a four-foot one. The Chicago and Northwestern Railroad put in a single track into the mine, and Salisbury Street would grow up on both sides of the track. Today the track is gone, but many homes remain.

By 1887 there was a second shaft built, and it was at pit three, and soon after, a shaft three on the south-east edge of pit three. This shaft re-opened in the 1950's when planks rotted, and the shaft hole now has a concrete cap over it. The railroad tracks were moved around to accommodate the shaft currently being used.

The Chicago and Northwestern shipped from its port in Escanaba, and much of the Salisbury ore was made into pig iron for shipping at their Pioneer Furnace in Negaunee and other furnaces in the Upper Peninsula as well, sometimes being shipped to St. Ignace.

In 1889, a new, large shaft Four would be built in a new area south of the shafts Two and Three. Many problems resulted at this shaft. Upon completion, there was a large cave-in. First the underground ledge that all the new mine was built on broke off and the surface fell quite a distance down. Several weeks were used, with many wagons, to fill in the pit that formed. The shaft was not in the best of shape, but useable. Machinery was also bent and had to be repaired in a surface pump house. Then a second disaster occurred. Along with other mining men of other mines, the men went on strike, the first ever. The mine decided to spite them and closed off the pumps. As some of the ore was a soft hematite variety, the flooding water really made it like oatmeal, and the shaft was so out of line that the entire mine had to be move again, back by shafts Two and Three, but a bit to the west. The newest shaft was largely built up from the bottom up from old drifts, as well as from the top down, and the two met within a foot or so of each other. It was a large shaft that changed direction several times, and it was quite an invention to run the hoist and its cables through the downward tunnel that was built at different angles. The New and Final Shaft had its hoist house high on Terrace Hill and began operating in 1899. The skip was unique with wheels to ride on tracks on both sides.

The Salisbury Mine hard and hematite ores were better and better the further down the mine went and also much in demand by the Pioneer Furnace in Negaunee in 1893. So that the reader will not be left in the cold as to where the furnaces were, we have put in a special section for them. In 1893 employment was 200 men at the Salisbury.. In spite of the many unemployed miners, and closed mines, including the Cliffs Shafts and Lake Angeline, the Salisbury hired 75 men for the night shift on February 24, 1894. We shall also note that the Salisbury Mine never used electricity underground, and when the mine closed in 1924, mules were brought up after many years of year-around life underground.

Total ore shipments for the Salisbury were 4,489,102 tons.

THIS IS A PHOTO OF THE MATHER A MINE OF THE 1940'S TO THE 1960'S. HOWEVER, BEHIND THE SHAFTHOUSE ONE CAN SEE THE REMAINS OF THE OLD NELSON MINE, WITH THREE ROCK PILES GOING OUT FROM A FORMER SHAFT IN A FINGER-LIKE PATTERN TOWARD TEAL LAKE.
THE PHOTO BELOW SHOWS A SHAFT HOUSE TO THE LEFT BEHIND THE BURT BUILDING STILL PRESENT ON SOUTH PINE STREET (JUNE, 1990, CALENDAR OF THE FRIENDS OF THE ISHPEMING CARNEGIE LIBRARY.)

Chapter 7:
Newer and Near-by Mines

Mines were soon numbering in the 30's, and beginning to flourish in Negaunee as well. We name here just a few of the ones closest to Ishpeming.

CLEVELAND IRON COMPANY THIRD STREET MINE

The Cleveland Iron Co. in 1892 sunk a shaft west of Third Street in the north part of Ishpeming. It was 80 feet down and meeting sand and boulders in February of that year. Work in the shaft was stopped and diamond drills took over the exploratory work.

THE DETROIT MINE

The Detroit Mine was located in the general area of the present US-41 in the area of the Ishpeming-Negaunee City Limits. The description is the NE quarter of the NE quarter of Section 3, T47N-R27W. In 1882 it opened as the Norwich, but operated by the Detroit Iron Mining Company through 1890.

We can note here that it was at this time in 1887 that the Detroit Mine flooded when a body of water was tapped at the 400 foot level and men rushed to surface but almost were swept away. There was 120 feet of water in the mine in three hours, but was running normally and pumped out in just a few weeks.

At the end of 1890 the new Detroit Mine Shaft was still progressing, but three months later, the Mine was temporarily closed with a decision to sell the mine.. Shaft work must have continued, however, because in March of 1891 we find that the old and new shafts have been connected underground. In August, however, even the exploratory work stopped. And in October, a note in the paper tells us that the "Detroit Mine is now filling up with water." This is the last mention of that mine. It shipped a total of 141,841 tons of underground soft ore.

THE EAST NEW YORK

The East New York Mine was opened in 1888 by the Ishpeming Mining Company and was taken over by the Ames Mine at the end of 1893. The Ames was owned by Mr. Braastad and had a shaft down 100 feet and twenty men were working there. Since his mine was just north and east of the New York, the two shafts were joined together by a lower level drift. In the hard times of 1894 the mine must have closed down because on September 9, 1899, we read that the East New York is getting de-watered so it will be ready to mine once again. Two other wonderful things were happening for this mine and the others. Lake Superior was higher in 1899 than it had been for the last 23 years, allowing more depth in the Sault Locks and heavier boat loads. The other nice item is the fact that all the mines decided to give a ten cent an hour raise.

The East New York was in the SW q. of the SW q. of Section 2, T47N-R27W. It shipped 327,604 tons of hard ore through 1895, all from underground.

THE HOLMES

The Holmes was opened at the Winthrop Junction Location in 1915 and shipped from 1917 to 1929. By 1930 the Section 16 Mine was caving to the south-east of the Holmes. The Cleveland Cliffs Iron Company sold the Holmes to the Oliver Company who transferred their

Section 16 work to the Holmes. The details of this mine are found in the yearly write-ups up to 1920. The mine operated until 1946.

IRON VALLEY MINE

A note in the September 7, 1889, paper tells us that there is also a new Iron Valley Mine in the Ishpeming Corporate Limits next to the East New York Mine, but nothing else is heard about it.

THE LAKE SALLY-IRON MOUNTAIN LAKE MINE

This mine was opened in 1865 as the Iron Mountain Lake Property. It only shipped 35,434 tons and was located on Lots 4, 5, 6, & 8 of the SW quarter of the SW q. and SE q. of the SE q., all in Section 14, T47N-R27W. From the SW q. it shipped 16,700 tons in 1915-1916.

THE MARQUETTE

Located near the Lake Sally Mine in the North half of the North half of Section 14, it opened in 1860 and shipped approximately 268,000 tons of ore by open pit.

THE MITCHELL

The Mitchell was also called the Braastad and Shenago and was located on the W half of the SE q. of Section 21, T47N-R27W. It opened in 1872 and shipped until 1888, and then again from 1908 to 1913. It was both open pit and underground and had a soft ore. Shipping was 233,750 tons.

THE MORO

The Moro Mine is located south of the Ishpeming Bell Memorial Hospital and its two shafts are still rather open and sitting right at the edge of Bluff Street. At least one of these was an air shaft for the Cliffs Shafts which ultimately also mined the Moro Ore. Extra shafts were always useful for sending fresh air down into the mines. Sometimes even 16 inch drill holes were used as fresh air conductors. It opened in 1890 and shipped until 1918. Up to 1899, the mine had been closed for some years, but at this time the shaft (evidently only a single shaft at this time in history) was pumped out and mining again was planned. It ultimately shipped 1,119,854 tons of hard ore before becoming part of the Cliffs Shafts. Its official location is the S half of the NE q. of Section 10, T47N-R27W.

THE NATIONAL

The National is mentioned here as it was just outside of the city limits to the south of the city on the original South Pine Street from Salisbury. The road is still there and walkable, but closed to traffic. This mine was opened in 1878 by Captain Samuel Mitchell. There were several larger mines in the same area, including the Mitchell and the Winthrop, but the new Post Office took the name of National. There were five pits and one shaft. It only shipped for six years until 1884, but in 1950, rock piles of salable ore were also sold.

THE WINTHROP

This originally was the Braastad Mine. It opened in 1869 and shipped to 1889. The total tonnage at this time was 832,445 tons. However it reopened as the Winthrop from 1890 to 1903 and shipped from underground and open pit, a total of 1,759,115 tons of soft ore.

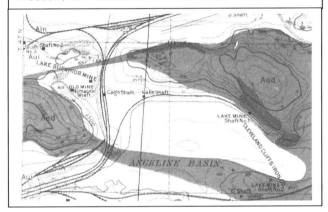

ABOVE IS THE CLEVELAND AREA MINE, AND BELOW SHOWS THE LAKE SUPERIOR, LAKE ANGELINE (UNSHOWN NAME), AND THE CLEVELAND LAKE MINE SHAFTS. THESE ARE FROM AN OLD GEOLOGIC MAP IN THE FRANK MATTHEWS MUSEUM, NOW THE NEGAUNEE HISTORICAL MUSEUM.

HERE IS THE LAKE SUPERIOR HEMATITE CAGE SHAFT ALONG SOUTH PINE STREET JUST SOUTH OF THE BURT OFFICE BUILDING. YOU WILL ALSO SEE IT LOCATED ON THE MAP ABOVE. THE MINERS USED THIS SHAFT FOR ENTERING AND EGRESS FROM THE UNDERGROUND MINE. THE SHAFT CAVES IN PERIODICALLY, AND EVEN NOW MAY HAVE A DIP IN THE CENTER AREA OF THE LAST FILL ADDED.

HERE IS THE 1911 ISHPEMING CO-OP STORE TRUCK.

CREDIT TO THE NEGAUNEE HISTORICAL MUSEUM AND MR. W. ROWE.

Chapter 8:
The Excelsior Peat, And other Furnaces

The first industries to treat iron ore were not very efficient and could not heat iron ore to a melting temperature, but could heat it up so that it could be worked, as in a blacksmith's shop. These were called Forges, and of course, the most popular one in Marquette County was the Carp River Forge where the Michigan Mine Museum now stands in east Negaunee, on the Carp River as it runs out of Deer Lake and Teal Lake and other tributaries.. Other forges followed, including the Collins Forge. As an experiment, the Collins was changed to a furnace, and it was a success, and then other furnaces followed. The job of these furnaces was to separate the ore from the rock and to make pig iron ingots. These were then shipped to the large Bessemer Furnaces in the lower Great Lakes where steel would be made. Steel soon was replacing iron in the rails, and wood in the building of ships.

For the process of making pig iron, heat from charcoal was used (Except for the original Excelsior Furnace). Wood was placed into specially-made Charcoal Kilns, the remains of which quite a few still exist, including a restored one on US-41 near the Marquette State Prison. Two other remains are west of Ishpeming, on the old US-41 just west of where the Gold Mine Lake Road turns off of it, which is also the road to the privately owned Barnes-Hecker Mine area.

The kilns used cords and cords of hardwood. Later, as hardwoods disappeared, they had to often mix in some softwood, such as spruce and balsam, and towards the turn of the century, hardly any kind of any wood was left in the Upper Peninsula for making charcoal. Often, a dozen or more kilns were built in hardwood groves of hundreds or thousands of acres, and the smell was a terrible stench. Later processes, including the large charcoal plant by the Cleveland Cliffs Iron Company in north Marquette, were able to treat the smoke from the burning wood and obtain several chemicals, including the liquid wood alcohol.

By 1900 there had been a total of 23 pig iron furnaces in the Upper Peninsula, and surprisingly, there were several also in the Lower Peninsula, and in Wisconsin. The Pioneer, in Negaunee, was by far the largest, producing over 637,000 tons in one year. It was operated by the Cleveland Cliffs Company for its mines. Furnaces in, or near, Marquette were the Collins, Northern, Bancroft, Morgan, Marquette & Pacific Rolling Mill, Grace, and Carp River. There were also furnaces in Champion, and Clarksburgh (The Michigan). The other near-by furnace was the Greenwood which produced 42,200 tons. The Ishpeming Furnaces were the Excelsior which produced 68,631 tons in its lifetime, and the Deer Lake Furnace which produced a total of 93,579 tons of pig iron.

THE EXCELSIOR PEAT FURNACE

The Excelsior Peat Furnace was built by the Lake Superior Iron Mining Company who owned the property, and was one of the most unique furnaces in America. In 1867 the first mention of peat being mined is at the east end of Teal Lake. Some pits may have existed there until recent development in the last 30 years. Those who moved to the area from England were familiar with peat, and its burning well when dried out. In Europe, it had been used to manufacture iron.

By 1870 a company called the Lake Superior Peat Works was operating on the property south of the Lake Superior Mine near Lake Angeline. It is noted that the Peat bed is 250 feet west of the works and the amount of peat is "inexhaustible". It was cut, ground, mixed, and put out to dry for five or six days and then put in sheds to dry for 6-12 more days. The Peat Works produced 25 tons of peat per day for burning. At this time, it was being sold for domestic use in homes.

Following the success of the Lake Superior Peat Works, the Excelsior Furnace was built in 1872, designed to use peat for fuel, and built in the same general area. The peat bed was estimated to be 200 acres, and nine feet deep. The peat bog was mined in blocks. The author has personally seen it mined this way in the Isle of Man in the Irish Sea. Shovels cut it as we formerly cut out blocks of snow in the winter, but peat was both more difficult and heavy, and often wet, when cut..

The furnace location is on South Pine Street, on the side of the hill to the north, now situated between two homes and covered with young forest. The property is privately owned. The address today would be in the 700's. This street, in reality, is two parallel roads, the railroad formerly having run between them. We are including some photos.

Peat is a very thick amount of roots and plant life and forms a bog, and locally is called "black muck.". In very dry periods, a bog can dry out and develop a soft, spongy surface, and deep holes that even a cow could fall into, and did. People who threw hot stove ashes out in bogs often started fires that were difficult to put out.

According to an article in the <u>Weekly Mining Journal</u> on October 26, 1872, we find the Excelsior Peat Furnace running on Peat alone and able to melt iron into ingots. After the ingots were formed, the rock slag, which also melted, was drained off into a slag pile and often looked like beautiful Tiffany glass. The Chicago Northwestern Railroad put in two different rails. One was to bring in the ore and the other to carry out the ingots to steel mills.

The furnace continued operating off and on by different owners and lease operators. However, it did not operate for a very long period using only peat. By 1880, the Excelsior Furnace was known as the "old peat furnace" and was running on coal, and charcoal. The largest problem to overcome was the spring water runoff and heavy downpours, that ran down the hill into the Furnace, and "swamped" everything. There was a good iron ore crusher. It was quite different from all other mine crushers, but worked very well, according to Mr. George Newett.

In June of the same year, 1880, the furnace caught on fire and was a $15,000. loss. The original equipment had been purchased and moved from the Greenwood Furnace. It was rebuilt. By December 11, it was again ready for "blast." With the new equipment, by April 2, of 1881, the Excelsior was producing 25 tons of pig iron every 24 hours. By the end of May, however, it went out of blast, with the hearth burned out, and needing six weeks of repair. This was the story of many of the furnaces and could be told over and over. In October the furnace was up and running again. Once it was sold to a man who had a lot of wood to burn and he ran the furnace at a good pace for a short period. In 1882 the furnace ran using 108 bushels of charcoal a day.

The furnace in the 1890's ran at full steam for several years with the top productions seeming to be in 1895 when pig iron produced averaged 63 tons a day, and 1,900 tons for the month of March. It is noted that it is making "Bessemer pig iron." For a few months that year, however, it was closed, and because of the great poverty in town at this time, people began to strip the machinery, including brass bearings. One of the last public items regarding the Excelsior in was when the Lake Superior Mining Institute toured the area mines, including the Excelsior Furnace. The furnace, being in blast, did a full charge with a cast of pig iron for the tour. The newspaper date was August 22, 1896.

One reason that no large pile of furnace cinders, or slag, exists at the site is that it was often taken for use in road fill, once being on the road to the National, and Winthrop Mines.

A further note in the <u>Iron Ore</u> tells us that the Escelsior Furnace was running yet in the summer of 1900, but its "days are numbered." The Furnace was purchased for the final time on August 18, of 1900. It was never opened, and on June 10, 1905, it was announced that the "Old Excelsior Furnace" has been torn down.

THE DEER LAKE FURNACE

The Deer Lake Furnace began in 1867 and went into blast in September of 1868. In the beginning, no railroad went to the Deer Lake Furnace, and wagons were required for everything. An original wagon road from the Deer Lake Furnace Road went to the New York Location road just north of the Peninsula Railroad tracks and went to Negaunee. This road was built in 1870. In addition, the Furnace built a second melting stack to increase production. This was in 1873, and it now took 39 charcoal kilns to feed the furnaces.

The Weekly Agitator began in October of 1879, and in February of 1880, tells us that the Deer Lake Furnace was in blast and was also producing 25 tons a day.

We must remember that Deer Lake was smaller at this time as the Cleveland Cliffs Company had not yet built a dam on the outlet's east end. Thus, most of the area where the Deer Lake Furnace was, is now under water, but was located just east of the bridge over the Carp River, where it enters the Lake on the south west corner. For power, the Deer Lake Furnace men built an eight-foot dam on the entering Carp River above the Furnace. They ran a large tube of water down to a separate building where the great force of water ran the turbine. The turbine powered large blowers of hot air used in the melting process. Water power saved the company a lot of money, except for the charcoal required to melt the iron ore. The water power was even greater than what was really needed by the Furnace, so the owners also built a Deer Lake Lumber company and also ran three saws with the water turbine. With a new Lumber Mill, in 1880, 15 additional wagons were ordered from Fond du Lac, Wisconsin.

The hauling by wagons was very inefficient. Wagons also had to haul the ore from the mines to the furnace. In 1880, the newspaper noted that the C&NW was surveying a line to the Deer Lake furnace from the Nelson Mine, "so that in the future ore can be conveyed by rail direct to the latter". The Nelson Mine was on Teal Lake's south side. The railroad never did come in from that direction, but a more efficient road did. In 1884 it was announced that the C&NW RR would be coming from the Ishpeming Cliffs Shafts, along the Carp river, to the Deer Lake Furnace, and Lumber Mill.

Usually an Iron Furnace would use limestone for flux. However, the Deer Lake Furnace was different in this respect, although some others also used the same type of flux. It used mined quartz for a flux. Mr. Ropes, later associated with the Ropes Gold Mine, was involved in many, many ways in the financial life of the city. At this time he was selling the rock that was used for flux in the Deer Lake Furnace from his quarry, located in the area of his gold mine

The Deer Lake Furnace was rather short lived, and it may have been because of the Ishpeming City sewer problem, the details of which are in Chapter Eleven. The city wanted to use the Carp River for sewage, but the drop in elevation was not great enough, and it certainly couldn't be used with an eight-foot dam on it. Thus, for $30,000.00, the city purchased the dam, tore it down, and lowered the falls six feet. This took place in 1890 and a few years following. The Furnaces of Deer Lake ended their life in 1891, after 23 years of existence. As was often the case, the remains of the equipment of the Furnaces and the Mill were all sold to a large Detroit scrap dealer.

THE CLEVELAND CLIFFS FURNACES

The Iron Cliffs Company built a Furnace that is not well known, and it was on the Cliffs Drive, when we had the Cliffs Drive. The furnace was across from the Foster Lake, at the base of the former TV-6 Television Tower at the Cliff Drive, but on the west side of the Lake. That is why many knew the lake as Furnace Lake, because of that furnace. The C&NW Railroad came in to the furnace area in 1867, from midway between Negaunee and Palmer. Construction of the Cliffs Furnace then began, but ended when winter set in. As times then got bad for the mines, the Cliffs was slow in getting completed but was producing pig iron by 1874. It didn't produce much, running only a few months at a time, and by 1879 it was closed up and the machinery taken to the Cliffs Pioneer Furnace in Negaunee. The Cliffs only produced 8,000 tons of pig iron. Much of this information is from the book, Flaming Brands, by Kenneth LaFayette. The railroad was not a total loss, as it continued running past the Furnace and on to the Tilden Mine just down the road a mile or two.

The large Pioneer Furnace in Negaunee was purchased by the Iron Cliffs Company a few years after being built, and became the furnace to which the Cliffs crushed iron ore went. The Iron Cliffs eventually became the Cleveland Cliffs Iron Company after merging with the Cleveland Iron Company. By 1896 this furnace had been dismantled, and the company built a large new furnace near Gladstone. According to details in the Iron Ore on February 1, 1896, the Gladstone Furnace was located on an island in Little Bay de Noquette (Noc), and was to go into production that spring. The CCI produced about 100 tons or more of pig iron daily, and sometimes averaged 130 tons. Near-by were 40 of the beehive charcoal kilns with each having a 65-ton capacity. Cleveland Cliffs had purchased 8,000 acres to supply the hardwood. The article also noted that 2,000 tons of crushed ore from the Ishpeming Cliffs Shafts were already at the furnace waiting for the first production.

THE GREENWOOD FURNACE

The Greenwood Furnace stack, just west of Ishpeming was still standing in the late 1940's. The author can remember the numerous pieces of colored glass and the gigantic stack that one could walk in at the bottom. It was torn down about 1950. It was located close to the present Wawonowin Golf Course, in a westerly direction in the Greenwood Location area.

According to Kenneth D. LaFayette, the Furnace was built by the Marquette and Ontonagon Railroad in 1865. It was repaired from time to time, and used quarried stone from right by the site for the large stack. By 1871 it was in "full blast" and burning up 125 tons of charcoal for every ton of iron ingots made. Soon the wood all around the furnace was gone, and a plank road that was 10 miles long was built to haul the wood from charcoal kilns in the forest. Ore used was from the Lake Superior and the Washington Mines.. The Michigan Iron Company, was forced to file for bankruptcy, and all machinery was removed by 1880.

Excelsior Furnace, Ishpeming. Built in 1872. Designed to Use Peat for Fuel.

THE ABOVE EXCELSIOR PEAT FURNACE PHOTO IS TAKEN FROM THE JULY 10, 1915, ISSUE OF THE IRON ORE NEWSPAPER. THE PHOTO BELOW IS PRINTED WITH PERMISSION OF MR. JACK DEO, SUPERIOR PHOTOS. LOWER RIGHT CORNER IS A SKETCH OF THE 1874 LAKE SUPERIOR MINE WORKINGS, AND THE UPPER CENTER SHOWS THE OLD ANGELINE STREET ON THE FAR SIDE OF LAKE ANGELINE, WITH HOMES (DOTS) ON THE TERRACE HILL AREA. THE EXCELSIOR PEAT FURNACE IS IN RIGHT CENTER AT SMALL BOXED AREA AT BACK OF CENTER HILL.

Chapter 9:
Julius Ropes and the Gold

On July 23, 1881, there was a newspaper story about Mr. Ropes and gold. At this time he had a shaft down 14 feet and had gold in some quart bottles. The next week the paper told its readers that Ropes found gold, silver, nickel, and copper in quartz veins which sometimes ran crossways with each other. In October of the same year, 1881, it was announced that Ropes expected to start mining under contract. In November we are told that more gold had been found. Visitors started coming out to see the mine. At first the rock was not crushed very well, and some visitors were finding gold in the "rock pile". Another shaft was begun and went down 30 feet. In February of 1882, Mr. Ropes sent some of his quartz with gold to Philadelphia for a trial run of the chlorination process. Early value showed up to $435.00 a ton.

Mr. Ropes had Mr. Sedgwick, a local attorney, obtain the financial aid of several Detroit men who agreed "to spend several thousand dollars in order to more fully test the value of the property." In 1883, mining began, along with processing the rock for gold. Mr. S. S. Curry, a very good supporter of Mr. Ropes' work had the main shaft named after him. The first 100 tons of rock treated yielded $705 in gold and $99 in silver. The first stamp mill was not very large and did not crush ore very small. It consisted of only 5 stamps that smashed the ore. The ore was heated and mercury used to attract the gold. Chlorine was also used in the process.

Through all this, many others began searching for ore and "prospecting". Excitement grew when in September of 1883, a brick of gold bullion was put on public view in town. This was done on several occasions at a bank, before the gold was sold to the United States Mint. There were about 20 men working at the Gold Mine. Julius Ropes, in October, then built houses for the miners as winter was going to set in. A school was also eventually built. Ropes rock was even put on display where one could see the "free" gold in it.

By December of 1883, 272 tons of rock produced $1,651.00 in gold and $358.00 in silver.

Financing the mine then became very important as cash grew short. A large block of stock was sold to the public. Money was used partly to enclose a new mill for processing the rock. Batteries were used to drive the stamps. The Curry Shaft also went down another 50 feet. A new hoist was put over the shaft. It was the old Dexter Mine hoist. By the spring of 1885 the Ropes was down 135 feet. During this time it also bought the Phillips' Gold Mine property next door on the west, and put a shaft down in it.

In June of 1885, The Ropes reported its best month ever of reclaiming gold. There was, however, a problem. Money ran short and shareholders were assessed ten cents a share for operational expenses in order to pay the 1885 taxes.

With taxes paid, the mine was now down to a fourth level by the autumn 1885, and Mr. Ropes was also busy doing assay work for other gold mines starting up. By Christmas the shaft was down to 250 feet, and by the summer of 1886 electric feeders were installed. In the meantime, not all stockholders had paid their ten cent assessments per share, and the names of those people were listed and printed and their delinquent stock put up for sale. A new hoist was also installed for the shaft, and in September of 1886, the mine produced a bullion brick weighing 24 lbs. and worth $4,000.

By April of 1887, the Ropes seventh level was being dug outward from the shaft. The superintendent of the mine left and was replaced. Diamond Drills were now being used to look for gold under the ground. In order to make more improvements yet, contracts were let out in October of that year for another new mill again. For water power, a dam would be built on the Carp River. In 1888, for the months of March through July, the income from the gold production totaled $20,120.

One must understand that no profit was being made, and never was. Disillusioned people began to try to sell their stock according to the August 18, 1888, paper. Still, many other local companies in the area of Gold Mine Lake were opening new local gold mines and putting down shafts. Even the iron ore companies were exploring. The other mines were soon in the news more than the Ropes. In the spring of 1889, however, more investment was made at the Ropes, and 20 stamps were ordered in order to reclaim more of the gold. This resulted in $9,000 in gold being recovered in the month of October.

Things went so well that the hundreds of stocks floating around for sale were all purchased. In the paper on May 2, 1891, Mr. C. R. Ely, a stock broker in the Jenk's Block had 500 shares of the Ropes stock for sale, but in a news column next to the ad, the note said that "of the several thousand shares of low-priced stock of the Ropes Gold and Silver company that were floating about a few days since not one is now to be found. Takers would be numerous if the offers were still being presented."

In 1891 the Ropes was down to a 12th level, and the paper stated that things were "looking well". And in April and May there were reports of more gold being found. The 12th level ore was running about $20. per ton in gold. By November the report was that the previous month's production was $2,300. of gold. The mill was also busy because, by January of 1892, the Fire Center Gold Mine was hauling its ore to the Ropes for processing. In February, however, the Rope's crusher broke down, and by July the mine was again asking for an additional assessment to shareholders for more funds. The mine continued to go deeper, however, and in July there was drifting on a 14th and 15th level. Nothing lasts forever, however, and at the end of the year the night shift was let go, and at the same time, the Fire Center quit sending ore to the Ropes because of a great fire at the Fire Center Gold Mine. This fire permanently closed the mine according to the paper on February 11, 1893. Little was said in the paper about the Ropes for the rest of that year, but on December 2, 1893 there was a note that only a small force was working there. Not giving up, in January we find that the shaft is now down to a 16th level, following the quartz vein of the previous levels. Gold was averaging about three to four dollars a ton. The yearly report in March showed that the Ropes had net earnings for 1893 of $2,000. Work also went back up on the 10th level which now had a 65 foot drift and had found more gold and silver in a westerly direction. A new shaft was sunk from the surface over that area by the fall of 1894.

The newspaper was finding the gold field a bit quiet on the whole, and no doubt the public was getting "dull" also about gold stock. In April of 1894 Mr. Newett wrote a message to his readers saying, "Idle men could be out searching for gold." Mr. Ropes, himself, went exploring for gold in November at the Eldorado Mine out west, and gave a report on his trip in the paper in the January 26, 1895, issue. Whether he saw his mine in Ishpeming coming to an end is not known, but it only had four years to live. In actuality, many thought the mine would have died some time before this, and in the paper for March 23, 1895, Mr. Newett gave much credit to Mr. Ropes that "while it has not returned to those who have invested in its shares any of their money thus spent, it has lived, and with life there is ever a chance of doing better. That it has so long continued has been surprising to the thousands who years ago predicted sudden collapse of the enterprise." The article also notes at this time the mine had produced $568,845 in gold and silver. Mr. Newett also printed the Annual Report of the Ropes Company, including work being done on several levels. He also noted that if gold would rise a bit in price, dividends could be given to shareholders.

The year's finances were also printed and the author notes that about half of the income went for employee wages of $20,429.

In 1896, the newspaper reported that the Ropes was producing from the 16th level "at a lively rate." But a note was also made that same year that gold coins were being replaced with silver coins and that the U.S. gold pieces were rapidly disappearing. A sad note appeared in the paper on February 27, 1897, that the Ropes could not afford to stay open. The last two gentlemen to be killed, died in June in separate accidents. In July, all of the men stopped working as none had received pay for a month. This, basically, was the end of the original Ropes Mine, but it would be resuscitated several times yet and die a very slow deat.

In September of 1898, Mr. Newett, the newspaper editor, noted that the local gold mines disappeared as fast as they had appeared. In the summer of 1898, however, there was still an article noting that the Ropes may still re-open. The reason was printed in the August 13, 1898 paper when it was noted that the Ropes was being leased by some "Detroit people", and that mining had resumed. In October the readers of the paper noted that the Ropes' work force was to be increased, and that pumps would unwater the bottom levels. It was only about six months later, in May of 1899 that the Ropes Gold mine stopped working again. In December of that year, the newspaper reported that the Gold Mine might yet go back to work, but it never did.

Still the gold mine was not dead. Out in the swamp where the stamp rock and waste tailings had been put for all those years of operation, there was a lot of unclaimed gold. Not long after this news, an ad appeared that there would be a receiver's sale of the company, and Mr. B. W. Wright of Ishpeming soon became the receiver. He also hoped to reopen the mine by raising $20,000.00. Again the mine did not reopen.

The story still continued. There was news in the spring of 1900 on reclaiming gold from the swamp tailings. By May the tailings were waiting for the apparatus required for being chemically treated. Gold would also be found in good quantity in all the mud and material collected on all the machines and plates that processed the ore for many years, and even fell on the floor, or through the floor boards. The new owners now were Corrigan, McKinney and Co. They believed, said the paper, that they can get $1.00 profit per ton from the tailings, and estimated that there were 200,000 tons of tailings that would yield $2.00 a ton, but that half of that amount would be used for the cost of retrieval and treatment. The process ran for several summers successfully. It used the Cyanide process and the process was explained in the December 29, 1900, Iron Ore newspaper.

While the tailings were being recovered, there was a note in the paper in May of 1901 that the Ropes may again work. The same message was voiced again in January of 1902. It was now, of course, realized that with the new cyanide treatments, that more gold could be recovered if the Ropes were to reopen, and which it ultimately did many years later by the Callahan Mining Company. However, in 1903 there appeared a very sad note that the Ropes was being dismantled.

In 1904, Mr. Julius Ropes died at age 69. His son, a graduate of the Houghton College of Mines always felt for many years afterwards that the Ropes mine still had possibilities and expressed that in letters to the paper from time to time, although he was living in a western mining area.

In the ten years after Mr. Rope's death, some work went on at the Michigan Gold Mine, and Mr. Trebilcock also did some work on a gold ledge in the Ropes area. By 1913, the operations at the Michigan Gold Co. were suspended. The Ropes Gold and Silver Mine Company came to an end on September 26, 1914, when Trebilcock Brothers bought the Rope's 24 buildings, old machinery and other equipment. The wood amounted to an estimated 250,000 feet of lumber, of which 75% was white pine. The mill was three stories high and the shaft house had much large square timbering still in good condition. The purchase price was $30,000. and it was reported that the Trebilcocks in turn, received $20,000. from the sale of the mill plates that contained gold. Much of the wood was hauled to Mud Lake for a large new ice house. They sold the machinery for scrap. In the end, Mr. Newett tells us that nothing was left on the surface of the mine but the waste piles.

THIS IS A SKETCH OF THE ROPES GOLD MILL DRAWN BY WILL BRADLEY FOR THE IRON ORE IN 1888.

Chapter 10:
The Town
From 1882 up to 1890

1882

The town had found that its original 1874 steam fire engine did not work too well. For two important fires, it did not perform. So the first item of 1882 was to obtain a new steamer, and they named it the J.P. Outhwaite, after one of the town leaders. Like the other Steamer, the Outhwaite was pulled by two horses. At first, when the bell was rung, the first man to arrive with his two horses got the job, but then the city purchased two fine horses at $275 each. A month after the steamer arrived, one of the horses died.

Also in 1882 is the first recording I can find of the dog races which would become famous with the kids. It was a "Dog Derby" planned by an organized "Dog Trotting Association." This will be covered in greater detail and became the morning event of the yearly Skee Tournament. The smallpox vaccination had been discovered, made from cowpox germs. It was discovered that people around cows seldom got smallpox. They had become immune. Now everyone could become immune. Mr. Newett's paper wrote that "many are being vaccinated against small pox." What people now seem to be getting are horses and wagons. This results in a desire for better roads, especially between Ishpeming and Negaunee. Miners are also tending to find farms on the edge of towns where land can be purchased and crops raised, and sold, or used at home in case of layoffs at work. And immigrants continue to pour in. 400 Tyrolese Italians arrive over a short period in 1882 and housing is filled "to overflowing".

On one day's train in May of 1882, 150 Scandinavian immigrants arrived, mostly Norwegian.. The paper makes this important note: "All are employed." New mines continue to open in Marquette County, and many are put to work on railroad construction and grades into new mines. We should also say that many went to work in the woods in the winter and lived in "timber" camps. In the spring they all came to town in great numbers and with lots of money, and the results were often great disturbances in bars and on the streets.

Bicycles are the new item, especially for women. Many thought it disgraceful for ladies to be riding a bike, even though they wore their skirts. One person reported to Mr. Newett, the disgusting habit of young girls playing leap frog. The great place for bicycling was on the new Cliff's Drive, which went to mines in that area from Negaunee to National Mine. Much of it today is under the present Tilden Mine. The new bikes looked pretty much like today's, but had no brakes at first.

Entertainment in this period often involved Cornish Wrestling, and men traveled large distances to come to town to wrestle the local winners. As in many sports, there were cash prizes, with $300 in prizes on July 4th of 1887. There was a local roller skating rink, and the girls asked for a special time when just they could skate privately. It was granted. On some nights a band played.

Telephones had been invented by Mr. Bell, but only because Mr. Edison had added the magic "carbon button" to make it work, and people were signing up to get one. The line was going from Marquette, and even to Champion and beyond. Mines were the first to get phones.

On the national scene, the paper reported the death of Mrs. Abraham Lincoln in July of 1882.

1883

Times were tough on some, and especially in January of "83", when both open pit and underground mines had lay offs. The winter was especially bad and the underground mines had gotten no contracts to buy their ore. Mr. Newett guessed that about 200 idlers were on the streets from mine closings, and that 300 were now unemployed from the city mines.. People were too proud to say they were poor, but in the January 27, 1883, issue of the paper there was a note about a Swedish family that was found destitute and that they were given help by others. The Winthrop Mine in National Mine could not pay wages again until the following June, but Mr. Braastad agreed to make provisions available to the men during the winter. Life insurance was coming into existence as an improvement to life, and men getting killed at work often left $500.00 for their survivors. The cost of the insurance soon went quite high, however, as the owners of the insurance companies did not expect so many deaths in the mines. In 1885 Mr. Newett suggested to the townspeople that there were quite a few poor women in the city who needed sewing and other employment and wrote: "You can help." Many women were left widows by mine accidents. Many men were often left unable to work, though not killed, from accidents. There was no such thing as a disability income for anyone, and no Social Security for old age.

Strawberry Hill, as steep as it is today was a favorite place for snow coasters, and even adults went out and had fun. At times, however, it made it very slippery for getting up and down walking on foot, or with horses.. In 1884, the practice of coasting on Strawberry Hill was outlawed.

The Upper Peninsula newspapers at this time pushed the idea of a separate state for the U. P., called "Superior". There was talk of a bridge between Lower Michigan and the Upper Peninsula. Groups of berry picking boys organized in 1883 and were asking for ten cents a quart this year, rather than seven cents.

There was a fine concert soprano who came to Ishpeming on a regular basis whose name was "Mari Litta". Returning from touring and singing in Europe, she came in the winter of 1882 and few seats were left for her performance. She came again in May of 1883, but upon arriving was unable to perform. She became very ill at the Breitung House in Negaunee, and her performance was cancelled. Her sister came by train the next week, and gave a benefit concert for Mari Litta to help with finances. Mari was able to leave two weeks later, noted Mr. Newett, "still very ill" and returned to her home in Bloomington, Indiana. In July, Mr. Newett reported that she had passed away at home.

By August of 1883 the newspaper reported that labor was getting short again and that the railways were advertising for emigrant help. The DM&M railroad was building a grade from Marquette to Ishpeming and was short 50 men. One man came to town and tried stealing and eating free. Upon being caught, he was put to work, and quickly left town. Another fellow joined a railroad crew at mealtime for several meals until discovered.

Every year there was the large "Fireman's Tournament" that continued into recent times. In 1883 it was in the Copper Country. The Ishpeming men were going, and sought to win some of the special races. They were given a big send-off by the city, and wives and friends. The report in the paper by Mr. Newett a week later noted that "word is that some passed themselves off a single while there. There is not a single one in the bunch."

The beginning of "The Cash Railway" had begun. It is my hope that some store, some where, has kept its "cash railway" for tourists and youngsters to see. The pneumatic tubes at bank drive-up windows have the last vestiges of these. In 1883 a store in Ishpeming installed the "roller coaster" type. . It had its tracks on the ceiling, and handled money from the wrapping area up to the business office. In the little cars a receipt and change would be returned down to the customer. The author remembers two of these, one at the J. C. Penney Store, and the other at the Gately-Wiggens Store.

1884

On the other hand, it was also tough for businessmen. One fine individual, Mr. A. A. Anderson was a jeweler in town. Like many others in the county, he got interested in opening an iron mine, and it was a gamble, and in early 1884, he lost. He was bankrupt, when his fellow businessmen came to his aid. Even Mr. Newett printed in the paper: "He will work his way up again." And with help and forgiveness, he made arrangements with his creditors and reopened his jewelry store. He did so well that he soon built and opened a jewelry store in Champion, and then built the fine new three-story building in town at the corner of Pearl and Main Street. On the top floor he built a large entertainment room, and rented it out to the AOUW that in turn, rented it out to other groups. The building still stands. He often ran large ads with an illustration of it at Christmas time. He later was more successful in finding iron ore and was also the county sheriff. But more troubles were ahead. In July of 1887, Mr. Anderson was in a carriage accident and was partially paralyzed. All of his newspaper ads after that showed his jewelry store being run by a manager.

In 1884, the city fathers decided, while waiting for electricity, to put gas lights throughout the city, to be converted later. The gas at this time was a reservoir of kerosene with a wick. Also, in 1884, the large Sells Brothers' Circus came to town at the "Driving Park" between Ishpeming and Negaunee. They not only would entertain, but bring good business to town as local arrangements were made to feed 260 people. Their train had 54 cages of animals, including two hippopotamuses. For the previous two weeks they ran full-page ads in the paper, and a special highly colored circus train car came to town and "Gay colored" posters were put up everywhere and included pictures of the animals. The week before the show, Sells Brothers sent another railway car filled with baseball players to play a free exhibition baseball game with Ishpeming men. When the circus arrived, there was an accident during the performance. Mile Claire, a performer, fell to the ground, and it was thought that the fall would be fatal. There was no further word in the paper. As was usual for the event, the MH&O railroad provided a special train and rates to the event from the Copper Country. All of the railroad tracks went right through the area of the park.

A new entertainment for boys was the invention of cap guns with caps. Mr. Newett was not entertained, and thought the guns with the "pungent smell" should go. Gum chewing was a new fad, especially for girls. Mr. Newett added, "Women maybe will talk less."

Also in 1884, the body of an American Indian was found at Pilgrim River in the Copper Country. He wore silver earrings and had a tomahawk.

A street addition came to town when Mr. Nelson decided to have a hotel further back from the railroad tracks. If he could put the hotel back a bit on the hill, there would be room for Canda Sstreet to be between his hotel and a new row of businesses north the tracks. The city decided to move Canda Street north, between Main and First Streets.

The Voelker block at Cleveland and Main Street was built in 1884, and one story still stands and has an active store. This was also the time the new and currently present cemetery was built, and this subject will have a special section devoted to it in Chapter Ten. The railroad gates that were still in existence into the 1950's were also installed at this time. They came down to regulate auto and pedestrian traffic. Often two or more trains were running at the same time, often in different directions.

Lots were being sold on 40 acres of Iron Cliffs land at High and Third Streets. Steel rails and steel nails were replacing breakable iron. The public schools had built some new schools, and the architect and building company convinced the city that hot water heat was what they needed, rather than the common steam boiler. However, in cold weather, the schools could not be heated. The contractor said it was because they leaked too much cold air. Evidently heating with hot air was bad, as Mr. Newett commented once that using hot air was why some people were burning so much coal.

1885

Mr. Newett announced two items in the first issue of the 1885 newspaper. First, he acknowledged that in the previous week he had made a bad error. The quartz found in large quantities in Palmer was not worth "nine dollars" a ton, but "none dollars" a ton. He also announced that the testing of well water in the

Ishpeming downtown area showed it was no longer fit to drink.

Stenography, or shorthand, was now becoming popular, and a School for Stenography opened up in town. The C&NW announced round-trip tickets to New Orleans for $40.00. The city band, called the Lake Angeline and Ishpeming City Band, had a February indoor concert. It was -40 degrees the week before, and the hot-air furnaces at the new schools were failing to heat.

Two new state institutions will be built in the U. P. They will be a School of Technology and a Prison. Ishpeming will try to get both of them. The road around Lake Bancroft was to be completed soon, and in March, a new state law was passed requiring all military companies to be on parade on Washington's birthday (February 22). Big news came when it was announced that the Marquette and Western Railroad was sold to the MH&O Railroad. Stockholders were shocked and claimed a sell-out by the M&W. It also meant a lot of changing of tracks. The C&NW reduced its hauling rates for iron ore to their Escanaba dock to 70 cents a ton, a reduction of ten cents. Railroads with Marquette ore docks are now charging 45 cents a ton.

In April, the newspaper announced the coming of the town's first roller rink, and that the Methodist Episcopal Church would be building a new building. However, in September, a decision by the church was to simply "undergo renovation." The first Circus announcement was made. The Coles Circus would be in town on the 19th of June. It was announced by the public schools in Ishpeming that the new schools would be changed over to steam heat, and teachers would return to their jobs with no raise in pay for the coming school year. By August 1, the new

steam heat was installed in the school buildings and the trial run worked well, noted Mr. Newett.

The state announced that the town would get neither the new technical school nor the prison. And, out in the western area of the U.S., the Apache Native Americans were having difficulties with the Government. Former General and President, U. S. Grant died and stores closed an hour early in his memory. There was a nice report also on cities that now have electric lights. Baseball managers in the U.S. have agreed to reduce player's salaries to a maximum of $2,000.

It was summer now, and in July the Notton's Opera House had a theatrical group performing the play, "Only a Farmer's Daughter." Drama must have not worked out well, and in September the hall was turned into a gymnasium with new equipment. The cost of having a telephone from the "monopoly" Michigan Telephone Company was reduced from $50 to $36.

In September, the City Library had a fire and closed temporarily. A business that failed in town was a Main Street Lunch Counter. Someone complained of an indecently dressed bicyclist, but Mr. Newett stated that the rider looked fine to him.

As the fall weather season began, Mr. Egan's Hardware store on Cleveland Avenue had a fine picture of a nice parlor stove in the newspaper. It was announced that Rev. and Mrs. Ashley, who served the Presbyterian Church in town for several years, and who recently moved to Nebraska have lost their eleven year-old son. And in December, there was a story of how several local miners started mines and became quite rich, including Joe Sellwood and his $250,000. The Iron Agitator, as it is currently named, has 1,600 subscribers, the city library has 2,800 volumes, and at the Superior Ice Rink, 6000 saw a Christmas tree with electric lights for the first time.

1886

1886 began with the city trying to plow the streets for the first time, but that the plow just skimed the surface. Up to now, rollers have been in fashion for "panking" down the snow. A month later, four horses were used to pull the plow with more success. The Ishpeming toboggan slide is now open, and it, too, has electric lights for the first time. Its location is still probably at Lake Bancroft. The Fire Department has a new sleigh which will be used to haul the hose reel. The Cleveland Mining Co. has put several 50-foot deep shafts along the north shore of Lake Angeline at an incline under the Lake and has found no water coming in at this time. Just a few weeks later, however, Mr. Newett tells his readers that Lake Sallie may be needed for city water, and that water used for drinking from Lake Angeline should be boiled. There are 370 water meters now in use, with 32 new ones in 1885.

The Swedish Lutheran Church has installed a pipe organ and a concert will be held. Iron miners all received a twenty cent a day raise in pay. So many people have arrived from Cornwall, England, that Mr. Newett will now have a special "Cornish Section" in his paper. For the first time, trains can now get to the north side of the Portage Canal by crossing on a bridge in the Copper Country. The newspaper has almost weekly notes about a miner's union trying to come here, called the "Knights of Labor."

By the middle of April, the woodsmen are coming in from the timber camps and the Agitator sold 400 extra copies of the newspaper. There are a great many complaints abut the bad road between Marquette and Ishpeming. The city tells the reader that Third Street will be extended to "the race course." (It is unknown where this race course was.) The Superior Roller Rink has been open for a year with great success and with a band on two nights a week

During 1886, the mines are all booming. There is a request by Mr. Newman for crossing guards at downtown streets as the DSS&A and the C&NW often have trains going on the tracks at the same time. The paper lists ore shipments weekly, and more ore could be shipped if there was not such a great shortage of boats on the great lakes. This will soon be solved by the building soon of steel ships, one of which in the current year is being built in England. One mine that seems to be having difficulty is the New Barnum which will be closed, just after recently having had a drift built between the A and B shafts. The Iron Furnace at Fayette also was "blown out" for the last time. Thoughts are to bring it to this area.

The Ishpeming public schools have advertised for bids for the new school at Third and High Streets. School bonds totaling $25,000 were available for sale at a 5 % rate. The slate roof will be from the L'Anse Quarry. The city library is making a $2 charge to use the facilities. In later years, this was dropped as there was no way to return the deposits made. As summer came in 1886, quite a few boats appeared on Lake Bancroft. A circus came to town, but Mr. Newett reported that it was more of just a side-show, and it charged 15 cents. Many gardens were lost about July 20 when a heavy frost occurred in the city. It must have been a cold year as in late September there were snow flurries as well. Ladies were cutting their "trusses" and men are delighted. In the summer, men and women are out camping in the woods, often in larger groups with several tents, such as "Camp Duffy" on the east branch of the Escanaba River. In the fall there is an outbreak of diphtheria with 15 cases in the city, and there is still a great shortage of housing. There is a worry about fires this winter as many new homes do not have any chimneys, but just pipes running up through the roofs. Schools reopened on December 6, when the threat of diphtheria subsided.

By the end of the year, the New Barnum had reopened, and Mr. Newett's newspaper's name officially become the Iron Ore, and Christmas came and went with hardly a holiday note or ad in the newspaper. 400 students were enrolled at the "convent school", and iron ore cars are now carrying 22 tons.

1887

Interest rates were going up, and in 1887, bonds being sold with an advertised 7% interest. The City expenditures also seemed expensive at times. Ishpeming purchased seven new band uniforms that cost indicated to be over $300 each.

One man was making money at old mines by buying the rock piles and re-picking out the rock that had ore in them that was now sellable. Lower percentage ore was now being mined in mines and purchased at the furnaces.

There is new discussion about the manufacture of piped gas fuel with a building to manufacture it. After several years, a Mr. Higgens came to town by invitation to show his "smokeless gas system." The city decided to build the gas system, and during the building state of the apparatus, an ad appeared in the paper for 300 cords of wood for the new "Gas Manufacturing Works." A cord of wood, of course, is four foot wide, four foot high and eight feet long. To build the building, laborers were

short, and several men sold themselves as bricklayers and when the building was completed, the gas chamber leaked so badly that no gas went through the pipes to businesses and homes. It was rebuilt by competent builders and joined the town's businesses. There was a problem eventually, and the entire system had to be shut down to control a house fire. The city immediately required shut-offs installed at every installation. Mr. Newett marveled at seeing homes and business lit up at night like never before. He announced that the Iron Ore now was lighted by gas. The reader may wonder how the early down-town gas lights worked if just now gas is being produced. The answer now comes to us in the paper on September 7, 1889: "The city adds more gas lamps to replace kerosene." (Kerosene had been called a gas.) And during the same weeks the vapor gas was being installed, Mr. Newett notes that the Cliff Iron Mining Co. is now illuminated with Edison's incandescent light bulbs. There is also now talk about an electric railway in town..

A big discovery in 1887 was that some Marl dug up in a mine at Norway, Michigan, contained petrified fish and sea shells. The biggest idea was a plan to build a canal from Gladstone to Lake Superior. The newest fad was hair dye, and not at all for women— at this time it was for men's graying beards.

Sports in the winter now involved belonging to a snow shoe club that has regular outings, often at night, with candles. There was a bowling alley, believe it or not. Eventually Mr. Braastad built a very nice one. Ice skating was very popular on Lake Bancroft many years, with live music and a charge for some evenings. Skee (that's the way it was spelled into the 1900's) jumping was so active, that the Lake Bancroft hill to the north had two skee jumps. All other types of skiing was spelled the common way. The same hill in 1888 had a large commercial toboggan slide with two chutes coming down on to frozen Lake Bancroft. Curling was also a very popular sport. However, notes the paper on the last issue of December 1886, "Dog racing seems to be gone, along with the prizes."

There seemed to be a lot of unusual mine areas in town. The Lake Superior mine did some work and built an "engine house" west of the Detroit Mine which was where U.S.-41 is today (2/19/1887). In 1891 the Cleveland Iron Co had a shaft down 60 feet north of the old Protestant Cemetery. That would be a shaft in the neighborhood of the Ishpeming Playgrounds. On May 2, 1908, there was a cave-in on Empire Street when the wood cover on an old timbered shaft from an old mine was exposed. It was filled in. .

In March of 1887, the mines decided to give raises to the men without the men even asking. The town was surprised. Those working on surface would get $1.60 a day, and Company account (contract miners) would get $2.15 a day. We read that in the very next month of April, many Finlanders arrived in Ishpeming. This is the first mention of Finnish immigrants. The paper noted on May 7th, a month later, that 600 Finlanders arrived on Tuesday and 400 went to railroad work, and that "Finland is trying to check the vast emigration, but cannot." Housing was still short, and although the Lake Angeline mine built 12 new homes, Mr. Newett noted that "100 new houses would find tenants in a day." There were so many new people that a man was found in the woods in Humboldt, and was still alive, but had never even been reported missing.

New rules are that no children under 14 can work and must be in school, and nothing can be posted on telephone poles. On man made a mistake of taking a lawsuit to court to sue over his wife's death and make some money. The Iron

Ore found out she was not even his wife, and further discovered he had other wives as well.

Some issues of the paper did not have much news, and in order to still any complaints, Mr. Newett noted on 12/17/1887 that this has been the "dullest week in some time."

1888

The Jenks Block was completed on Front Street between the Miner's Bank on Main Street, and Pine Street. Front Street was the continuation of Bank Street, and still followed the railroad tracks and Partridge Creek..

On May 5th, there was still no iron ore shipping and the ice in Marquette was "still firm". The Cleveland Iron Company was considering a pipe line from Marquette for the shipment of fuel oil, rather than overland shipping of coal to Ishpeming.

In 1888 the Sells Brothers' Circus returned in a similar fashion as before, but the paper announced that everyone "should be careful to lock up everything when you go to the Circus—Thieves come also." All the Upper Peninsula newspapers subscribed to each other, and thus they could read from week to week what was happening in other communities, and pass it on, good or bad. Mr. Newett gave a nice report on the two performances, even though they didn't put any ads in his paper this time around. The Barnum and Bailey show also came that summer, and though it charged $2.50 for a reserved seat, Mr. Newett thought it was worth the price. The B&B shows sold tickets early when they sent a railroad ad car with a steam calliope playing circus music in the middle of May. Each circus provided a ten a.m. long parade through the down-town for all to see. Without any movies or television yet, the parade was an extra special educational event, even a traveling zoo. A special "excursion train" was sent for the B&B circus from the Copper Country.

Many of us remember the fireboxes located around town. These date from 1888. There were boxes before this, but they did not work so well in telling the fire department where the fire was. The new ones cost $50. To operated, one broke the glass and turned the key and the message went through to the fire department. They must have run on battery. Telephones also did.

In October there was the sad death of Mr. James Harris who died but cutting his throat with his razor. He was 35 years old and had been in a mine accident and was unable to work. He was found in the closet of his room. There were some problems with a school teacher who kissed one of her students. She quoted a scripture, "My mouth shall show forth thy praise." Another time Mr. Newett noted that the Salvation Army met at the Indian statue drinking fountain at Main and Bank and preached. They also sang the song "There is a Fountain Filled with Blood."

At Christmas time, Mr. Tillson put an ad on the front page of the Iron Ore with a picture of what Santa Claus looked like in 1888.

1889

1889 began with the 30-some sketches of the soon-to-be famous illustrator Will Bradley. Bradley came to Ishpeming with his mother from Massachusetts after his father died. He was only eleven years old, and soon went to work for Mr. Newett and his paper, which was then located on Division Street between Main and Pine. Will was an expert illustrator and not only did he do 30 sketches, some of which are in this book, he also did at least three beautiful mastheads for the newspaper, combining art

with the words "Iron Ore." He left Ishpeming eventually, and went to Chicago and then the New York area, and became head editor for Collier's magazine, and did covers for many other leading magazines of the time, being a leader in the "Art Nouveau" field. He even designed several new type styles. His specialty, however, was posters, and they are today among the most valuable of his works.

Mr. J. Maurice Finn was also active in town at this time, publishing a daily Ishpeming paper, The Lake Superior Democrat, the only daily paper Ishpeming ever published. He also was involved in owning a gold mine near Gold Mine Lake, and running for the U.S. Congress. He made a lot of enemies during his campaign, and Mr. Newett, in his paper publicized some of Finn's financial problems with borrowed money. He lost the election badly and quickly closed the paper and left the area with a lot of debts left behind as well. He eventually showed up in Cripple Creek, Colorado, where he also invested in a gold mine. He became friends with Teddy Roosevelt, who was campaigning at Victor and Cripple Creek. Teddy returned as Vice-President, and came and visited a new home Finn had built with Michigan white pine. Finn had a sad ending with his leaving his family behind in Cripple Creek and dying of alcohol in Denver. (There are separate books on both Mr. Finn and Mr. Bradley by the author.)

Mr. Tom Edison came through town in 1889 on his way to the Sampson Mine in Humboldt to build his iron concentrating plant, using magnets. . It was right on the corner of old US-41 and the road that went to Clowry (The first road west of the Wolf Lake Road on U.S.-41, but to the south on the old highway). Although misplaced a bit, a State Historical Sign commemorates the concentrator today. It eventually burned down. He returned to the area but decided not to rebuild. He was now interested in building an electric chair, which he did. The first one did not work well at all, and the death of the inmate was a tragic one.

In June, the Adam Forepaugh Circus also showed, and came with 200 Sioux Indians and cowboys and their horses. The parade had five sections. The newspaper had a nice ad as well.

Here is the 1889 statistic for school children in Ishpeming, stating that the current enrollment in schools was 2,564, an increase of 194 over 1888. At this time the Salisbury School was built and is still standing on South Pine Street. It was built with a cost of $9,400.00. A new high school also was built, of which the west end is still part of the present High School. The Swedish Methodist church was also built at Cleveland and Fourth Streets.

Word was received from New York regarding the building of an electric street railway in Ishpeming. The city voted to receive a deposit on the project idea, but no deposit was immediately made. Plans were also being made to build a large race track and driving park between Ishpeming and Negaunee. It was called Union Park. And in town, the city had purchased land at Division and Main for a new city hall, which still stands in daily use.

ON THE LEFT IS A PHOTO OF MR. OUTHWAITE. ABOVE IS THE FIRST MOTORIZED FIRE TRUCK IN 1923. IT HAS JUST BEEN REPURCHASED BY THE ISHPEMING FIRE DEP'T AND STILL HAS MR. OUTH-WAITES PICTURE ON IT.

Chapter 11: The Old and New Cemeteries

Most people in Ishpeming never knew that there was a cemetery problem. And they don't know that the present cemetery is not the original cemetery.

In the May 20, 1882, issue of the newspaper (the town as a city is only 9 years old), Mr. Newett informs the reader that a new cemetery is needed. The city had hoped for land two miles from the city at Deer Lake, but that the Cliff's Iron Company will not lease any of its lands. Mr. Newett further noted that the present cemetery has only three feet of dirt down to solid rock and that citizens of town will either have to be cremated or quit dying.

After several months of discussion of new locations, it was announced on April 21 of 1883, that a new cemetery might be possible on Deer Lake Road. That September the newspaper informs us that the present cemetery "is packed full." Nothing happens all winter, and again in June of 1884, the paper once again says "The Cemetery is full," and in August, "Cemetery decision not yet made."

The reader is probably wondering where the first cemetery was. We even have a photo of it in this book. It ran from about the corner of Main and North both west toward Lake Bancroft, and north towards the present playground.

In those days, people left flowers at the grave-sites also, and like today, for some strange reason, people would rob them.

The new cemetery was purchased. At the end of 1885, in November, the announcement was made that the new cemetery is graded and will be soon divided into lots. In the spring, grass was planted as well. It looked like things were moving along, but in May, 1886, plots were not yet available for burials, yet deaths continued.

One sad death that month was a young widow whose husband had been killed at the Winthrop Mine. She hung herself, leaving two children, ages five and three. There were many such deaths of widows and single women who had no way to support themselves and their families. There were deaths of men as well, often from gunshot, who had been maimed from injury and could no longer support themselves. And there were those who committed suicide in old age who could no longer work and had no other income. In any case, the old cemetery had been filled, with many who died before their time had come. And, in spite of the old cemetery being full, people still had to be buried there.

The new cemetery opened finally, and in the summer of 1887, a wood sidewalk, 4,960 feet long from High Street to the new cemetery was built. However, it was still difficult to get to as there was a large ravine at the end of Second Street that had to be crossed. In September, work began on a bridge over the gully "south of the new cemetery." In 1891 a vault to store bodies in the winter until ground thawed was built. For the next three years, Mr. Newett hammered away at the city to do something about the old cemetery. As you can see from the map inside the cover, there were both a Protestant and a Roman Catholic Cemetery next to each other. The Roman Catholic people must have done a fine job of fencing theirs in, as a newspaper article only notes that cows have been overrunning the Protestant Cemetery. In 1890 Mr. Newett noted that the old Protestant

Cemetery is going badly into decay, including the fences. During that time, however, many removals of the dead were being made from the old to the new cemeteries, as stated in the paper on October 13, 1888.

The old French Catholic Church Cemetery west of Pine Street was moved to the new cemetery in April of 1891, and which was enlarged in 1896. The Protestant Cemetery continued to have unclaimed bodies in it. . Mr. Newett reported on November 18, 1893, that the condition of the old cemetery is very bad and that headstones are strewn all about. In 1898 citizens are still removing bodies from the old cemetery. It was at this time that the city started to require a permit for such action. Perhaps there was some grave robbing?

In 1902, at the new cemetery, a fine steel fence was put up, with a lovely gate that had on it the name of the Cemetery. . It is not the same gate that is there at present. In that year, trees were also planted. To further improve the new cemetery, there was talk of a new bridge the old one being almost 20 years old and was condemned. No bridge was built, however, and instead, the ravine was filled partially with dirt to provide a valley crossing.

In 1905 the city announced that the old cemetery would be sold as home building lots. The city petitioned the judge for permission to remove bodies from North Main Street between Pine and Maple. Judge Sloan granted the request and between 1905 and 1911, and during that time period, 3,000 bodies were removed. In 1910, Mr. Newett, in September of that year, still is complaining about the fact that what is left "shows no sign of respect for any bones that may still lie in its bosom." The paper also noted that the old Ishpeming Cemetery is a disgrace with overgrown weeds and is used as a playground by the boys. Many bodies were missed as there were so many single immigrants and those who could not afford headstones that often there was no way to tell where all bodies were.

Finally action started to take place in 1911 when the city of Negaunee began to move its cemetery to its present location.. The Negaunee railroads and road to Marquette were also moved from the downtown north to a newly made Prince Street. It was discovered that the ore body of the Negaunee Mine was under the cemetery, railroads, highway and city homes, and had no rock roof over it, and sand could pour into the mine and sink the surface. In Negaunee, letters were sent to all grave owners. Many came back as undeliverable, but this quick work of Negaunee in getting all the graves moved also seemed to move the Ishpeming people to get going toward emptying their "first" cemetery as well.

Investigation showed that the Catholic Cemetery was under their ownership but still had graves at the head of Main Street. Plans were made to remove all bodies remaining, and make 13 lots to sell on the property and the profit would be used for the new Convent school for 450 younger students, using frontage on Pine and Pearl Streets

The city wasn't sure they owned the Protestant cemetery. After all they had sold lots and the lots were private property of those who bought them. Thus the newspaper emphasized that those who owned lots should turn them over to the city for its ownership. Evidently there were some burials being made yet in the old cemetery by those who owned lots there, and this practice came to an end when the City passed action to "prevent the burial of the dead within the city limits." On May 20th, 1911, there appeared a note in the paper saying, "See if you have anyone to identify in the Ishpeming Protestant Cemetery." The city also offered

ideas for opening Main Street northward, and Michigan to the West.

In solving the existing problems, the city bought 20 feet on the south side of the Roman Catholic Cemetery, while the Catholics bought 40 feet of the south side of the Protestant Cemetery. This allowed the Roman Catholic Church to sell 20 lots for homes. In 1912, North Street was widened by the old cemetery. However, evidently no homes were built on the properties yet as the new Ishpeming Advancement Association suggested in 1913 the north half of the old cemetery north of Main Street be used for a much needed city playground. This came to be.

Houses were eventually built, and an article in the Mining Journal on July 13, 1954, noted that when houses were being built in the area in 1938, "it was not unusual for workers to find coffins while making excavations."

HERE IS A PHOTO OVERLOOKING LAKE BANCROFT TOWARDS THE EAST, AND SHOWING MANY TOMBSTONES STILL IN THE OLD CEMETERY. HOWEVER, HOMES HAVE BEEN BUILT ON PINE AND OAK ON LAND ORIGINALLY SET ASIDE FOR THE CEMETERY (SEE CITY DRAWING INSIDE FRONT COVER.) COURTESY OF FRIENDS OF THE CARNEGIE LIBRARY FOR THIS APRIL, 1986, CALENDAR PHOTO.

HERE IS AN 1874 DRAWING OF THE CLEVELAND MINE. IF YOU ARE CONFUSED, IT IS DRAWN FROM THE AREA BY "PILOT'S KNOB" ON THE NORTH SIDE OF LAKE BANCROFT AND LOOKING SOUTH-EAST. ROAD AT TOP GOES TO NEGAUNEE. STREET BELOW MAY BE HIGH OR NORTH.

SKETCH COURTESY OF JACK DEO, SUPERIOR VIEW GALLERY.

60

Chapter 12:
A City Sewer

Just about the time Partridge Creek rose over its banks in 1881, Mr. Newett noted in his paper, that the city was realizing that there was a need to lower Partridge Creek, and clean it out. One couldn't stop it or drain it. After all, it went through the city of Ishpeming. In October of the same year there was a very heavy rain and the river rose and rose. It covered several of the "lower ground" streets in town and their buildings in up to 18 inches of water. Two weeks later the newspaper read: "Partridge Creek being dredged and widened between Main and First Streets.

Knowing the dredging to be a temporary solution, a survey was done of the Creek in December of that year and sewers were studied. The ground was pretty flat. In April of the next spring, the solution was still to make "Partridge Creek deeper and wider." Then a bottle-neck was found. The Creek ran into the Carp River west of town, which ran into Deer Lake. Near the mouth of the Carp was a waterfall. It was decided that the falls needed to be lowered in order to get Partridge Creek to drain better. In fact, it was discovered in the survey that if the River rose 11 feet, that the Creek would back up into Ishpeming. It was decided to put in sewers before improving city streets, but first of all, the Carp River Falls would have to be removed. Property also had to be bought from the Deer Lake Furnace which had an eight foot dam on the River for water power. This, too, had to be removed.

In late April of 1890, the task began of lowering the Carp River. The article noted that there had been a mine in that the area of the River, called the Perry Mine. The paper noted also that not

only will the lowering prevent backing up of a sewer system; it will result in a faster movement of raw sewage water into the Deer Lake, until the 1950's. The Sewer Committee report also noted that the sewer would drain water from the down-town swamp and make the town drier. In the meantime, in the spring of 1891, Partridge Creek again flooded parts of downtown. Mr. Newett also commented several times in his paper that Lake Bancroft was filling up with sewage. He lived on the NE corner.

An election in 1891 passed a $50,000. sewer bond to blast the Carp Falls down and lower the river. By 1893, sewers were indeed carrying off standing water that formally flooded the downtown. It wasn't until 1896 that the rock cut lowered the Deer Lake Carp River six feet, and it was noted that it will prevent sewer back-ups.

By the turn of the century, the Partridge Creek was running into the city sewer starting at Third Street, and through a pipe under Bank Street, and Front Street.. The ditch was filled in, and the Roman Catholic School was put in just west of Pine, right in the area of the old Creek. The newspaper editor worried a bit about the children playing in that area, but it all seemed to work out very well for the entire town. Brick caissons were built down in the ground all along the path of the creek to drain surface water and lateral sewers as well.

DEER LAKE FURNACE AND FALLS

THIS IS WILL BRADLEY'S JANUARY 1, 1889, SKETCH OF THE DEER LAKE FURNACE AND FALLS. BOTH WERE REMOVED FOR A SUCCESSFUL ISHPEMING SEWER SYSTEM. NOTE THE FISHERMAN ON THE LEFT NEAR THE FALLS.

Chapter 13:
Lake Angeline and Lake Sallie Water

In the 1880's the city put in a water main to Lake Angeline. It was tough going said the paper: "lots of stumps." A pump was installed, and then a second at the Lake Superior Mine "Cage Shaft". The pipeline was made of wood, rather than metal, as it was thought that the wood would handle the frost better. The town, having a larger population than it has currently, thought that the lake might be drained dry by the users. Bathers weren't too happy, either. The Lake was a favorite bath place, and now it was off limits. Quite a few were now going out to the Carp River, west of town, to bathe, according to the July 28, 1883, paper. Some were arrested for indecency. Soon, the near-by mining companies caused the quality of the Lake Angeline water to go down-hill. The public put up with a diamond drill on the ice, drilling down in over 27 feet of water in 1887, and Mr. Newett noted in wonder what would happen in the spring when the ice melted with all the manure of the horses on it. He noted wryly, "The Lake Angeline water is getting pretty thick."

Running water allowed for the wonderful invention of fire hydrants, a God-sent gift for firemen. Although they often would freeze up in the winter, when running, they would allow unlimited water to be put on a fire. It was wonderful for the city residents as well, and from time to time for many years, more were added to the system.

At first there were no water meters, just a basic charge. However, it was found that several families would get together and install one water line to one house while they all used the water. Mr. Newett, himself, abused the system by installing a water motor" that ran all his presses at one time, using constantly running water. He was even able to lower his printing prices by 25%. After water meters were installed, he didn't say much in the paper about his water motor or whether it was still in use. In any case, it was his luck that electricity soon followed. The Lake Level got lower and lower, and water consumption increased so much that by May of 1889, a new water pumping engine was installed that pumped even more water a day, up to 380,000 gallons. However, mines were getting ready to go under Lake Angeline, and the Lake's days as a water supply were numbered. Considering also, the Lake's lessening purity, in 1890, the paper noted that "spring water was being peddled all over."

The first discussion of Lake Sallie for water was on November 5, 1887, but it was noted that there were large deposits of iron ore on two sides of the Lake. And after serving the city for 100 years, the Lake was required to stop furnishing water and is now a part of the Tilden Open Pit Mine. The Lake, however, exists as it always was as of a visit by the author in 2003.

On August 3, 1889, the route of the piping from Lake Sallie to Lake Angeline was announced. It would leave the south-west end of Lake Sallie and follow the north side of Grass Lake to the Salisbury Mine, where it crossed through the south side, then across Dawson and Douglas Street (That is why one lot still has no building on it. In fact, Douglass Street was not made yet.). The route continued to Salisbury Street and around the Lake Angeline west side to the Lake Angeline Pumping Station. The distance would be two miles with no rock cuts. However, it was soon announced that there would be one rock cut on the east end of the line. In October of 1889, the number had grown to "several rock cuts." The laying of pipe on the shore of Grass Lake was a very difficult job because it was very wet and the path was a long curve.

Today, people are surprised to find out that the pipes were made of wood. Actually all the water pipes in the city were wood. When a leak developed, the city would dig up the ground and tap a wood plug into the pipe. The plug would get wet and swell up and plug the hole perfectly. This was true into the 1950's. The pipe from the lake was large. The logs were 22 inches with a 14 inch passage. 11,000 feet of pipe were ordered. Bands went around the pipes periodically and at joints. By the end of November the project was completed and tested. At first, the water just poured into Lake Angeline, and already Mr. Newett noted, "That water is now improved."

During the winter, Lake Sally (we will jump to the present spelling) was hooked up directly to the water mains of the city and it was discovered that the people on Strawberry Hill had good water pressure without any of the city water pumps running. As Lake Sallie was 28 feet higher than the present source, the water pressure to the city would now be greater. However, the city desired an emergency pump building, and it was built at the corner of South Pine Street and South Angeline Streets where it is today.

The city had continued to grow and there was worry by 1891 that the new Lake might run out of water in a very dry summer. Two items were instituted: A dam was built across Lake Sally, raising the lake five or six feet high by 80 feet wide at the outlet end. Also, it was decided to tie in two more lakes to the system, the Lake Miller and the Iron Mountain (Ogden today). Dams were also added to those to store up extra water. Lake Tilden was also piped in eventually.

It was time to drain Lake Angeline. By July 9, 1892, a launder, or flume, was completed from Lake Angeline through the Salisbury Location to a ditch from the Salisbury Mine. It would drain Lake Angeline of its water through Winthrop Junction to the Carp River.. The paper noted that one-third of the Lake's water had been removed by a ditch, but it is unknown where the route of the ditch was. To remove the other two-thirds of the water, the Launder pump was run. It worked so well that by August 20, a pipe had to be laid further into the lake 1000 feet to get the remaining water at the deepest point.

As the lake got lower, it was seen to be full of nine and ten pound trout. One night a duck went through the pipe and came out okay on the other end. City personnel also tried it with a goose, and it also survived. Sometimes when the launder pump closed down, large fish were found in the pipe. When the lake was pumped out by the end of December of 1892, the mud on the bottom was 22 feet deep in places. We will print a photo of the flume in this book.

A postscript to the Lake Sally pipeline is to note that the route was soon changed. After the pipeline went through the south end of the Salisbury Mine property, the mine decided to build a new shaft in that area. All worked out okay until a good size cave-in of surface near the shaft took place. Although the surface was quickly filled in and the reason for the cave-in was discovered, the city was nervous. They saw two problems. One was that if the cave-in broke the water main, the city would be out of water for some time period. People had gotten used to taking showers. The other problems would be that without any shut-off, the Lake Sally would flood the mine by running down the shaft until the lake was empty. The pipeline was then moved to the back of the hill behind the shaft and around the west end of Salisbury Street and Douglas Street, meeting the old line near the pump house.

As you will note by now, many of these subjects are all taking place about the same time of the 1880's and 90's. You will come to realize why it is called the "Gay 90's." It was also the time of the great electric street railway.

Chapter 14:
The Electric Street Railway

On July 19, 1890, the newspaper reported that an electric railroad between Negaunee and Ishpeming is being planned. The Electric Railway was to operate four to six individual cars on the route. In October the news said that the railroad would be ready by the spring of 1891, but it was October of 1891 before the tracks began to be laid. As it was being constructed, plans were announced that it may go all the way to the Winthrop Location in National Mine. 125 men were at work on the project.

The newspaper, on August 8, 1891, gave the route as follows: It will not cross any railroad tracks in Negaunee and leave for Ishpeming by way of Cyr Street. It will run north of Union Park and cross the railroad going north to the Detroit Mine. It will enter town on the south side of the bluff of the New York Mine property and come down High street past the high school building to First Street. It will turn on to Canda, and then go south on Main to Division, west to Pine, and out Pine to the Lake Angeline Location.

In spite of the progression in the use of electricity at the mines and now for an entire railroad, the city in the same year ordered 30 more gas lights for the streets at a cost to run of $10.00 a month. Work on the Electric Street Railway continued into the winter, and by February of 1892, the street cars were running part of the route and were very popular. Around the end of that month a record was set of 2,230 people riding in one day, and it was a Sunday. Even the city councils of both Ishpeming and Negaunee took a ride.

By July 23, 1892, the Electric Railway was going from downtown Negaunee to Ishpeming, and then south out to the Lake Angeline Location. At first it stopped where the end of the "high sidewalk" was and where Excelsior Street began. The sidewalk is now a blacktop strip in the same area. Later, it was extended several hundred feet further to the Section 16 Mine. It was suggested that a store be built on the end of the line by someone so that people would have a place to go if required, and a store was built, known in the 1940's as Nault's Store That building is still there.

In the summer of 1892, the Street Railroad was surveying for the "line" to go yet further to Winthrop, and noted that it will cross the railroad tracks just west of the Section 16 Mine, which was just west of the Angeline. In Anticipation, lots for homes were developed and sold on the south side of Badger Hill, between S. Pine and Saginaw Streets south of Ishpeming (by the National Mine) as the new proposed Electric Railway addition was to go right by there, following the old Winthrop railroad grade into National Mine. In September the newspaper reported that the extension would be as far as the Salisbury School House in a month or two. In actuality, the Electric Street Railway never got past the Section 16 mine and Mr. Nault's Store. When the State of Michigan informed the Street Railway that it would have to cross all the Railway tracks (the DSS&A going to the Copper Country, and others) with an overpass, the extension project was cancelled.

What is heard of next is that the Street Railway has extra electricity available and wanted permission to sell it to buildings in Ishpeming. It was a direct current. The present City Hall was built about this time, and there was discussion to wire the building for future electricity, but nothing more was printed of when or what kind of electricity was used when it was lighted.

From time to time, new companies bought out the Electric Street Railway. The company that built the railway eventually was doing so badly that owners were trying to sell their stock. New buyers relied on larger and more beautiful cars to entice riders, but after about 1905, autos were purchased by the hundreds, and greatly affected business. Yet it hung on into the 1920's. The cars did not turn around at the end of the line as in San Francisco, but the motorman would just reverse the boom that rode on the electric wire above the tracks and then seat himself on the other end of the car and drive in the reverse direction.

THIS DEMOCRATIC NEWSPAPER WAS ONLY IN BUSINESS FOR THREE YEARS WHEN MR. SOULTS WENT TO MENOMINEE AND MR. J. MAURICE FINN WENT TO COLORADO. A SEPARATE BOOK ON THE EXCITING LIFE OF ISHPEMING'S MR. FINN IS AVAILABLE BY THE AUTHOR AT MARQUETTE COUNTY AREA STORES.

Chapter 15:

General News
From 1890 to 1900

1890

The post office was thinking of giving free mail delivery to homes. This entailed the naming of streets that had no names up to this time, especially those outside of down-town, and of giving each residence a house number. And in early 1890, the Iron Cliffs Company was bought by the Cleveland Company and formed the Cleveland Cliffs Company. Miners that same year were offered an eight-hour day, but turned it down as their pay was based on either the amount of footage or tonnage mined.

We should also remember the respect that people had for holidays back then. The mines and the stores closed for Memorial Day to honor the veterans in 1890. They often all closed on Good Friday, and for special events like a ski tournament. 1890 saw a new U.S.A. flag with five more stars, and new states continued to join the union.

Many children died from illnesses, and from drowning. Some fell into old open shafts. Several were run over by trains backing up while they played baseball on the tracks. One girl's screaming led police to find her father was trying to kill her. The paper one week noted in a tavern that "many saw a tear-filled eight-year old boy pleading with is father to quit drinking and return home."

The mines are working at such a full speed at this time that most of the news in every edition is about mining, and far less is about town activities. The mine news was listed under the individual mines.

A new store was built at Pine and Division by a Mr. La Londe. It was 25 x 60 feet and two stories high. The French are planning to replace their church. The new Union Park is completed and the Main and Franklin Circus will appear there on June 19. This circus may not have appeared, however, as an advance man selling tickets in May, left his employment and stole the money. The Union Park was a great success, however, and in July, 60 more feet of grandstand was added on. School enrollment jumped by 472 children this year. Enrollment now is 2,976.

It was in December of 1890 that Mr. Edison's Plant at Humboldt was destroyed by fire. It was the following June that he came to Humboldt to see the fire area and decided not to rebuild.

In December, 1890, the men drilling at the Lake Angeline Mine, in a drift 330 feet underground and going in a northerly direction hit a stream of water. The next month, a shaft at the Winthrop as it was dug further down, touched a large pool of water. The Detroit mine had also hit a stream of water some time before. What happened at Barnes-Hecker in 1926 was escaped from many times at other mines. At the Hungerford Mine near Crystal Falls, the entire Michigamme River one night ran into the mine and the river dried up for some hours. Later investigation showed that a stope hole from the first level had come to within 11 feet of the surface, encouraging the river to enter.

A 16 pound baby was born in 1890. The Winthrop Mine now had a medical doctor in residence at the National Mine Location. There was a pop bottling company now in Ishpeming and it was "doing great business". A large steel boat was being built to haul iron ore that will be 318 feet long and have a draft of 25 feet. 65 steel ships are now on the Great Lakes. The Ridge Street School is about to open, but it is called the Strawberry Hill School on Ridge Street. It is currently an apartment building. Ishpeming had a Northern Michigan's Business College, and it did well for many years. 170 buildings now have gas lights, and the town has 81 fire hydrants.

1891

A good Skee Tournament took place at Brass Wire Hill between Ishpeming and Negaunee. It would be a favorite hill. The Presbyterians built a new church, and Mr. A. A. Anderson's new building, still on Main Street in 2005, will have three floors. In the Salisbury Location, a new Methodist Church is being built in the area of west South Angeline Street. The Division Street Methodist Church wants to build on Third Street but is having problems with a deed and then financing, as times were tough by 1893. In the end, they rebuilt where they were, and Mr. Trebilcock's greenhouses went on the foundations which were to be for the new church.

The city was adding a lot of "nice rock for roads, but it disappears in the muck." Later, some people will complain that a lot of the rock was rich in iron ore and now could have been sold. In April the lumberjacks were returning to town, as well as about 150 teams of horses that were loaded on trains and shipped out for the summer. Partridge Creek flooded again, and at the Chicago and Northwestern Depot, about 25 railroad cars a day are unloaded of freight for businesses and private individuals. Many are ordering from out of town. Mr. Newett commented that one grocer has complained that people are not giving their business locally, while he himself was getting his printing done elsewhere.

There are miners out of work and men are standing around at all the mines, hoping to get hired. Still in the same month, 20 Norwegians arrive on the DSS&A Railroad and are met by a large group of friends. The Lake Superior Mine has obtained a large 60-ton steam shovel for loading ore into cars. Two girls give some of their skin for a man burned badly in a Barnum Mine accident. An alarming number of peddlers are in town, and a lamb was born with five legs. Baseball is big, and is even played in the winter in some local buildings. Up to 1891, Ishpeming had a professional baseball team, but that year attendance was bad, so the club closed with $1,500. of debt.

Business booms and busts. A note says that a city merchant had to close his doors as he had too many unpaid accounts on the books. The amount owed by customers was $27,000. Sometimes the merchants met and decided to be cash only for certain periods. Mr. Braastad had cards out and people charged and earned "green stamps" for gifts. However, he also recalled his cards eventually and allowed only cash purchases. When lights arrived, several stores agreed to be closed in the afternoons and open every week-day night for the summer. One time they all agreed to be open on payday nights. Mines got paid once a month and several got paid on one day, and several another day, etc. Paydays meant paying out thousands and thousands of dollars, and the quicker the businesses got the money before the bars did, the better. At this time in 1891, Christmas was still not a big thing, and there are few Christmas ads, and no after-Christmas sale ads. Even Mr. Newett himself wishes a Merry Christmas to his readers with two or three lines of small eight-point type written in with the other local news in the issue before Christmas. (This is 14 point type.)

At Vine and High Street there was a frog pond. After July 11, 1891, there was not. It was filled in forever. No restrictions in those days we are sorry to see.

Some women left their husbands. In August of 1891, a woman of an Ishpeming Lake Superior miner left him for the far west. Another lady with two children left her husband and ran off to the Copper Country with his brother. She soon came back when he wanted to hire a young lady for their house cleaning.

In 1891, the Ishpeming Michigan Gas and Electric decided to buy an Edison General Electric dynamo to make its own electricity. It was housed in the old Lake Angeline pump house. Electricity will be used to continue lighting arc lights.

The trains were getting more competitive. The Minneapolis and St. Paul was serving breakfast on its morning train going south from Champion. The Milwaukee and Northern added a Pullman car and meals as well, on its route from Ishpeming to Chicago. And the Chicago and Northwestern announced that it plans to build a fine new depot in Ishpeming. And of course, that is the depot in the Anatomy of a Murder film. The C&NW was also putting gas lights in some of its passenger cars.

A miracle that happened was that Mr. Al Olds, as a youngster in 1891, fell into a shaft and went down 150 feet and recovered. Two mining companies, the Iron Cliffs, and Pittsburgh and Lake Angeline are planning to build a hospital on Fourth Street by Division. It is still there and serving well. A hospital might be needed, said Mr. Newett in his paper, because the ice in one's soft drink probably was cut from contaminated Lake Angeline ice.

Two Italian "wanderers" came to town and entertained children and adults with their two trained bears. These two entertainers and other people now had to be licensed at $10.00 a day, or $50.00 a year. There was now far more control over peddlers. In the same newspaper was a note that people can now buy Traveler's Checks, which were a new invention of American Express.

The Detroit Mine, having stopped operating, was now filling up with water. The new city hall is in the process of getting built and the Library will also be located there. Mr. Anderson's new three-story building is now up at Pearl and Main.

1892

The Cleveland Iron Co. has a shaft now down 810 feet and will soon be the distance of three football fields. And then this drastic change came: The Barnum Mine will begin paying its employees with checks. The new French church is completed and the pews will sell for $11.00 a seat. The Episcopal Church is also planning a new edifice and rectory. Eight new buildings have been built on Jasper Street, where a pit was filled in. The Baptists are going to build a new church on Third Street. Other old buildings are being of repaired. 75 Screw jacks were under the Horse Livery Stables to make corrections, and in July of 1892, another building was found to be tilting by seven and a half degrees in the "swamp."

There was a very large Fourth of July celebration at the Union park, right by the Electric Railway route, and a new record of 9,700 paid receipts was the railroad attendance for the day. Those attending saw people earn $1,000 in prizes.

There were many railroad accidents around this time. Once when an iron ore train was going over a hill fully loaded, several railroad cars became disconnected from the rest of the train. They made it over the top and then sped up and hit the train causing quite a bit of derailment. In 1892 there was a smash-up of two engines. A rare photo was in the paper. There was also a huge 64 railroad car pile-up in front of the Ishpeming Railroad Station. The large cars were pulled up on each other higher than the roof and took out the boarding dock. There was also an accident of two engines of the DSS&A Railway colliding head-on. One engineer did not jump and was killed.

Lots of cows are brought by train to Ishpeming to sell every spring. By May 30 of 1892, 21 carloads of them had been brought and sold. Many were killed for the beef in the fall. Cows played such an important role that Chapter Eighteen is devoted to them.

Men were also leaving the city. 60 miners left for the silver mines in Lead, South Dakota. Many were single men. However, many were staying and the school population in town was now 3,430 students, up 272 from 1891. This figure, notes the school, does not include 292 five and six year olds.

Up to 1892, the Iron Ore has been setting type by hand with individual letters. The difficult thing was that after printing the paper, the type had to be all placed back in their little type case cubicles. Now, new type-setting machines had been invented to set type by the line, and after each use, to simply melt down the type to be ready to make new type. The line-o-type could make an indefinite amount of each letter, like a typewriter. Whereas in previous years, different newspapers had employees race each other to see who could set the most type, now the best typesetters raced the Line-o-type operators of other newspapers in contests.

The Electric Railway was bringing electricity to Ishpeming and lines were going up and those getting electricity used the new incandescent light bulbs, like we use today. Ishpeming also now has its first dentist, and he is being kept busy.

In October, a farmer and his wife came into town to sell their potatoes. As they went by the Division Street School, they were "preyed upon by boys." One threw a large rock and hit the man, but police scattered them and the onlookers, and no arrests were made. In December a home in town was robbed of all its Christmas presents. Kids with dogs had a good time during the holiday, racing their sleigh pulling dogs at the dog races.

We should also note that many areas of the town are being built up with homes at this time, and real estate lots are being sold by the mining companies. Evidently, with diamond drill work, it was determined where there was ore and where there was no ore, and the ore-less land was being divided into lots. 128 lots were sold by the Cleveland Iron Company from Main to Oak. They were $500.00 each. 215 lots, size 50 x 120 were being sold in north Ishpeming by the Deer Lake Company. There were others as well.

1893

An ad appeared in the paper for people to sell Edison phonographs. An Ishpeming man has invented a ski that steers and has brakes. The Finnish people are raising money to send to help those in Finland. One Ishpeming resident who has built homes here is moving to Galveston, Texas. Wolves are killing many deer.

Death statistics for 1892 were 294 deaths in the city, with 84 of them being under two years old. 24 died from typhoid, and 18 from mine and other accidents. The mine accidents were not as great as many have made them out to be in their writing of history. When things were booming there might be a death every week, but things were bad at the mines this year, with many lay offs, and several mines closing at least temporarily. Still the city had a fine July fireworks presentation, spending $1,000. for the display. Marquette also had a new steam boat, giving rides to the Munising Pictured Rocks.

The Cleveland Cliffs Company, for their part in the Chicago World's Fair, has made a complete model of its Lake Shaft Mine at the former Lake Angeline. It is on glass plates showing all the different levels and paths in the mine and is a tremendous educational project for the public. There was a suggestion to put it afterwards at the Michigan College of Mines in Houghton, Michigan, but it was instead sold to the Columbia College School of Mines in New York City when the Fair closed..

An added note regarding the city water supply from Lake Sally was that the water line, that formerly went through the Section 16 Mine area on the west end of the Lake Angeline Mine to town, was caving. The city, therefore, also moved that part of the line all the way west from the Salisbury Water Works building to Winthrop Junction down to the Barnum Location to hook up to the city at that point instead.

At the Red Jacket Mine at Calumet, there was an accident of ten copper miners who rode a disconnected ore skip 3,050 feet down an inclined shaft to their deaths.

Although Ishpeming tried to get the County Courthouse and didn't, tried to get the

Michigan School of Mines, and didn't, they are considering trying to get the new State Insane Hospital, which we know now that they also didn't. The city will also this year buy a steam roller at a cost of $500. In June there were 12 who graduated from high school.

1893 was a very bad year for mines, businesses, and the workers. Many were leaving to go back to England, and going west. Several Finnish miners left to work in Wyoming. Many families are buying farms in the area after being laid off. For the first time there is a note in the paper that there are some empty homes in town. It was decided to not hold a county fair this fall. Mr. Mather in Cleveland presented a plan to help the local needy, so the city decided to do some street work to help the unemployed, and hired 150 men from over 300 applications and paid them about $5,000. "Well worth it," said Mr. Newett. . The annual tax sale in the newspaper ran three full pages of unpaid taxes. One man wrote to Mr. Newett's paper and informed others not to come to Burke, Idaho, as there was no work there either. (Burke is a little town just off of interstate 90 to the north on the east side of the state. It has no population listed today.) Also, some men returned to town after leaving to work in coal mines. Their complaint was that one "cannot stand up" when working.

Dogs are a large problem in town, so big that the problem will be covered in Chapter Twenty-four. Winter is coming on and wood is selling for $5.50 a full cord. Another train wreck happened at Thanksgiving time when a train, in order to get up a long grade, went extra fast, but then came to Negaunee and could not stop and hit another train. And during the holiday, Mr. Newett suggested that many remember Thanksgiving by helping the unfortunate by kind thoughts and deeds.

In December, for the first time, the DSS&A came to town by clearing the tracks with a large rotary plow. There was lots of excitement, especially when it ate up part of the Ishpeming's railroad station's platform. It was also announced that a new book on the life of a lumberman has been published, with the title In Big Timber. Also, the unemployed are being hired to shovel snow. Maybe it was good that it was a stormy Christmas Day.

1894

For the first time, ore from the stopes and drifts of a mine will be brought out using electricity. The Cleveland Lake Shaft Mine will replace the trammers who push the cars by hand to the shaft.. Through this invention, a new record was set of 1,303 tons of ore being lifted from the shaft in one night shift. Except for the Salisbury which hired 75 men, and a few other mines, there are more mine layoffs and closings. . Lake Superior stock which was selling for $80.00 a share is now down to $50. The Saginaw mine closed after an investment of $140,000. and it produced only 5,000 tons of ore.

Suits for men have been reduced from $15.00 to $12.00. At the Nelson House, rates are now only $2.00 a day, down fifty cents. Union Park is having horse racing, bike races, and horse versus bike races. A cash purse was $700. Employment was advertised for wood choppers, and pay was sixty cents for splitting a full cord. And in spite of the slow mining, the Excelsior Furnace was running full steam and making 50 tons of pig iron a day.

Ishpeming, Negaunee, and Marquette are now all connected by telephone. The Ishpeming Library in the past ten months loaned out 8,088 books. Julius Ropes went on a trip to Colorado to tour the great Eldorado Mine. Boys in town

are making ice boats and sailing them on Lake Bancroft, where ice is also being cut. Ice blocks were used in Ishpeming almost to 1960 and chipped to put in pop and other cold drinks. Men working in the woods this winter will make $26.00 plus room and board. At Christmas time, Ishpeming got a new Dentist, W. I. Bell. At the same time, Mr. Will Bradley left the Iron Ore and the city behind to go on and become a famous "Art Nouveau" illustrator in New York.

The year ended with tough times still existing. Two boys had to be arrested for stealing coal. Someone broke into Mr. Egan's Hardware Store to steal a gun. People are collecting and selling used newspapers for 50 cents a hundred pounds. Mr. Dunstan on Vine Street had 15 chickens stolen. Forged checks are being passed and a warning given to area businessmen.

1895

Statistics show 429 Ishpeming births for the past year with a doctor assisting, and 60 or more without a doctor. There were 233 boys and 196 girls. Telephones now total 187.

People will be able to ride the new Lake Superior and Ishpeming Railroad to Marquette in their new passenger cars next summer and picnic at the Island.

Mr. Mather is in town and says he will donate money towards a new high school, providing that there is a section for manual training. With the help of other mining companies as well, a public vote was taken on Saturday afternoon, March 23, 1895, to build a new high school with the mines paying $19,500 of the cost and the public paying $5,500. It passed, 109 for and 9 against. Remember that only property owners could vote at this time. The first High School will be at First and North Streets and later became the middle school

Grammar School. It would have an 8 foot dial clock and a 1000 pound bell.

Women are seeking the right to vote. Someone wants to sell a Columbian bike with only 200 miles on it and it has a self-oiling chain. While Mr. Mather is in town he announced a contest of prizes for beautification of the Cleveland Cliffs Mining Locations. At the mines, part of the surface over the incline shaft at the Cleveland Mine caved in.

The first circus that came in 1895 was the Leeman Brother's Circus. Its ad tells us that they have "Rajah, an elephant larger than Jumbo 2, and 3000 pounds more." When the circus day arrived, the Leeman train collided with an iron ore train, twenty miles north of Escanaba. It was very foggy and two horses were killed. There was no report as to whether the show was cancelled. A month later, in August, it was reported that the Ringling Bros. circus would arrive on 50 railroad cars. Only one show was presented as it arrived late from the Copper Country, but the show had a full tent in spite of the low employment, and a rare mine strike going on. It was going next to Menominee.

Because of the strike, the U.S. Militia was sent in to Ishpeming and they camped on the hill just south of the Lake Superior Mine. The strike affected all the mines, and after the men refused an offer, the Salisbury Mine closed down its pumps, which flooded the mine and the shaft, The shaft went out of shape because of the water soaking the soft hematite ore body, and a new shaft, and in reality, a new mine, had to be built. This was far more costly to the mine than the strike. The strike was ultimately over, but no one, as is often the case, really won. Miners settled for the previous offer. The militia was to hold the peace when the Lake Superior Mine

decided to hire others to help ship out ore during the strike. One soldier died.

Bicycling was in high gear, and there was to be a bike tournament with $3,000 in prizes. Often the prizes were presented by stores as many people would come to the area to see the tournament and then spend time shopping and riding the trains and electric railway.

This was one of the periods where grocery men met and would do business only for cash, and other merchants were also going to stop extending credit. By the fall of 1895, however, with the strike over, all mines were hiring.

A note regarding the Quincy Mine in Hancock appeared on October 5. A mass of pure copper, weighing an estimated 300 tons was found down on the 33rd level and was 33 feet thick. A note also tells us that a Calumet and Hecla copper mine shaft in the Copper Country is down 4,900 feet on an incline.

Mr. Mather gave his awards for his mine locations. None went to the Salisbury Location where he noted that there was "no attempt at improvement." The individuals who did win prizes were invited to be his guests at the Mather Cottage.

1896

It is January and the Tucker Theatre Company has been playing to crowded houses all week. Typhoid is quite high, and there is a notice not to use ice from Lake Bancroft in ice boxes for cooling as it is filled with bacteria.

Ishpeming now has night schools for immigrants at the Salisbury School, and it will be continued. Courses include English, reading, writing, and business courses. Cost is $1.50 a month. It later was increased to $5.00 for ten weeks. As to regular day school, several people were arrested and fined $5.00 plus court costs for leaving children out of school, or truancy.

One downtown store will give away three nice bicycles. All one has to do is shop there and get a free ticket with every dollar spent. This is also the year that pianos became popular, the big uprights. Over 60 were sold in town.   A new rule kept bikes off of sidewalks and they can travel no more than ten miles per hour. The city of Republic has a newspaper, the Republic Record. The Penglase Building, while getting a basement, discovered the original "Corduroy Road", the first wood log road through town. Mr. John Penglase moved away from Ishpeming in early December of 1894 for Montana, but just a month later, on January 12, 1895, he died in Alaska.

Silver coins are replacing gold, and Mr. Newett's notes that the U.S. is stamping $1.00 on coins worth only 50 cents of silver.   On the Fourth of July, the city used some 16 inch fireworks shot from a cannon.   The Lake Angeline Mine is working full speed, but the Lake Superior has an ore pile on the ground of 250,000 tons still unsold.   Because of caving ground, the Lake Angeline Mine also moved several houses from Angeline Street. The city of Negaunee is going to get its own electric plant. It has its own city electrical system still today.

The Salisbury Methodist Church held a picnic and had music by a band. A big bike race was held on the Cliff Drive road, and Cornish wresting matches are held in town for cash prizes.   Schools grew by another 250 students this year.

At Christmas time, the newspaper notes that a "Santa Claus" appeared in a store window. We take it that it was a "real" one.   At a local lake, a one mile ice skating race was held. There is

talk that maybe Ishpeming could get the new State Normal School that is planned. And, for the first time, there are no ads on the front page of the newspaper. Up to now, advertising filled the left two or three columns of the front page.

Crime has been a large item with robbing of railroad cars, of stores of guns, etc, and opening of safes. The police seem to solve none of them. In fact, one policeman was discovered committing a robbery of food at the Co-op store on Main Street.

1897

THE FIRST "MOVIES" began in this year. At the end of February of this year the first Cinematoscope Exhibition takes place for one week. People are coming to watch a movie film. The newspaper noted that the pictures "are animated and life-size. " Wow!" . Admission was 25 and 35 cents. So popular did movies hit town that on Saturday afternoon, 1800 children were invited to watch one. It must have been done in shifts as the town had no building to hold that many people.   After it left town, an announcement was made that it would return to the Opera House again for two more days. This report was made by Mr. Butler, the Opera House Manager A few weeks later, the show returned and added new pictures, and also phonograph music.

We don't know how the new Cinematoscope affected the live theatre performances, but a burlesque show came to town at this time and its manager skipped town with the money during the performance, and the girls were all stranded in Ishpeming.   The girls did an extra show courtesy of the city and raised the $40.00 necessary to get to Negaunee.

This was also the time the Carp River sewer was finally being lowered to improve the city sewers. A new law was passed prohibiting selling of tobacco to anyone less than 17 years of age. A local pharmacy installed a "Soda Water Fountain". "A beauty" noted Mr. Newett. Those were the days! A wonderful one still existed in Johnson's Drug store when I was a boy.

Upper Peninsula organized outdoor sports were held in the summer at the Union Park for the first time. A Sioux Indian doctor was at the Voelker Building selling Indian Medicine and entertaining. People from the Isle of Man in the Irish Sea met in Humboldt in July for a gathering and sports. Area gold mines have disappeared as fast as they appeared. Employment is good again, and the paper reported in October of 1897 that "All men can now find work in woods or mines."

Ishpeming Football now is in the news. The boys won at Calumet and then defeated a Milwaukee South Side Team. They ended up undefeated, and the game was played with few rules. When several new rules were instituted, the players refused to play anymore. Rules evidently made the game too tame. For a few years, Ishpeming did not have a team

The large Salisbury United Methodist Church was moved in October from the area of west South Angeline Street, across a long swamp, to be next to the large Salisbury School. Downtown, on New Year's Eve, the Division Street Methodist Episcopal Church provided entertainment for non-alcoholic drinkers.

December news from the Klondike in Canada reported that there was plenty of gold in camp, but no food. The Carnegie Steel Company is now making steel 30 ton iron ore railroad cars that are lighter than wooden ones. For comparison, today's railroads carry iron ore in 70 ton cars.

1898

The Cliffs Shafts, having been closed since 1894, are being pumped out so that mining can take place again. First Street has been cut through the bluff just north of the new High School. The Finnish Apostolic Church is being built at Cleveland and Fourth Streets.

"Uncle Tom's Cabin" returned to town and the show is good, says Mr. Newett, but adds that there was no calliope or donkey this year. A Mr. William Caine slipped on the ice and fell 100 feet down the Salisbury Mine Shaft and was only bruised. However, the mine inspector fell into a shaft and was killed after falling 444 feet.

Mr. Outhwaite is selling his seven room house at 604 North Third Street. The Ishpeming High School baseball team played the Minneapolis High School in a home game here at Union Park. The LS&I RR began its passenger traffic to Presque Isle in Marquette and it proved so popular that they added two more passenger coaches to their equipment. A new circus came to town. We don't know if it came by rail or by wagon, but it had the famous name of Skerbeck. This family name eventually moved on from being a good one-ring circus show to the present day amusement carnival show and still thrives in the Upper Peninsula.

During this year, a request came again from the Chicago and Northwestern Railroad to the city to eliminate the Second Street railroad crossing so that they can build a new station. The city agreed to do that. However, the station was eventually built and the street was never closed off and there seemed to be plenty of room for both.

The newspaper is cautioning people against buying stocks without studying them in detail. Many townspeople are purchasing them, and there is a list of many copper company stocks in the paper every week by a local broker. In September of 1898, the Calumet and Hecla stock was selling for $570.00 a share, the Quincy at $116.00 and the Tamarack at $172.50. By November 19 the C & H stock was up to $640.00, and gave a quarterly $10.00 dividend per share.

The Iron Ore was beginning its 20th year of production and still sold for its original subscription price of $2.00 a year. This will still be true twenty years later yet, in 1920.

The fountain pen is invented that can load ink into itself and write without an "ink-well" for a long period of time. Locally, a new "invention" is golf, and the Ishpeming Golf Club was formed. The Milwaukee and St. Paul Railroad now will not only have lighted passenger cars, but heated ones as well. Cameras are now being used at "up-to-date wedding ceremonies." One bank invented a new way to get business by offering 2% of its gross profits to Ishpeming churches between November 24 and Christmas Day.

A new film company, the New York Biograph Co. came to the Opera House with moving pictures of the latest boxing fight and a war movie of Cuba. Seats are 10 and 25 cents. The next week the newspaper announced, as usual, that the film attendance was very large.

At this point in his research, the author was surprised to read that a Mr. John Kotajarvi had an eye accident at Lake Angeline "C" Shaft, and was taken to the hospital where the eye was removed. This was my grandfather whom I knew as a little child. He left mining and ran a 120 acre farm in Humboldt, using horses into the 1940's, and I knew he had a glass eye from a mine accident. He died in 1948.
The Electric Light Company of the Electric Street Railway is selling more electricity and

will get a new, larger, G.E. Generator that will be 2.5 times greater than the present one. In the schools, the little children were visited by Santa Claus before going on their holiday, and the Star Bank, true to its ad, awarded local churches $7.42 each. Yet it was a sad holiday for nineFinnish families at the Lake Superior Mine. An accident claimed the lives of six men and badly injured three others. The deaths were all ruled "accidental" as usual.

1899

Slot machines have been a big and illegal problem at the town's taverns. The taverns have been a large problem in many ways. The previous fourth of July they were open when they were supposed to be closed. They are open on Sunday afternoons when they are supposed to be closed. Nothing seemed to be done about it, but the police did report that they got rid of a few of the "town's slot machines" to start the final year of the "Gay Nineties." Mr. Newett investigated this announcement and reported a week or two later: ""Not one slot machine is gone."

January 28: Calumet and Hecla Stock hit $750 a share. February 11: C&H stock is at $800 a share. A dividend was declared of $40 a share, and the total dividend paid to stockholders was $4,000,000. It kept going higher and in April it was at $815 per share. Then in October, the copper stocks came down and many lost quite a bit of money. In Negaunee, it was thought the people there lost a quarter million dollars.

An "ice walker" came to town and bet that he could out-walk an ice skater. The contest was held and the walking man won on Lake Bancroft. The city, which had been plowing sidewalks, but rolling down the snow on streets for sleighs, for the first time is using wooden plows on the streets with good success. The new state Normal College for teachers is in the planning works, and once again the city of Ishpeming hopes to be in the running. In March, state officials arrived in town to look at the site proposed by Ishpeming for a Normal College. Of course, it was not built here. The Lake Superior Mine was sold to the Oliver Mining Company of Minnesota. The Oliver was purchasing land of several operating mines, and kept it until recent times when it was all sold to private individuals, --- including entire mines such as the Lake Superior. The author and his wife are now living in a home on former Oliver property (Including an old paved 1940's US-41 highway in their yard).

The Marquette County Telephone Company now had 1000 subscribers and issued a phone book. For the past several years, the Michigan Bell Telephone Company had been pushing to also have a phone company here. An Ishpeming firm will start a profit sharing program with its employees. The Ishpeming Public Schools held an exhibit of all the work that school children have been doing and it was well attended. The Columbian Bike Company has eliminated a chain on its bikes and replaced it with gears and a drive shaft,, similar to an automobile. The bikes now sell for $60 to $75.00. The Ringling Bros. Circus is returning this year, with half-page ads in the newspaper. There was the usual large street parade and two performances. Two other trick bicyclists came to town and were stopped by the police for doing their tricks. Mr. Newett, who liked entertainment, noted that it was certainly "not illegal." And in this year the first carnival ride ever, appeared in Ishpeming. A large merry-go-round was unfolded and put together on West Division Street and had a "liberal patronage nightly".

Mines are booming again, and neither railroads nor wood cutting companies could find enough local workers. In Ishpeming, 200 men arrived on the train to work for the Cleveland Mill Company in the woods. A group of black men even arrived in the Copper Country to help out with the labor shortage in the mines there. Cleveland Cliffs moved their offices from Division to a new building on Lake Bancroft.

Here is another first: the FIRST CAR visited Ishpeming. Mr. Harry Pickands brought his car to Ishpeming on a trip from Marquette. It must have been the first automobile to ride on an Ishpeming street. Six new residences (cottages) are being built on W. Empire, N. Second, and on the north shore of Lake Bancroft at a cost of $2,000 each. For a second time, mud and water broke into the Cleveland Lake Mine from the old Lake Angeline Lake Bed. The ore piles at all the mines are quickly disappearing to be shipped before the Sault Locks close for the winter. Thus ends the decade for the "Gay 1990's."

THIS IS ONE OF THE FENCED OFF SHAFTS OF THE OLD SECTION 16 MINE. SOUTH PINE STREET CAVED IN AT THE LAKE ANGELINE MINE IN DECEMBER OF 1906, AND SEVERAL TIMES DURING THE WINTER OF 1907. A NEW HIGHWAY WAS BUILT NEXT TO THIS SHAFT WITH THE TRESTLE FROM THE SHAFT TO THE ROCK PILE CROSSING OVER THE NEW ROAD. THE SHAFT WAS IN SOFT ORE, AND EVENTUALLY WENT OUT OF SHAPE AND WAS UNUSABLE. A NEW HOLMES MINE TO THE NORTHWEST WAS BUILT .

10,000 PEOPLE ATTENDED THIS ISHPEMING SKI-JUMPING, 1907, TOURNAMENT. JOHN EVENSON MADE A RECORD JUMP OF 122 FEET (PHOTO FROM COLLIER'S MAG.)

THIS BIOGRAPHY ABOUT FREDERICK BRAASTAD SEEMS TO BE IN ERROR, REGARDING HIS LEAVING THE ISHPEMING AREA, AS WE CONTRAST IT TO WEEKLY NEWS IN MR. NEWETT'S IRON ORE. THE AUTHOR IS UNABLE TO TRACE THE DISCREPANCY. THIS ISHPEMING CENTENNIAL ARTICLE APPEARED IN THE MINING JOURNAL. NOT ALL OF THIS BIOGRAPHY IS PRINTED.

mine operated by the Winthrop Iron Company, of which he was general manager. He also was a director of the Peninsula Bank of Ishpeming and a director of the Negaunee and Ishpeming Electric Street Railway Company. He served two terms as alderman of Ishpeming, held the office of mayor and in 1890 was elected state treasurer, serving two years under Governor Winans.

In 1904, after 16 months of remodelling and enlarging the great new store was opened, with Braastad as manager, assisted by Arvid Braastad. But two years later, Braastad decided to dispose of his interests in Ishpeming and leave this city to go into business

to an industrial concern which would benefit the city financially. The businessmen succeeded in getting the Gossard Company to open a ladies garment factory on the site in 1920.

in Canada. In addition to the store Braastad owned several farms comprising nearly 300 acres in the Carp River Valley and 60 acres in the Dead River district. When he planned to leave, however, he offered for sale all his real estate, farm, timber lands, equipment, etc.

Dissolved In 1919

A Chicago firm negotiated for purchase of the store block, merchandise and a large stone warehouse on Front Street. The store continued to operate until 1919 when the Braastad Store Company was dissolved.

Ishpeming's businessmen then decided to raise funds to purchase the Braastad block and turn it in-

THE AUTHOR AND HIS WIFE, ROBERT D. AND ETHEL DOBSON

Chapter 16:
And There was Crime

We have mentioned several crimes thus far in this history, but there were many saved for this special section. The readers can judge for themselves in which direction the world is going. And note how much the invention of the telephone a bit earlier might have changed these crimes.

Two bartenders used guns to chase a husband away from his wife and then tried to rape her. She was saved by her screams. (1882) Also in 1882, Jesse James was killed, and before the police could arrest the Ford Brothers for the murder, Jesse's brother Frank had a band of outlaws out to get whoever killed his brother. Two women were arrested for stealing and were found to have special coats with extra big pockets. In another case, although he hadn't been yet arrested, the newspaper noted that there is a man calling at homes of women alone, under the pretense of selling pictures. Another man went around selling subscriptions and saying he was from a down-town drug store and that their magazines could be picked up there. He had no drugstore endorsement and put the money in his pocket.

Several quack "doctors" were coming to town giving free lectures and then selling health items. Ishpeming was often flooded with these people when spring broke every year. Ishpeming also had a real "Chinese Laundry" and in 1883, the Chinaman from the Laundry was attacked by hoodlums. At Thanksgiving time that year a "seedy" individual came to town and was found to be stealing. He was caught by the police and the police chief put him to work. Mr. Newett notes that the man was gone "quickly." There was the problem of

young boys shouting and whistling in the balconies during theatrical entertainment. In 1884, Mr. Newett writes that several youth have been finally arrested for constantly disturbing the performances.

In 1885 a man was arrested for taking advantage of someone else's wife. A person soon found out the he was the same man who had been calling down the skating rink on Lake Bancroft as immoral. Another man escaped to Alaska after having been discovered that he stole money from two local financial accounts. The newspaper notes that he will be arrested if he returns, and then also says that he had been appointed as postmaster of Humboldt, so that tells you how much the government knows. In October of 1885 there was a Saturday night wife beating. No mention of an arrest. Locally, several boys formed a gang and robbed a keg of beer and were found at their hideout west of the Barnum location. The next month there was an article about the University of Michigan, saying that the 1,200 Ann Arbor University students think they own the town.

In 1886 three peddlers arrived in late February, and not one had a peddlers' license. Only two were arrested, and one allowed to go as he was blind. Many of the readers may remember blind men going house to house with an assistant and the author remembers buying some needles and a threader from one when a youth.

One man came to town with a $200. draft, and wished to cash it, asking several to sign for him as to his identity, but no one would. He seemed to also have an alcohol problem. Another man was killed in a saloon----he fell. Four boys, aged 9, 10, 11, and 12 were arrested for robbing homes in the summer of 1888. In Iron Mountain in 1889 a man with two guns robbed the passengers on the Milwaukee and Northern Railroad just south of town. He was later arrested by the sheriff and was awarded with two nice new pistols.

In 1890, a circus employee came to town a few weeks before the Main and Franklin Circus, to put up posters and sell advance tickets (they were cheaper earlier). After taking the money, he left town, and the Circus. Two employees of the Michigan Gold Mine were arrested for taking gold, just as they were leaving Ishpeming on the next train. Voelker's Saloon was robbed by safe crackers.

In this period, $1,200,000. was the spent for a 36-mile railroad that went bankrupt in Champion. No one was ever arrested, but some individuals from Lower Michigan sure lost a lot of money. The Iron Range and Huron Bay Railroad made many, many rock cuts, including a large sixty-footer at the 1,900 foot summit of the Huron Mountains, built a large 112 pocket ore loading dock, and kept about 1500 men working for three years. .

In 1893 four men robbed the train between Calumet and Hancock of its payroll, probably in gold and silver. They got $75,000 of the pay being sent for the Calumet and Hecla miners. They were arrested. A mind-reader appeared in Ishpeming and was determined by his audience and Mr. Newett to be a fake. It appeared in the paper and the man received his own punishment in Marquette when only a small crowd came "because of the publicity."

Boys were often caught for stealing. Some abandoned buildings were often stripped bare of wood, taken home for the stove. Mr. Eggan's store on Cleveland Avenue was robbed a second time. Guns were taken on both occasions. This period was one of the hardest of the hard times of employment. Even forged checks were being passed.

A confectionary store worker, a woman, was "molested" by some boys and they were later arrested in May of 1895. In September of that year a young boy was arrested for stealing shoes when cold weather arrived. In October, Mr. Jochim's Hardware Store on Main Street was robbed of guns. Although there were many fights, and often knifings at local saloons, there was a murder in one on Pearl Street on the Fourth of July in 1896. In August, three boys were arrested for burglary. Somehow, the punishment news rarely made it into Mr. Newett's newspaper. In September, a man on the Cliffs Drive was held up and robbed by two men. In October the Seldon Hardware safe was robbed. In November, there was another robbery of guns and knives at a local store.

Some people were caught. Mrs. Lord had her name printed in the paper. She was guilty of shop-lifting in the winter of 1897. In the spring of that same year, the police caught some store robbers, but in the next week there was another burglary. During that summer there was an interesting arrest of a new business owner in town who ran a Second-Hand Store. Police came all the way from Altoona, Pennsylvania, to arrest him for the rape of a fourteen year old girl. He had jumped bond and came here and secretly used post offices in Marquette and Canada so he could not be found.

I don't know if there was any arrest or not, but on Thanksgiving week of 1897, two men roughed up the Mayor of Ishpeming, Mr. Trebilcock. 1898 saw the mines pick up in employment, and at the same time, there were a lot fewer burglaries, with the only one being the robbery of a confectionary shop. The largest crimes in 1899 seemed to be that "Cheap Johns" were arriving in town to sell "cheap merchandise." Not really a crime in that, but Mr. Newett put out a warning to his readers anyway so they wouldn't get "robbed".

WHEN THE INDIAN STATUE WAS PLACED IN THE ISHPEMING CITY SQUARE, WHERE IT STILL STANDS, IT HAD SEVERAL DRINKING FOUNTAINS. THE SMALLEST HIGHER ONES WERE FOR HUMANS. THE NEXT, AND LARGEST FOUNTAIN, WAS FOR THE MANY HORSES OF BUSINESSES, AND CUSTOMERS IN TOWN. IN THE NEXT CHAPTER YOU WILL ALSO SEE THAT THIS FOUNTAIN BECAME THE MEETING PLACE DAY AND NIGHT FOR THE COWS OF THE TOWN AS WELL. DOGS AND CATS USED THE LOWER FOUNTAINS.

PHOTO: THE OCTOBER, 1981, CALENDAR OF FRIENDS OF THE ISHPEMING CARNEGIE LIBRARY.

MARQUETTE COUNTY MINES.

ANTHONY BROAD, *Mine Inspector, County of Marquette.* Office at Negaunee. Telephone.

AMERICAN IRON CO.—W. H. Johnston, Pres.; T. F. Donahoe, V. Pres.; S. K. Wambold, Gen'l Mgr., Treas.; C. R. Ely, Sec.; W. C. Reed, Supt. Lessees Boston mine. Sec. 32, 48-28.

BLUE IRON MINING CO.—W. D. Rees, Pres. Location one mi e east of Negaunee, S.W. ¼ of the S.W. ¼ of section 5, N. of main track of C & N. W. R'y, also that portion of W. 10 rods in width off S.E. ¼ of S.W ¼ of section 5, N. of said railway. Sam Mitchell, Negaunee, Gen'l Mgr.

THE BOSTON MINE.—Located a few miles west from the Dexter. The property consists of 80 acres—the S. E ¼. S.W. ¼, and S.E. ¼ sec. 32, 48-28.

THE BARNUM MINE—And Cliff shaft; belonging to the Iron Cliffs Co. Sec. 11, 47-27. S. L. Mather, Pres.; Wm. Sedgwick, Supt.; A. Mather, Negaunee, Agt.

THE CHAMPION MINE.—At Champion. W. E. Stone, Treas., Boston, Mass.; A. Kidder, Agt., Marquette; W. Fitch, Supt., Champion; James Cundy, Mining Capt.; Wm. Williams, Master Mechanic. Sec. 31, 48-29.

NORTH CHAMPION IRON CO.—Mine in the E. ¼ N. E. ¼ Sec. 29, 48-29, being a mile north of Champion station. W. Fitch, Champion, General Managerr.

THE CLEVELAND MINING CO.—F. P. Mills, Supt., Ishpeming; S. L. Mather, Pres., Cleveland, O.; F. A. Morse, Sec'y. Sec. 10, 47-27.

THE CAMBRIA MINE.—A. Maitland, Negaunee, General Manager; Chas. Koch, Supt. Sec. 2, 47-27.

WE SHALL PERIODICALLY, AS ROOM ALLOWS, PRINT THIS 1891 CITY DIRECTORY LISTING OF ALL MARQUETTE RANGE IRON ORE MINES. THIS IS NO. 1 OF 5 PARTS

Chapter 17:
When Cows Ran the Town

For most of the time period covered in this Mining Town History, downtown Ishpeming provided cows with an open range. Many people in town wanted a cow, but no one had any land on which to keep it. So it was that all land became "cow-land."

If I could have written this book entirely as a news item, by news item history in chronological order from the summer newspapers, this would have been the subject. The Iron Ore showed many articles about cows, popping up almost as a regular feature. Some stories were sad, some were humorous, and often they were complaints.

The first article in Mr. Newett's paper was in 1880, that "Two cows were run over by an ore train at the New York Mine…" A butcher from a near-by store was called to end their misery. The mine also paid for damages done, which might be to say that the owners were reimbursed for their cows by the railroad. We often note that when miners were killed in the mines, almost 100 per cent of the time they were declared accidents, and no compensation seemed to be given to wives and children.

Two years later, in 1882, the town's newspaper noted that the pound master, Mr. Blewett, had posted around town, signs "notifying people that if their cattle, hogs, geese, etc. are not kept off the public thoroughfares, they will be immediately impounded." We shall see that this attempt was absolutely useless for about the next 40 years. In fact the problems would get far worse as railroad cars full of cows were brought to town and sold every spring starting in 1883. It was the same year that bars were required to close on Sundays, so the arrival of so

many cows was reasoned by Mr. Newett as "Something had to be done, you know, to supply liquids for suffering humanity on Sundays."

Cows got very numerous, so Mr. Newett put in this humorous news item: "The Ishpeming cow should be allowed to register this spring (to vote). They associate with the people so generally that they should be allowed all the privileges of citizenship."

More humor resulted by a cow herself. One of the new cows just arriving in town "made a fine record as a climber.…going up the long stairs leading to the Opera House Hall from the bottom to the top. She drew a larger audience than most of the shows." Mr. Newett added: "She is of the same breed of animal that jumped over the moon.…"

In 1887, 300 cows arrived in town and were sold. The reader might ask if 300 cows come every year, how many cows were there, actually. Well, not as many as you might think. In the fall, many people killed their cows and feasted on beef all winter. Some may not even have had barns to keep them in. That same year, several cows also died from drinking water from Mud Lake which turned out to be poisonous by chemicals from a "glucodine works" nearby. The owners sued, but the judge decided that the cows were trespassers and the factory owner was not responsible. (Note that this Mud Lake was also the lake that ice was taken from for cold drinks in the summer.)

In all of the articles, there is no mention of cow bells. I should think if the cows each had a bell that the entire town would have been tinkling all day, and even more at night. I grew up in the city of Ishpeming in the 1940's, and our cows, even calves, had a bell, even though we had fenced-in fields for them. The bells helped us to know where the cows were and the bells were a beautiful sound on a quiet day as the cows chewed their "cud" while lying down. I still have our cow bell and ring it now and then, but only a cow knows how to ring a cow-bell.

On October 6, 1888, Mr. Newett decided to write an entire essay about the cows, and titled it simply, THE COW. It was his best article yet, of putting a real problem in a humorous light. Here are some excerpts: "The cow still enjoys the autumnal shrubbery in the lawn of the average citizen........Who has ever gazed into the eyes of a brindle cow and has not been moved---or tried to milk one from the wrong side and not been moved........Last spring when the council got out its notices stating that the cows must be kept off the street, it was a heart rending sight to see a number of the poor bovines standing around the city flag staff, in the public square, reading a poster that was intended to deprive them of their former enjoyment and liberty."

The very next week, Mr. Newett tackled a problem he forgot in his "Cow column" of the previous week, and that was the "cow pasty." They weren't called that at this time, but the manure was the same. "Monday morning she left a bundle of tracts in front of the post office door that remained there for two days. Looked real pretty until some unfeeling wretch stepped on them." The next week Mr. Newett tackled the problem of the filthy condition of the sidewalks on Main Street and that the city did not clean them up. He suggested that people use the streets and let the cows use the walks.

Cows went everywhere. "Yesterday morning a big black bovine tried to get into the recorder's office, probably wanted a license to operate a lottery....." The same month of October, 1888, the new city Indian Statue and water fountain was to arrive, and Mr. Newett noted that it should be protected with a neat fence, "else the cows will make a nuisance of the spot. They will

roost there nights and gambol about throughout the day."

The cows were quite smart and evidently people argued from time to time as to which was smarter, a cow or a dog. Mr. Newett once noted that a cow learned to open his master's safe after watching him do it a few times. He also recorded this story, also in 1888 of watching a cow open up the gate of the Reverend Mr. Jacobs: "She would take the latch in her mouth, lift it and pull the gate open a little way, but it would go back too quickly for her to get in when she would release her hold upon it. Finally, after many trials, she gave it an extra big pull, dexterously placed one horn between the gate and post and went in to enjoy the green grass of the pastor's lawn. Mr. E. C. Colley saw a part of the performance and can vouch for the truth of what we have said."

The same year a train locomotive hit another cow, but in this case, a brakeman on the train was accidentally killed. A cow crossed the track and an empty boxcar being pushed by a C&NW engine hit it and went over it, the car leaving the rails. The brakeman, riding the car fell off and the next car ran over him. "He was a single man abut 27 years of age, a steady hard working boy, the main support of a large family," reported Mr. Newett. Mr. Newett reported the death, but also the fact that the railroad people have been in "constant dread of such an accident."

The next year, in 1889, someone poisoned three cows and a heifer. The month was January, so these cows evidently roamed town all winter without any shelter. Four months later, the city again is encouraged by Mr. Newett, to hire another pound master. He ended the article by noting that the "cow is enjoying herself, promenading the streets, tasting of the new buds, and looking out for forage work to be done later in the season." Lost and found ads regarding cows were also being placed in the paper from time to time.

By October of 1891, the city had a pound master, and a pound for cows. That month he captured and confined 30 cows, and the city derived revenue of $36.50 from the owners. "The cow question is receiving proper attention," said Mr. Newett in the November 7, 1891 edition of the paper.

Here is an example of a "Female Chorus": "Quite a congregation of cows held service last Sunday on the plateau....where north Third Street is intersected by Vine. They bellowed out their hymns of praise in tons more voluminous than musical..... They pawed the earth, licked their chops, swung their tails, tossed their horns, and strained their eyes to gaze beyond the blue above." He noted that the service ended with prayers by the onlookers in a forcible language.

One day, Mr. Newett sat down and figured the financial picture of owning cows. The date was April 30, 1892. 420 cows had already been brought to town and sold to residents. The average price of a cow was $45.00 and so people have paid out $18,900. If every family had enough milk and products to use and were able to sell a quart for 10 cents, then the 420 quarts a day for every day of the summer would amount to 75,600 quarts for $7,560 of income by cow holders. If the cows are slaughtered, the 420 cows will amount to 210,00 pounds of meat at ten cents a pound, and would mean a savings of $21,000 for not having to buy from a butcher.

In 1899, almost 20 years have passed since we listed here the first cow story, and the record sounds about the same regarding the cow: "she is the most careless animal, and considers not the feelings of mankind, showing utter disregard of the opinions of pedestrians and

growers of shrubbery and flowers." The newspaper editor then goes on to say that the pound master during all this "continues to draw his salary with great regularity..." It seems that the pound master and his friends seem to be the owners of several of the cows running the town at night, but that citizens are requesting "to the village cowboy that he give some evidence that he is yet alive."

A new pound master now was Mr. Mike Tasson, and he impounded quite a few cows, with some interference from owners who tried to stop his driving their cow to the pound. Once he had to use his billy-club twice when a knife was used against him by a cow-owner. He did such a good job in the early 1900's that by 1908 people felt free to take down their fences of their yards. "There are still a few cows to bother, and gardens will have to be protected by fences until the bovines have all disappeared from the streets," wrote Mr. Newett.

Autos started coming to Ishpeming after 1903, and by 1910, there were quite a few—enough to start cow-auto accidents. "Some reckless auto driver killed a cow on the highway near Negaunee, Wednesday night. ....There are several places on this road....where cows are not taken proper care of, being permitted to remain on the road all night.....The public highway is no place to pasture cattle....." There was no report of any injuries from the accident, nor were there any from this following auto-cow collision. It was always an amazing fact that when cars overturned for one reason or another, that there were no deaths, considering the early cars often had no tops. This report from 1915: Mr. Charles Korppela was driving down the hill at West Ishpeming and noticed some calves on the highway. All but one got out of the way, and that one was hit by Mr. Korppela, with his car almost going into the ditch, and overturning.

All of the five people were pinned underneath. "Fortunately no one was seriously hurt."

In 1914 the health of cows became a concern, with tuberculosis (TB) testing of cows coming into practice. Ishpeming, however, seemed to lag behind such communities such as Munising: "Munising has tested more that 200 cows and found only five afflicted with tuberculosis. That's a small number providing you were not getting milk from one of them, in which case it would be too many." Mr. Newett also was concerned that milk was still being sold and delivered by individuals and dealers, in open pails. "We have noticed that several of the local dealers are now using the bottles, having discarded the pails, and are trying to sell milk that is clean," said Mr. Newett on December 8, 1914.

Many of our readers remember Northern Dairy. School classes took trips there and got a free Dixie-cup. That building was built in 1916, when the Meen Brothers opened a creamery. Because they were buying milk, it became a boon for farmers which encouraged keeping cows, and more cows, year around. The building stands today at Second and Ely. The author's mother was born in 1914, and she remembered going to Ishpeming on Saturdays by horse and buggy from Humboldt to Meen Brothers to sell their cream. She, too, got some ice-cream.

Our final article is from 1917. One would think that the down-town cow problem would be long gone, and cows would no longer be running the town. Wrong!! It was like time had stood still since 1880. "Not a few gardens in this city have been much damaged by cows and horses that are permitted to run at large in the night time. The mayor lost his garden several nights ago. .... Will Minnear, who had a fine garden, found a cow devouring everything within reach and her reach was good."

And Mike Tasson on August 25, 1917, is still the pound master and is at work in the city of Ishpeming. "The pound master will get very busy now, he tells us, as this is the time of the year when cows are the most destructive." . A year later, Mr. Tasson had to use his gun when attacked by a huge gentleman whose calf was found in someone else's garden. After being knocked down, Tasson drew his gun on a second forthcoming attack, and shot Mr. Joe Lami in the hip. Mr. Newett's paper noted that "Spectators said he was within his rights as he was attacked without reason and stood in danger of great punishment from this burly Joe."

Regarding the entire cow problem, Mr. Newett was able to end his last article with almost the same words he used 40 years before, regarding cows: "This is a country in which law and order must be preserved." In actuality, I believe the problem continued for at least 40 years more, as two people, older than I, have told me similar stories of cows still roaming the town when they were young.

DEXTER CONSOLIDATED MINING CO.—Organized to operate the Dexter and Dey, contiguous mines. The former being the E. ¼ N. E. ¼, and the latter the W. ¼ N. W. ¼ of Sec 3, 47-28. Supt, Thos Walters.

THE DETROIT MINE.—Lee Burt, Gen'l Manager and Sales Agent, Detroit, Mich.; Joseph Thomas, Supt. Sec. 3, 47-27.

EAST JACKSON MINE.—The property is the west part of the S.W. ¼ of Sec. 7, 47-26, formerly the Pendill mine, leased by Hon. J. Q. Adams, Capt. J. F. Foley and others of Negaunee.

THE FOSTER MINE.—Sec. 23, 47-27, east of the Branstad, on the estate of the Iron Cliffs Co. A. Maitland, General Manager, Negaunee.

THE GIBSON MINE.—Is in the N. ½ of S. E. ¼ of Sec. 29, 48-29. Mat Gibson, Supt., Champion, Mich.

GRAND RAPIDS IRON CO.—L. H. Whitney, Pres.; J. C. Holt Sec'y. and Treas., of Grand Rapids. Sec. 7, 47-26.

HUMBOLDT MINE.—Humboldt, Mich. J. B. Maas, Agent; Ed Maas, Supt.; G. A. Garretson, Sec. and Treas., Cleveland, Ohio. Sec. 11, 47-29.

JACKSON IRON COMPANY.—Mine at Negaunee. Major Fayette Brown, General Agent, Cleveland, Ohio; Samuel Mitchell, Pres. and General Manager. Sec. 1, 47-26.

THE HARTFORD.—Property in the E. ½ of lot 5, and lots 6 and 7, in Sec. 35, 48-27, on the east end of Teal Lake, on the south margin. S. R. Bell, Secy., Milwaukee; Ben. Neely, General Manager, Negaunee.

THE KILWORTH MINING COMPANY.—Mine on S. W. ¼ of S. W. ¼ of Sec. 22, and N. W. ¼ of N. W. ¼ of Sec. 27, 47-27, two miles north of Ishpeming. Officers of company, T. J. Dundon, president, F. W. Merritt, vice president; J. H. Quinn, secretary and treasurer.

Chapter 18:

Entering the
20th Century: 1900 to 1905

1900

We have partly entered the 20th Century on several occasions in the several chapters already covered, including the cow problem. However, for the hundreds of minor topics that cannot have a chapter of their own, we now enter 1900 as a citizen of that time, and in that place, and relive history week to week.

In February of 1900 we have three items of note: First, typewriters were being advertised in the paper for the first time. Secondly, people were asking about High Schools, "Do athletics in high school pay?" Thirdly, we can also ask if the big timber and trees of the Ishpeming area are gone, when we read that a carload of timber has been received from Seattle. Times are a-changing.

In March we have word that the new high school is to be built (the one that almost totally burned in 1932.). Mr. Mather is also still giving prizes to the best looking homes in the CCI mine locations, and the summer contest is to begin. Cleveland Cliffs has been putting more land on the market for homes, and building lots are being sold for $100 to $150 dollars. This year was also the 50th CCI celebration, with photos including the mines and the Mather house in Cleveland Location, and the CCI agent's residences below it.

For recreation, people can race their bikes at Union Park between Ishpeming and Negaunee and earn some money as well. The State Fish Car arrived by railroad in town and will distribute 100,000 trout to nearby streams and lakes. For people who wish to travel, there is a sight-seeing trip advertised to Custer Battlefield, Yellowstone, and other western stops, including Medora, S. D., where Teddy Roosevelt's hunting camp was. The LS&I railroad will offer special passenger trains during the summer for those wishing to go to Presque Isle to picnic. 1900 also saw the Skerbeck Family Circus at Ishpeming. At the Opera House, Vernon the hypnotist was entertaining large crowds. For those who like wrestling, there was a match at the Opera House. "It was the worst calamity in several years," said Mr. Newett, and people were "fleeced out of their money." The Opera House also had a theatrical play during the summer entitled, "Ten Nights in a Bar Room." Ishpeming also has a female baseball team this year, called the "Bloomers," and they will play games at Union Park.

It was quiet at the mines in general, with little news, so with the railroad tracks rather quiet, it was a good summer for the Ringling Brothers Circus to return to town.

Mr. Finn, of Ishpeming notoriety in the 90's has been found in Victor, Colorado, and is "still in legal trouble." School teachers wishing to continue to teach second and third grades in public school will have to take this summer's Teacher's Exam for recertification. Ishpeming posted new rules in June for the use of hoses. Too many people using water at one time causes lower water pressure to other homes. The Manx residents had an annual Manx Picnic. And this was the summer that the Ropes is treating the swamp tailings, and the Iron Range and Huron Bay Railroad is dismantling its $1,200,000. project. South of Ishpeming (presently road 581) a nice bridge is being placed over the Escanaba River. As to advertising, Garland Stoves had a fine ad each week showing its wares.

A fine new group was formed that would serve the city well for many years. The businessmen of the city in 1900 formed the Village Improvement Association. They encouraged new projects and publicized present ones, such as the Angeline Mine has painted its properties and they now match "Hematite color." We will hear much of what the VIA will do.

The Ishpeming football team played Marinette. The Ishpeming boys were evidently then called, "The Rough Riders," at least by Mr. Newett. The large Salisbury School is still running out of room with six current rooms, and another for a second kindergarten will be built in the basement.

Here is a look at mining figures for the past ten years on the Marquette Range: In 1891 there were 38 mines operating with 8,000 men working, in 1895, 19 properties with 4,650 men working, and in the current year of 1900 there are 31 mines, and six explorations, with a total of 6,627 men working. Between Oct. 1, 1899 and October 1 of 1900, 23 men were killed in the Marquette Range mines. The copper mines in the Keweenaw currently had 13,971 men employed.

Recreation continued in the winter. A popular play called, "Two Married Men" did a return engagement. The Golf Club contracted for a new golf club-house between Ishpeming and Negaunee. McKinley and Teddy Roosevelt were elected as President and Vice-President in November. The Ishpeming Library decided to renumber all its books as it was closed anyway due to the spreading of small-pox.

1901

Having a lot of English men and women, the Salisbury Methodist Episcopal Church held a New Year's Day Oyster supper. We note here for the reader that railroads were now getting refrigerated cars, aiding in the transportation of sea food.

Here is the first news about a pension system. The C&NW Railway devised a pension system based on the years worked. The Cleveland Cliff's Iron Company will soon also offer such a plan in 1909 for their workers.

For what its worth, a former Ishpeming miner who moved west is now a United States Senator from Utah. One can travel on the Chicago and Northwestern to Grand Rapids, via Chicago, for a round trip price of $15.75. For $40.35, one can ride the railroad from Ishpeming to California, and many people were taking such trips. And this year, of 1901, is the first we hear of motors to be used in mines that will run on gasoline. This will spell the end of steam engines. Mr. Donnahoe, a local businessman, has purchased a new item that will keep things cold using ice. These items will become known as "ice boxes." People are doing well and saving money. The Miner's bank has purchased the National Bank in town, and currently has over a million dollars in deposits. The Miner's National Bank stock was up to $150 a share.

After a meeting at the Braastad Club Rooms, it was announced that a ski tournament will be held. There will be no admission, and some Minnesota skiers will attend. It will be the only "race" in Michigan, with the last big one in 1891. It will be held on Sunday, March 17th, at the old Lake Superior Hill just south of the Hematite Mine and to the east of South Pine Street (It may have been on the opposite side of the hill, however, facing south and the Section 16 mine).

One would be surprised by the number of adults and children run over by trains. In the April 13, 1901, paper the story is told of a little child with the last name of Cox that was run over by the Street Railway car. Although it was not the Railway's fault at all, the company sent the family a check which was accepted. Another child, a Johnson, age eight, died when he fell in a pit while fishing by Jasper Street.

In 1901, the Methodist Episcopal Church on Division Street was hoping to build a new church on Third Street. The land was found to have some legal snags, but eventually the foundation was built, on the downhill side of the street. Hard-times then set in and the money could not be raised, and the project was abandoned, with the church staying on Division Street into the 1960's. The foundations became the base of the Trebilcock Greenhouses.

There was a Schubert Concert Co. presentation at the Anderson Hall on Main Street, but the paper noted that it was poorly attended. Mr. Voelker, suffering from some ailment, was said to be recovering nicely at home at Pine and Barnum, the present place of the home yet today. St. Joseph's church, still standing as a shell on south Lake Street at Johnson, installed two electric chandeliers. Mr. I. E. Swift, an important Ishpeming businessman moved to Houghton, where the copper business was evidently as important as the iron ore business. An ad appeared on July 27 for 23 waitresses for the Huron Mountain Club.

We have mentioned that the city had to eventually install water meters as several families would use water from one installation. What caused this to happen in the summer of 1901 was that there was a fire in one of the Cliff's shafts and, it being summer, there was not enough water pressure to fight the fire. The very next week, the headline read in effect: City to Install Water Meters. There was worry about their freezing, but it turned out to be only a small problem.

Cleveland Cliffs was busy in 1901 building homes on its land. It let out bids for 20 homes in July, and in August it built 18 new homes at Lake Bancroft. About a week or so later there was an ad wanting to hire 50 carpenters. Surprisingly, the houses were up and being painted in November.

A report on the Lake Angeline Mine reported plenty of ore. In September, newly elected President McKinley was assassinated. The Nation was in mourning and Teddy Roosevelt became the President. Ads in the newspaper are about a new fad: wallpaper~~ not just to make a house look prettier, but to keep out the drafts and keep the heat in. It replaced newspapers glued on the cracks. Other ads are made to look like news items. One has the heading, "Prisoner Set Free," and was an advertisement for a medication that relieved pain. In the Salisbury Location, Rev. Casler is sent to the Methodist Episcopal Church. His son later become a well-known physician in Marquette.

The first mention of a death from electricity at a mine is printed in September, with Robert Conibear dying at the Section 16 mine from 2000 volts. The Trembath Brothers buy the Grace Episcopal Church in town and move it across from the Nelson House on Canda. When completed, the ladies of Grace church held a "Rummage Sale" and plans were made for the new Grace Church, still in use.

The farmers and gardeners ended their growing season early when a killing frost came to town on September 28. Every week the births are listed in the paper, and they range about 12 to 15 a week. Weddings are now also written up in the paper, but without any photos yet. Carpenter Cook of Menominee made a decision in October of 1901, to come also to Ishpeming. Their building was at Front Street and the large Indian Tee-pee for their Wigwam brand of foods was on their warehouse into the 1950's.

Two young men have come to Ishpeming from abroad to live here, but found out on arrival that their trunks had been broken into. There was a cave-in at the Lake Superior Mine, and it took twelve weeks to locate the body of Edlord Ribardy. Albert Proulx had his grocery store closed by creditors. Mr. Braastad's store went to a "cash basis only" and the passbooks being used were being collected. A great explosion happened between Ishpeming and Negaunee at the Anthony Powder Company, and not only was it felt by residents in both towns, but many windows were broken.

There were good things happening as well. Slot machines were being removed from area businesses. A great violinist, Camila Urso appeared at the Ishpeming High School Auditorium, in football, Ishpeming won the U.P. Championship. The ore shipped for the year from Ishpeming Mines ranged from 635,000 tons by the Lake Superior, to 486,000 tons from the Lake Angeline, to 32,000 from the East New York, and although the Cleveland Cliffs Company showed the largest amount of 861,000 tons, it was from four city mines, the Moro, the Cliffs Shafts, the Salisbury, and the Cleveland Lake. The city's grand total was 2,014,800 tons.

1902

In January, a number of students were expelled from the Michigan College of Mines in Houghton for poor class work. At the Negaunee Mine, a large cave-in occurred when two pillars of ore, holding up the roof failed. Eight men were lost. In Ishpeming, Mr. Gust Winsaufe on Angeline Street lost two children to measles. Good news in January is that there is a possibility of a bowling alley in Ishpeming. The Ishpeming store owners met and stores will stay open on Monday, Saturday, and payday nights. And for some reason, there is a town discussion going on as to when the steamer boat, the Pewabic was lost. The next week it was announced that it was lost on August 8, 1865. Mr. Newett thought we would like to know.

An interesting sports note is that women, yes, ladies, are playing basketball on Wednesday evenings and on Saturday. The Ishpeming Elks are working towards building an Opera House for the city. After two months, the eight men who died at the Negaunee Mine cave-in were found. Water had to be pumped out for several weeks. In March, 90 men are discharged from the Lake Angeline Mine. A Motion Photography Show Exhibition returns to town using a new system called "Kinodrama". The street car line is building track into Cleveland Grove and to the Golf Club. (The author has never found out where Cleveland Grove was located.)

The Ishpeming Library got more publicity this year and the news tells us that 40 per cent of the users are children, and that book use is so great that many books have to be rebound. The next year the library reported that it would close for a week to re-catalogue books. We note that this was also done just a few years before.

Ringling Brothers will appear on June 18th. Large ads appeared in the newspaper for two or three weeks. It is hard to imagine the size of this

1902 traveling railroad show. There were 500 horses, 30 elephants (One plays the drum), 40 clowns, 50 musicians in the band, aerialists totaling 60, three rings, and a ¼ mile race course in the tent. A giraffe and seals were also included in the large menagerie of 100 cages. We can only note that, for many, this was the first time to see animals in motion and in real life. There were no movies yet, really, and no television and no one got to visit a zoo. It must have been a marvelous educational function, as well as entertainment. An adult could attend and see everything for fifty cents, and children under 12 were half price. There were two shows, at 2:00 and 8:00. This does seem, however, to be the first time there was no parade mentioned.

Another exciting item for the summer will be the appearance of Buffalo Bill's Rough Riders at Union Park. They appeared in July, and did have a large street parade which was "watched by thousands." Mr. Newett said it was "a first class attraction" and many groups came from all around the U. P. The first show was said to have 2000 persons in attendance. (July 19, 1902.)

The other Ishpeming newspaper for many of the past years was the Peninsula Record run by a Mr. West. It was the chief Iron Ore competitor. Mr. West sold it at this time to a mine captain, Captain Walters. This confounded Mr. Newett for some time, and he wrote several notes in his newspaper about it. It evidently had him worried that a Democratic paper might gain in strength and popularity. The old Ishpeming daily paper by Mr. Maurice Finn and Mr. Soults only lasted for about two or three years in the early 1990's, and so it was no longer a threat. There was a Finnish paper and a Swedish paper at times, but these, too, were seldom mentioned in the Iron Ore. In this same year, Mr. Newett began building a large two story wood building that was the newspaper's home until it ended in

1954. It was on the 100 east block of Division Street and moved from a building just to the west of it, which became a laundry. The competition may have helped also to improve the paper, as for the first time in its 23 year history; it has many Christmas poems and stories for the readers. Mr. Newett must have had another jolt, when on May 23, 1903, Mr. West was telling people that he may go back into the printing business.

A new store is now in town, called the A. W. Myers Mercantile Store. New gates were put on the cemetery with the name of Ishpeming on them. Trees have also been planted. An Oldsmobile "Knockabout automobile" is on display in town. In Marquette, the new courthouse will soon be built. The planned street railroad from the Lake Angeline location to National Mine is canceled because the state is requiring a very high trestle over the steam railway tracks that must be crossed.

Mr. Andrew Carnegie, who has made millions in the steel industry has become a philanthropist, and will provide half of the funds needed for a new Ishpeming library, and has also set up an Aid Fund for miner's widows, children and others for the United States. He will also set up a special financial gift award fund for people who do heroic feats to save the lives of others, and another for those badly injured in accidents.. On May 23rd of 1903, Mr. Andrew Carnegie suggested to American companies that they use revenue sharing with employees. It is amazing how long it took for this to start happening, much of it in recent years.

Telephones continue to increase in numbers, and a new set of equipment will allow 500 telephones in Ishpeming. Note was also made soon after this article that Marquette has only 300 phones. Two notable people also come to town in October. They are Cyrus McCormick, and his accountant, Mr. Bentley. They are looking for some land on which to build a club-house. After searching the Baraga area, they found uncut property near the defunct Huron Bay Grade of the Iron Range and Huron Bay Railroad, north of Lake Michigamme. It became the famous White Deer Lake estate into the 1960's.

In the same month of October there were four deaths from diphtheria, including an eight-year old. The Finnish people are raising money to send to destitute people in Finland. In football, Ishpeming played Duluth, but a big "row" resulted because of poor refereeing. By November, campers were going to the woods to hunt deer. Joe Carlson of National Mine also shot a large wolf at Flat Rock. The state is trying to get rid of wolves and word was that a bounty might be offered of $100.00 an animal. Mr. Newett concluded at that price, people would start to raise them.

Tillson's Drugstore was a popular place and it also became a book store, and a school supply store. As yet there were no "dime stores" or "5 and 10's". In November a large indoor baseball game was played and a special railroad car carried Ishpeming people to the game. Another game of baseball was played the week before Christmas with the Ishpeming Printers, versus the Marquette Printers. Marquette won. The big news was that Mr. Braastad would build a new store building on Cleveland Avenue, and it would be of such size as to take up the alley. A few weeks later the size was given as 78 x 100 feet, and three stories high.

Many people must have been investing in stocks during this period, and Mr. Newett notes now and then that people should study stocks carefully. In the December 13, 1902, issue he notes that some stock companies selling stock

"carelessly use the words 'Ore in Sight' which may mean very little.

There is new action in the mines. Low-grade ores are being mined for the first time and much of it is going to furnaces. The Cleveland Cliffs large Gladstone furnace produced over 100 tons a day for over a year without stopping. The Moro Mine on Bluff Street, between the Cleveland Mine and Mr. Mather's cottage, built two shafts. The Section 16 mine had a fire and to put it out, it had to be sealed up so oxygen could not get in. When the mine was re-opened, many dead rats were found. This was the year, as well, when the Ropes was dismantled. The deepest U. P. mine is now the Tamarack Copper Mine that is now down 7,800 feet on an incline. The temperature some distance from the surface has gone up 1 degree for every 110 feet and to go deeper is about impossible.

HERE IS AN EARLY MOVIE THEATER ON MAIN STREET, CLOSE TO THE ANDERSON BUILDING. THE LYRIC WILL BE MENTIONED IN THE TEXT AS MOVIE HOUSES BEGIN TO FLOURISH. THIS IS A LATER PHOTO AS THE NICE FIVE-GLOBE LIGHTS HAVE BEEN INSTALLED DOWNTOWN WITH INCANDESCENT BULBS, AND THE SIDEWALKS NOW SEEM TO BE BUILT WITH CONCRETE, WHICH CAME AFTER 1895. FRIENDS OF THE ISHPEMING CARNEGIE LIBRARY PHOTO, AUGUST, 1985, CALENDAR..

1903

The Division Street Methodist Episcopal Church was completed, but it was built on the original Division Street site, rather than on Third Street. It will seat 1000. Just two months later, the pressure of building may have gotten to the Rev. Polkinghorne as he was granted two months of rest at the Battle Creek Sanitarium. The Salisbury M. E. Church was also reopened after repairs and it may be that this is when the large false ceiling was installed. The city library is having an architect draw up plans for a new building. People complain to Mr. Newett about how expensive it will be. The planning continued.

Word was received that lumberjacks in a camp with small-pox had left camp in spite of a quarantine.. The Elks are still raising funds for a new Ishpeming Opera House. Mr. Mather, as usual, gave out awards in his mine locations for the "Prettiest Houses." Word was received from Arizona, that some former Ishpeming residents are already driving automobiles out there.

The newest invention here is the making of CONCRETE, and the Trebilcock Brothers will soon be building concrete sidewalks and cement blocks for building homes and buildings. The Lake Superior Main Office on South Pine had a sidewalk built between the building and the street. The first large concrete mine project would be the 1897 new hoist house foundation at the Salisbury mine, located on Terrace Hill. The contractor was the same man who just completed the new concrete Iron Ore dock in Marquette for the LS&I Railroad. In 1903, Mr. Newett reported that "Cement made in Ishpeming last year is working well."

One can wonder at the amount of power the mines had over what happened in a community.

In April of 1903 the Forpaugh and Sells Circus announced that they would be coming to Ishpeming on June 24. One would think that their schedule was unchangeable as the route was set in order geographically, and posters were already printed. However, the Lake Superior Mine would be celebrating 50 years of mining in Ishpeming on June 24th, with a large celebration. The Circus changed its date of appearance. A brand-new circus act was the appearance of three bicycle trick performances. In August another Forepaugh show came to town, the Forepaugh-Fish Wild West Show. Nothing more was mentioned about it in August.

The Lake Superior Mine Celebration was just like a large circus itself, and was held on top of the hill south of the mine. The tent being used was 80 feet by 120 feet. There were other tents as well. A good newspaper report was given on the history of the Lake Superior, the Section 16, and section 21 Mines.

Another important date that happened in the May 16, 1903, issue of the Iron Ore. My notes read this way: "Ishpeming man buys FIRST AUTO in town, a 1200 lb. Elmore, made in Ohio with 6 hp. He had visited an auto show."

Mining is moving along in the area, with not a whole lot of news. The Hartford is being built on the edge of Teal Lake. The Maas Mine in Negaunee has put down a new shaft, but also encountered much quicksand and didn't find a rock ledge until the shaft was down 120 feet. When the shaft was down even further, the shaft house was found to be sinking into the quicksand. The Ogden Mine on the Cliff's Drive was going to resume mining. Iron Mountain Lake would now be called "Lake Ogden." Since lean ores were now in demand, the owners of the Palmer Volunteer Pit sold to new owners. Today, it has now disappeared into the Empire Open Pit mine. The Mines were doing a project together and would have their own large building at the St. Louis World's Fair. The Gold Mines seemed to show some life, as well, when the Michigan Gold Mine was purchased by the Tribulon Company and announced it would sink a shaft. By September it was down 110 feet and the mine was being unwatered. The Cleveland Cliffs Company bought the Negaunee Mine and might put down a new shaft. At the Cleveland Lake Mine there was quite a cave-in, taking part of the road on the south side of the lake, breaking the launder and a city water main. By October of 1903, things are also slowing up a bit at the mines. Furnace orders for ore are slowing up and ore is piling up at all the mines. Some CCI mines, however, are still working two ten-hour shifts a day. In fact, Mr. Newett tells us, the Lake Angeline Mine is the only one working an eight-hour day. In November, the CCI announced that it was building a large new power plant near the Lake Angeline former shoreline, and also a new shaft, new buildings, and a tall chimney.

Voters turned down a school bond issue for a new school, but the library plans continued. Mr. Carnegie turned down the first plans and a more beautiful building was designed. Requests for bids went out during the summer, along with Mr. Carnegie's directions for building. The library plan was described in the paper. Announcement was made that it would be built at Main and Barnum, where it still stands. There was some problems with the lot, purchased from Mr. Tillson, in that it was actually two feet shorter than described, and so the new library was planned to be two feet shorter as well. A bid was accepted and by August, the foundation was under way.

Another new building also got underway-- the Ishpeming Opera House on Cleveland, next to Mr. Braastad's new store. The basement would be filled with rooms for theatrical groups, costumes, bathrooms, and the stage would be large and accommodate many varied performances. The basement work was soon halted because the construction of the footings "have not been up to expectations." A new post office would also be built that summer, but it would be on Division Street. The new city hall was having settling problems and the foundation required some work. It had been built only on wood pilings, and now would get a foundation. The C&NW RR wishes to put a large, new depot in town, but is requesting that second street be abandoned in the track area. The city was building fences around Lake Sallie, Iron Mountain Lake (Lake Ogden), and Lake Miller, to protect the city water supply by keeping cattle out. (and bathers and fishermen) The cost was over $5,000 and gave the water works a large deficit for the year. Up to about 1950, there was also a daily watchman at the lake. The city finished the road around Lake Bancroft. The Salvation Army was residing in its building a 111 Third, at the corner of Cleveland Ave. It was there into the 1960's.

A small article one day made the first note about tennis, and that some local residents were building private courts in their yards. Camps were being broken into, and the removal of stoves was a really "hot" item.. . The Skerbeck Family Circus would return for two days of entertainment. For some reason, store owners became negative toward street carnivals, and the city denied licenses often for such groups, which then had to set up outside of town. The Salisbury School now had seven teachers.. A new eye doctor in town was discovered to be a fake, being unlicensed.

In late October, there was a large gun battle at the Winthrop Junction Location. Two men who had robbed the post-office in Superior, Wisconsin were found to be traveling in a railroad car and a gun battle ensued. The newspaper described women and children crying and screaming as the guns fired. It evidently was a DSS&A passenger train. The men were arrested.

A larger accident in town involved Ishpeming's hook and ladder "truck" being pulled by horses. It had 15 men on it when it overturned. There were no serious injuries.

In spite of ore piling up at mines in the fall, things on a local level continue at a rather full employment. The "Old East New York Mine" is sinking a new 7th level, 700 feet down. The Section 16 mine has installed a new 12-foot drum for cable and a three-ton skip.

The December 5, 1903 paper announced that the new Ishpeming Opera House was ready and an opening night was planned with a theatrical play "We are King," and seats would be $10.00 each. The newspaper noted that one of the background scenes available at the new opera house was a scene from Lake Sally. Regular prices to see a play are one dollar, fifty cents, and ten cents. The old Opera House would feature seats at half-price on its last performance, the play of which would be "Reuben in New York."

Mr. Braastad's building is not yet completed, and he reports that "There will be little setbacks from time to time." He eventually enlarged his building.

By the end of 1903, the mines were beginning to slow production, with layoffs at the Lake Angeline. The Champion Mine, currently the deepest of the iron mines in the USA (stated Mr.

Newett), with 34 levels, closed down entirely. The Section 21 mine was operating with only 47 men, down 760 feet. Some mines were reducing wages, but not the CCI so far.

1904

The first discussion topic of the year is Sunday shows at the new Opera House. Mr. Newett will eventually write a column saying he is in favor of it. Even worse was the holding of a large sports meet on Memorial Day. Mr. Newett wrote an editorial on that, too, but not positive.

Ski jumpers are looking forward this winter to a big tournament, and have 56 jumpers already lined up. It will be billed as an International Ski Tournament. There will also be a boy's ski contest held with the big tournament. There would also be a very fine dog race with children on sleds early on the morning of the tournament.

There is a new Finnish Methodist Church on Division Street, across from the M. E. Church. This is where the current Salvation Army building is located. We should also note that the annual Fire Department report was in the paper, and informed the readers that there are several actual fire stations existing in the city limits, one of which was at the end of the street car line in Lake Angeline. It was there into the late 1940's.

Mr. Newett had several editorial battles in his paper in 1904 with the Peninsula Record newspaper competition. Mr. Braastad installed four Brunswick bowling alleys.. Each week the paper will list names and scores. The new city Carnegie Library was completed in March, and the Library closed temporarily for the move from City Hall. A large new steel ship has been built to haul iron ore. It is 500 feet long, 56 feet wide and has a 32 foot depth. And

Upper Peninsula roads are still hardly passable or usable. Many more ads are appearing in the Iron Ore. An ad appeared in the paper for C. W. Jarvis, a dentist in town. Another ad was for Mr. Deadman, a dentist, but also a veterinary surgeon. The Iron Ore advertised a seven room house for sale, noting that it was wired for electric lights. Mr. Newett, things being slow, took a trip to visit mines in Bisbee, AZ. It was while he was gone that Mr. Ropes passed away. In May, a fire wiped out much of Republic, even with the sending of Ishpeming's Steamer by Rail Car. To control dust on downtown streets this summer, the city has ordered two street sprinklers, comprised of a large tank with a pipe at the back with holes in it to pour out water on the sand and gravel. A cement contractor also came to town and built five-foot wide walks for seventy cents a foot.. It had been eighty cents a foot the previous year.

Photos are starting to appear in the newspaper, and the first place homes in Mr. Mather's 1903 contest are pictured. First place went to 915 N. 5th Street. Other location's best homes were also shown in weeks that followed. Addresses were 611 Cleveland Ave, 727 Empire Street, and 530 W. Division. CCI says Ishpeming is the "Nicest Kept Mining Town in the U.S." (May 28, 1904). So houses are looking nice, but buildings are getting old, and in June Mr. Newett notes that the Nelson House needs a good coat of paint.

A new toy was a toy rocket, but a three year old was killed by one in town, just outside the store where it was purchased. A large circus came to town on July 21, called, "Walter Main's World's Exposition." The ad said it would have three trains of double-length cars, seating for 10,000 and have a ten a.m. mile-long parade. The report on the show was that it was "very good." My, what we have missed!

With "modern life" setting in, people already seem to miss "roughing it." Mr. Newett said in a summer editorial that "Half of town seems to be out camping." To improve water pressure, the city is looking for water leaks. To improve streets, the city is building concrete curbs. Some went in on Oak between Euclid and Ely. The old rule of residents paying part of the cost was true from the start as those lot owners paid two-thirds of the cost.

The Barnum and Bailey Circus also returned to Ishpeming in 1904. The circus that came was fine, but a street car hit a carriage of people going to the circus at Union Park. No deaths. We can add that the Street Car Company has been bought by new owners and although the stock-holders were forced to sell stock at a greatly reduced price, something was better than nothing, and with a $50,000. debt wiped out for them, the cars now look better than before.

In Sheridan, Wyoming, a young girl who is from Ishpeming now has the head nurse job in a local hospital there. Rev. Polkinghorne, who has served the M. E . Church for six years, resigned because of continuing health problems.

Dr. Van Riper became the head doctor of the Champion Mine when Dr. Beach left for Baraboo, Wisconsin. Dr. Van Riper fell so in love with the U. P. that when the Champion Mine closed in later years, his wife was delighted about it, only to find out that her husband was going to stay in Champion anyway, and die there as well.. This information is from his son, Charles in his book, My Father, Dr. Van.

There will be special trains to the World's Fair in St. Louis by the C&NW from Ishpeming, on Sept 4, 12, and 26. The Ishpeming Theater (the name changes from the Opera House) is presenting the Inez Forman and Co. play, Romeo and Juliet. The Theater is making money and paid a dividend in its first six months of operation. The city also placed a fire-alarm box outside the theater. In September the Marquette County Fair had a poor attendance. The new County Courthouse, with a marble staircase was dedicated in Marquette..

Mr. Braastad's store is now open there are several departments on different floors. In June of 1905, he turned the store over to his son Arvid. The store may have been too big, especially after it had an addition to it, as after a few years, gradually the departments are reduced, and finally it becomes the Gossard Factory in less than 16 years.

Another International Ski Tournament is planned for Ishpeming, to be held on Washington's Birthday, February 22, 1905. The take-off is being built up higher than the hill for faster take-offs. The take-off then was called a "trestle," obviously borrowed from the local mining vocabulary. In 1905, when it came time to ride the new hill, several local men would not ride, reporting it was "too fast." Note that President Teddy Roosevelt is being invited to the tournament. He replied that he can't fit it in this winter, but he will eventually to the area, and did.

In October, the newspaper had a nice Winchester Gun advertisement with a picture. There were some tragic deaths by trains that fall, with two of them being men trying to get on the train while it was moving. Both fell under the wheels, one being decapitated with his mother in his presence. The other was Mr. Leonard Sundblad who was campaigning for an office, and fell getting off the train before it stopped.

There was a picture ad in the paper for the first time for a Treadle Sewing Machine with four drawers. It was another fine invention that could do a day's work in a matter of minutes. The name of it was the Eldridge.

One wonders where the money came from or whether the person was full time, but the Ishpeming City band reached out all the way to the Western states to find a new band leader. Fr. Keul at St. John's Catholic Church is preparing a nice Christ Mass Tree. So is Pastor Refsdal of the Norwegian Lutheran Church. Since Christmas falls on a Sunday this year, stores will close on Monday. A sad Christmastime note is that the dry at the Section 16 Mine burned down and the clothing of 200 miners was burned up. An old boarding house will temporarily act as the dry. A death resulted also in the holiday season when an Argall boy ran his sleigh under a street car as it came around a corner.

A report on students at the Michigan College of Mines in Houghton showed the origination of its students. Mr. Newett noted that it looks like we are annexing Canada. The famous unsinkable whaleback ship is disappearing from the Great Lakes as the shipping season at the locks ended on December 17. Iron Ore was a difficult to unload from whalebacks.

The end of the year mine news is that the Lake Angeline Mine has 300 men now working, but the Moro Mine is presently closed. The U. S. Steel Company is now the owners of the Lake Superior Mine Company. The Superior Hematite Lake Mine and Section 16 are doing well, as is the East New York which is busy diamond drilling. The Republic and a dozen other mines in Negaunee are doing fine as well. Even better news is printed about local mines when the first issue of the next year comes off the press.

1905

On January 7, 1905, the first issue of the Iron Ore for the new year had a front page story that the CCI would add 475 men to its employment. The next week the news got even better as The Lake Superior said it would add 450 men, and the Lake Angeline Mine said it would add between 75 and 200 men at their new East End shaft. In March, the paper continued to say that there were steady additions to the mine work force. Also in March, the CCI purchased the Negaunee Jackson Mine and 20,000 acres of land. It had closed in 1898, originally going under the city of Negaunee, and then going west. In April, the Champion Mine re-opened. By October, the Cliffs Shafts got a night shift with 175 new men hired to work at the mine.

The city has purchased a snow plow, pulled by horses, and it is working well on South Pine Street. With the coming of automobiles, plowed streets, rather than rolled and pressed snow streets, was required. Many people began buying Franklin cars as they had no radiators and would not freeze up in the winter, and thus were quite drivable in January. The city also was thought to be ready for the sale of old cemetery lots for homes, but this was, in reality, a long way off. Mr. John Jochim, who owned a hardware store died at the early age of 60, of diabetes.

At a meeting in Ishpeming, a very important event happened in February. It was the forming of the National Association of Ski Clubs during the ski tournament week. Over 60 ski riders participated. An exciting feature was a double jump with two sailing off the jump at the same time. Children's dog races once again preceded the tournament.

In the printing business, Mr. Newett was constantly getting new type faces, and letting the public know the new machinery obtained for their printing needs. He was even able to print stock certificates and bind books. Then came the most modern of newspaper equipment, a six font, two-magazine Merganthaler's Linotype. He announced that it was the "Only one of its kind in Michigan," and invited the public to come in and watch its operation. He even put a photo of it in the newspaper. He was printing more photos also with the new half-tone technique developed, and two weeks after the ski tournament there were several photos of the event and of the dog races as well.

For deer hunters there was a new law on the book: Deer meat could no longer be sold. The Carnegie Library now gets 1 mill of taxes, and is open until 9:30 at night. Mr. Newett writes an editorial on the fact that Ishpeming needs a new school building for the large amount of children.. Shakespeare has become common at the Ishpeming Theater and after Romeo and Juliet a few months back, a show in April was the Merchant of Venice. People are also gathering in the cold weather at the depots to stay warm and watch trains come and go, as there are several passenger trains in both directions each day. The Railroads ask Mr. Newett to print their complaint about this viewing habit of the public.

How about a SOFT DRINK? They are the new rage. Pop companies will exist in every town. Mr. Newett printed an article about them. Most businesses closed for Good Friday Services. A local ski rider went 60 feet this week when he fell off a ladder painting a home.

Anyone wishing to do research on the gold and copper mines out west from Nevada to Montana can find a lot of information in the Iron Ore at this time in history. Mr. Newett is using his front page often for mines out west. Recently he has covered North Butte, Arizona, Silver City, New Mexico, and the Bonanza Circle group. Leadville, Colorado, and Tonopah, Nevada are also studied in detail.

In June of 1905, the High School on First Street graduated 33 persons. The high school went to local Record Print to get its high school annual printed, and Mr. Newett says they farmed it out to printers out of town, and it is a "punk job." The Excelsior Furnace is being torn down. If you own a car now, you must pay $2.00 a year and get a number to post on the car. As for deer hunters, the license cost is now $1.50, and you may kill two deer.

There was another person killed by a train, when John O'Neil jumped off so he could get to work while the train was moving. His clothes got caught as he jumped. Mr. Braastad has invited people to bring their own groceries and purchases home and save delivery, and bring delivery wagons to an end, which could save money. A month later, Mr. Braastad put a "motor launch" (boat) on Teal Lake at his property on the west end, and will give rides this summer.

The July 4th celebration in 1905 was very large. The parade was estimated to be two miles long, and there were games, races, prizes and fireworks on Lake Bancroft's west bluff.

The Adam Forpaugh and Sells Bros. Circus came in the summer. The combined show had a morning parade of three miles long but Mr. Newett said it was not as good as the July 4th one. He did add that the Circus was good and clean.

The first AUTOMOBILE AD appeared in the Iron Ore. It is air-cooled, a four cylinder, aluminum body, and sells for $1,400.00 to $3,500.00. The agent is Mr. Newett himself, in a new sideline. More and more car ads and articles on the auto appear in Mr. Newett's paper. Names of new car owners appear almost weekly. Mr. Maitland has a "nice new Buick with a double opposed engine." The Franklin auto has the most ads, probably because Mr. Newett puts them in free. The county in 1905 decided to name important roads "County Roads." We will also see a large new industry of building and re-building roads and new highways because of the automobile.

The old Opera House Theatre will reopen as the Bijou and have three one hour shows a day of Vaudeville. The old Opera House is the upper story of Wm Leininger's Building on Main Street. In July, there was a large earthquake felt in the U. P. The date was Wednesday, July 26. The next week, the beginning of August, there was a killing frost and gardens and potatoes were destroyed. Mr. John Anderson cut his hay on North Third Street. The remains of the farmhouse and barn are still in the gully between second and third just before US-41. It was still known as the Anderson Farm in the 1950's.

The Ishpeming Theater continues to have drama groups appearing. Two September shows are: "Her Only Sin" and "Our New Minister." An Ishpeming saloonist, Mr. Talo was put in jail for opening on Sunday. Gately's Store has come to town, but is at Main and Bank Streets.

The Methodist Conference of Michigan was held in Ishpeming, and 200-400 pastors were in attendance for five to eight days. One pastor wrote the Iron Ore, upset with the poor rooming arrangements when several people had to sleep in three shifts of eight hours each in the same bed.

In November there was a bad explosion at the Miners' Bank. The entire building was in fragments, three children were killed, and many dozens injured. A new building was built with the telephone company on the second floor. When a second explosion occurred some years later, the second story was removed, leaving the building at Front and Main as it is today, although the bank is no longer there.

It is time to think Ski Tournament again, and word has been received from Mr. Mather in Cleveland, Ohio, that he enjoyed the tournament last year and this year will make two gold medals to present to winners in February of 1906. In the sport of football, Ishpeming won Grand Rapids to once again take the State Football Title. It was noted that there were no injuries and they received a big "Welcome Home." Mr. Newett was not too much for sports, and in an earlier editorial said that sports are more emphasized than the academics. An ad for the academic job of being a stenographer appeared in the paper with the wages to be $60.00 a month.

If you want to travel, you can get away from Ishpeming during February and March and tour California for $350.00 a person. For those using the Carnegie Library, you will have to ask for the periodical you wish to read. Too many are carrying them off and out.

Braastad's store ran the first ad of its kind seen, saying, "Avoid the Christmas Rush" on December 16. The next week, December 23, Braastad's ran an ad saying "Our clearing out sale has begun" and Christmas had not yet been celebrated.

For some reason, the Lake Angeline Company decided not to raise any more ore from its East End (of former Lake Angeline) shaft, but would raise all ore now from its old shaft. The East

Shaft equipment will be moved to the Rolling Mill Mine in Negaunee.

The after-Christmas issue of 1905 has the news that merchants report a successful Christmas season.

THE LAKE SUPERIOR IRON COMPANY.—Mines at Ishpeming. Jas. S. Fay Jr., Treas., Boston; C. H. Hall, Agt., Ishpeming; W. H. Johnson, Supt., Ishpeming; H. B. Sturtevent, Mining Engineer; Jno. McEncroe, captain Hard Ore mine; James Trebilcock, captain Hematite mine. Sec. 10, 47-27, sec. 9, 47-27, sec. 16, 47-27.

THE LILLIE MINE.—The estate consists of 70 acres in the N.E. ¼ Sec. 2, 47-27, owned by the Teal Lake Iron Co., leased by the Lillie Iron Co. A. Maitland, General Agent, Negaunee; Chas. Koch, Supt.

LUCY MINING CO.—W. H. Barnum, Pres., Lime Rock, Conn.; A. Maitland, Gen. Manager, Negaunee; Jas. R. Rough, Supt. Sec. 7, 47-26.

THE MICHIGAMME MINE.—At Michigamme. J. C. Fowle, Supt.; Geo. Orr, Mining Captain. The estate covers 1,400 acres of land. Mine in Sec. 10, 48-30.

MICHIGAN GOLD COMPANY.—F. P. Mills, Ishpeming.

MILWAUKEE IRON MINING CO.—H. H. Brown, Pres., Cleveland, O.; W. E. Stone, Sec'y and Treas., Boston; A. Kidder, Agt., Marquette; Jno Carmichael, Supt. Sec. 7, 47-26.

THE NEGAUNEE MINE.—In the center of the N. W. ¼ of Sec. 5, 47-26. Capt. Sam. Mitchell, General Agent, Negaunee; Capt. Albert Newcome, chief local officer; Wm. Chisholm, Pres., Cleveland, O.

PITTSBURGH & LAKE SUPERIOR IRON CO.—Located at Palmer, Mich.; Joseph Kirkpatrick, Agent.

THE PHOENIX IRON MINING CO.—Property in S. ¼ N.W. ¼ and N. ¼ S.W. ¼ Sec. 29, 48-29. For information apply to Hon. Peter White, of Marquette.

PITTSBURGH & LAKE ANGELINE IRON CO.—Jas. Laughlin, Jr., Pres., Pittsburgh, Pa.; W. G. Pollock, Sec'y and Treas., Pittsburgh, Pa.; Alfred Kidder, General Agent, Marquette; Thos. Walters, Supt. Sec 15, 47-27.

QUEEN MINING COMPANY.

SCHLESINGER SYNDICATE.

QUEEN MINE.—Sec. 5, 47-26. F. Schlesinger, President; Jno. Jeffrey, Mngr.; T. Cole, Superintendent.

SOUTH BUFFALO MINE.—Jno. Jeffrey, Mngr.; T. Cole, Superintendent.

NORTH BUFFALO MINE.—T. Cole, Supt.; Jno. Jeffrey, Mngr.

PRINCE OF WALES.—Jno. Jeffrey, Mngr.; T. Cole, Supt.

THIS IS LIST THREE OF FIVE LISTS OF IRON ORE MINES ON THE MARQUETTE RANGE. FROM THE ISHPEMING CITY DIRECTORY OF 1891 THE ISHPEMING CARNEGIE LIBRARY

HERE IS A PHOTO OF A CARBIDE LAMP THAT REPLACED CANDLES AND PRECEDED ELECTRIC LAMPS.

CARBIDE IN BOTTOM, WATER IN TOP WITH REGULATOR

Chapter 19:
Ski Jumping Tournaments

People awaited the ski tournament of 1906. Would President Teddy Roosevelt come? The Ski Club planned for a lot of people said the January 27 issue of the Iron Ore. The Duluth Ski Tournament had been held in January, and Ishpeming's Wesphal had the longest jump. A young fellow from town also had the second prize, a fellow with the name of Holter. Skis for sale from Finland were being advertised by Peter Koski, and put on display.

The following week's paper, February 3, contained an even larger article about the upcoming tournament. The slide was described and it was expected that jumps over 100 feet would be possible in 1906. Even Menominee had a ski club that would attend. Escanaba wished to form one, and asked Ishpeming to show them "how to ski jump", and they meant business by joining the National Ski Association. Note was made that the high, built-up trestle was 60 feet above the hill and had high sides to prevent distraction of the jumpers coming down the chute. The name for the ski hill at this time was the "Brass Wire."

On February 10, Mr. Newett gave the announcement to the readers that President Roosevelt had written to the Ishpeming Ski Club, informing them that he could not attend the ski tournament which would again be on George Washington's birthday, February 22. Undiscouraged, the Ski Club reminded people to dress warm and to come early to get a seat. There were no warm cars to sit in at this time, and sedans with a top had not yet been invented. There was also a note that many would be attending by coming on special excursion trains from many towns. Often the trains were giving special rates. An advertisement in the same issue notified people that reserved seats were now on sale.

The February 17th issue of the newspaper had the final details of the tournament. We are told that the ski hill is only a half mile from town, and a few blocks from the street car. People are also told that there will be some stunt skiing at the tournament, and possibly two or three men skiing down at one time. The Ski ad was real big in this issue. As this was a National Tournament, there were no cash prizes given, but awards were. We also realize that the fine publicity in the newspaper is partly because Mr. Newett is president of the Ski Club.

The day of the tournament had rather bad weather, and many who did come, did not pay any fee, but watched from behind the fence which had been erected. The Ski Club reported that it needed 2000 people to pay for the prizes, and that if it broke even, it would be doing well. In March the Ski Club concluded that paying the expense of visiting ski riders is too much for a local club to do.

In October, the Ski Club was again working on a new ski hill. The new hill would be east of the old one and nearer the Wawonowin Golf Course. There were tall trees to shelter from the wind, and the new trestle would be bigger and longer than the old one.

During January of 1907, tournaments were held at Ashland, Wisconsin, Duluth, and Cameron, Minnesota. Ishpeming is also mentioned because the juveniles jumpers under 16 also have a new ski hill and had their own tournament. A Carlson boy won with 256 points. There were nine other jumpers.

The February 9, 1907, newspaper tells us that there are lots of reservations at local hotels, and that although there will be no cash prizes, there will be fine medals, made by Tiffany, awarded. The dog sled races were held in the morning as usual, and school must have been cancelled for the day as Washington's Birthday seldom fell on a week-end, and this year it was on a Friday. There was a note that this year, a new route has been made to the ski hill. One can get to it from the Standard Oil Storage Warehouse on the Negaunee Road, rather than from Wabash Street as in the past. It was really an improvement for Negaunee attendees. We note that the Standard Oil facility until the present year, 2005, was still in the same location, and that "new" road is still there as well.

An Ishpeming man, Mr. Lokken took second place in the tournament, with a man from Bovey, Minnesota taking first. The report on the dog races was just as interesting. The race this year came down Main Street's Strawberry Hill. Twenty dogs were running, with a large number of spectators at the sides. A note was made by Mr. Newett that "Judge Uren did a spectacular somersault. It was the best entertainment, and he was not even on the program."

Up to now, ski jumping was a semi-professional sport. Often there were cash prizes and people rode for cash. About March 9th the National Ski Organization voted against cash for tournaments. Mr. Newett adds that clubs planned to disregard it. In April, the local ski club held a meeting on the third floor of the Anderson Hall, with a large turnout. In October, Mr. Newett notes that the Ski Club still has not heard from Mr. Roosevelt, but if he makes it, he noted, "We hope he is not shot as a bear". This, of course, is referring to his bundling up his larger size with many clothes. In the fall, the Ski Club had a new clubhouse at Deer Lake. It had a 16 x 28 kitchen, and a 28 x 65

downstairs room with a fireplace to hold four-foot logs. On the second floor was a huge hall.

Practice jumping on the new hill was taking place in January, 1908, with jumps up to 108 feet. People were asking about cash prizes, and the ski club stated that they would follow the new rules and there would be no money anymore. Whether the ski club was paying for outsiders to attend or not is not known, but they did publicize that the "best riders in the country" would be present. A February article noted that this year, Mr. Mather, himself, from Cleveland, Ohio, would be present to award the medals at the tournament.

February 22 arrived, and the results of the tournament were told. The youngest jumper to ride the big hill was only nine years old, by the name of "Dud" Kean. It was said he gave a "wonderful performance and surprised the spectators. He hit 40 feet on his first jump. His father was Dr. Kean. The dog derby was even more popular with youth running 30 dogs this year. The winners of the tournament were published in a special Sunday edition of the Iron Ore, of which there was no microfilm print.

There was some controversy after the tournament when the Duluth Ski Club, at their meet, claimed to have broken Ishpeming's Ski Jump record. To even the score, Mr. Newett proudly printed a fact in April, that in Duluth, the highest ski jump in the world had collapsed after a storm. And in an April meeting of the Ishpeming Ski Club, it was announced that they were out of debt and that dues were five dollars.

In all this, President Roosevelt did come to our U. P. and Mr. Newett ended up getting sued by "Teddy" for saying a few words about his drinking habits. The President won the charge, and Mr. Newett faithfully paid the five or six cents he owed. Both men were staunch

Republicans. There was not much about it in the Iron Ore. The last word about ski jumping in 1908 was the fact that the "Big Ski Hill" was made even faster for the coming February. In February, in Chippewa Falls, Wisconsin, a tournament was said to produce a jump of 138 feet. Mr. Newett reported that some skee (The spelling at the time of the writing for this entire chapter is still skee, but the author has updated it to the present spelling.) experts claim that the jump was a fake. In any case the Ishpeming jump was once again all set for Washington's Birthday which in 1909 was a Monday. Forty-four riders were listed.

In 1910, the tournament was on a Tuesday afternoon, and one rider jumped 133 feet. Railroads made special low rates and the Street Railroad offered $10.00 in prizes to younger boys who would jump following the regular tournament. The Street Railway used eleven cars to transport people to and from the jump. At the dog race in the morning, an eleven year-old took first place, using a big dog. There was one dog-fight noted Mr. Newett. At the afternoon tournament, a new American Skee record was set in Ishpeming with a distance of 140 feet by a visiting ski rider from Superior, Wisconsin.

In 1911, there were two categories of riders-- Amateur and Professional. The amateurs were all local, including Tuomy, Hall, and Asplund. The professionals were all from Wisconsin and Minnesota. In March a discussion ensued about the problem again of two categories of ski jumpers. There was no mention of any tournament the next February, although there may have been one, but late in the month in 1912, the National Skee Association took the stand that its tournaments will be for Amateurs only "in the future." In 1912 there was a small mention about the jumping and the dog races, and a note that jumps of up to 160 feet were

expected. There was some excitement in 1912 at the Ironwood tournament when a skier there did a single somersault and repeated it, and landed fine on both jumps. Mr. Hendrickson, the somersaulter, came also to the Ishpeming tournament and repeated his performance. The tournament always didn't have real good weather, and this year they had a very large snow storm. The Tournament was held the day after Washington's Birthday.

A note in the newspaper of November 4, 1911, makes us aware that even Chicago is getting in on the Skee act by building a Ski Jump in Indiana. On the day of the jump, conditions were very poor, and jumping was difficult. It was tried for two years and given up.

In 1914, the only new item was that after the successful morning dog race, it was decided to hold another one the following Saturday in town on Cleveland Avenue between Mr. Braastad's Store and Main Street.

There is not much in Mr. Newett's paper after this period. It might be that he was no longer the President of the skee jumping organization, or that the Club was now using a different paper to publicize the event. With the large number of automobiles on the roads at this period, and the improvement of roads, The Daily Mining Journal may have been now the town's newspaper of choice.

HERE IS A 1906 PHOTO OF ISHPEMING'S BRASS WIRE SKI HILL, BY UNION PARK, NORTH OF M-28 BETWEEN ISHPEMING AND NEGAUNEE. PHOTO BY CHILDS ART GALLERY ON AN OLD PENNY POSTCARD.

Chapter 20:
1906 Through 1910

1906

How old is "The Wizard of Oz"? Well the drama play came to Ishpeming in January of 1906, with tickets prices from 35 cents to $1.50. A larger production of it came from Duluth that November, being carried in seven railroad cars. It must have been popular from the first. Other entertainment the winter of 1906 included Mr. Randall building a bobsled ride from the ridge of Strawberry Hhill down onto Lake Bancroft. For those wishing to travel, low train rates are offered for a trip to New Orleans this winter for the Mardi Gras. The Ishpeming Theater in March hosted Mr. John Philip Sousa and his band for one night. The next issue of the paper noted that the Sousa concert was both filled to capacity and "was up to expectations."

A project for many of the single men may be a Young Men's Christian Association, a YMCA, and plans are to possibly build it at the corner of Division ("the great highway") and Pine. Mr. Mather wants to help fund it, but the city is being slow to accept the challenge. A picture of the proposed building appeared in the paper.

The new Chicago and North Western Depot will be built. Second Street will not be closed, and the South Shore Railroad (DSS&A) will also use the depot on the other side. Mr. Newett will get more involved as he is rewarded with the job of being the new city postmaster. The iron ore companies were giving raises to their employees.

Trebilcock's Greenhouse was selling Easter lilies in April, and the LS&I RR was purchasing six new passenger coaches, with the old ones to be used for the Lake Independence route.

We will start to read much about Howes Moving Pictures. This company will come several times, preceding permanent theaters, and show many types of films, especially news type features.

A bad cave-in occurred on South Pine Street area by the Lake Angeline Mine and Section 16 mine, between Salisbury and Lake Angeline locations.. Timbers fell in and luckily blocked the hole thus preventing more dirt from going down into the mine, and one house was hanging over the edge, but safe. Several houses were moved, and in 1907 there was an additional cave-in of 60 x 130 feet. A brand-new 2,500-foot road was built during 1907. The new road was built in 125 days and was 22 feet wide.

Youth can make money now, "up to $100 a year," by selling the Saturday Evening Post. Upstairs of the Heyn Block at Main and Division (Now Buck's Restaurant), there will be a new Finnish Hospital. The latest play in town is "Why Women Sin.". Ishpeming police will, for the first time, be getting dress uniforms and helmets. 31 graduate from Ishpeming High School located on First Street. At the same time, the Ishpeming School Board decided that the school on Division Street was in very bad condition after an engineering study, and needs replacement.

In 1906, the town got its first Cement Block factory and the blocks lock into each other. A house built with them will never need paint. The city also has a new ore carrier named after it by the CCI. The "Ishpeming" will carry 10,000 tons of iron ore. Wood sidewalks in town are quickly being replaced by concrete.

In the summer, the Sun Brothers Railroad Show came, with a Grande Parade and Family Fun and no games of chance. Indications seem to be that it was a carnival. In any case, it was the first recorded show to come to town with its own generators for electricity. A small circus also came to Union Park, was good, and had a parade in both Ishpeming and Negaunee. In August, the Ringling Bros. circus returned once again, now with two giraffes, the "last of almost an extinct race." The parade has grown now to three-miles, and will also have Bengal tigers, 40 elephants, and a two-horned rhino. Mr. Newett reported on the band wagon at the front of the parade, and drawn by 24 horses, saying "It has grown in size." Attendance was estimated to be about 13,000.

Not much has been said about sports in the <u>Iron Ore</u>, although the baseball teams are covered well, and scores of several sports are listed weekly in the paper. One big item in 1906 was the new rules for football. In November, probably because of numerous penalties, the Ishpeming Football quit playing because "Roughness has been removed." Winter baseball was played often in Braastad's Hall.

Here is the Mine Inspector's report in brief for the year 1905: 22 fatal accidents, with 5,500 men working at 25 active mines (six not producing currently but exploration taking place.) This is for the Marquette Range. Killed were 12 Finnish, 1 Polish, 2 Italians, 1 Irish, 1 French, 2 Swedish, and 2 English. (note absence of Americans as a nationality.)

The mayor and some policemen toured the bars at 2:00 a.m. that year and found many open yet. Six arrests resulted. Builders of new homes are finding a replacement for plaster and lathe. A new "plaster board" has been invented.

In October, voters had passed the new High School Bond issue, and the basement soon was going in on Division Street. At Mr. Tillson's Drug Store, he had decided to not sell books anymore and some $2.50 ones were going for 50 cents. Plans are also proposed by the end of the year for a new fire hall. Soon there will be fire-trucks. In December there are many Christmas ads in the paper, and many toy departments open. There is also another large cave-in at the Lake Angeline Mine near the Lake Superior southern-most shaft. Both the railways and South Pine Street were affected and the main city water-line was only eight feet away from the caved ground. The Ishpeming pipe supplying city water was temporarily rerouted with pipe shipped from Chicago.. Mr. Carnegie a week later sent a Mr. J. B. Betters a "Carnegie Medal" for flagging down a locomotive in time to keep it from going into the cave-in.

The 1906 records showed 176 deaths in Ishpeming, and 407 births..

1907

Cleveland Cliffs has begun to buy land around Deer Lake. It will dam up the Lake for water power to make electricity. The lake will become larger, with a new road around the west end. A high walking bridge will be built over the dam area on the east end..

A study of wages shows the average factory wage in Marquette is $2.50 a day, while Detroit is only $1.90. The State Average is $2.85 a day. Rates at the Nelson House are $2.00 and $2.50 a night.

It was a cold spring, with frozen water pipes, and it was said in the paper about Ground-hog Day, "The groundhog saw his shadow which froze to the ground, and he went back to sleep without it."

More ground again fell at the Lake Angeline Cave-in at the NW of the NW of Section 15 into Section 16. Many are worried if the caving in will be even greater in the summer when the ground is no longer frozen. The Lake Superior portion of the cave-in has been filled in.

Asbestos is being recommended over heating pipes to insulate and allow more heat into the house. Some raw asbestos has been found north of Ishpeming and there is wonder about mining it in the future. The fire department in March made a run to a fire, after being notified by telephone. In April, the city had elections and many of the "People's Party" were elected to local offices. In May, 32 saloon owners were bonded to operate in the city.

Alternating current electricity is now also available in town, and people have a choice between it and direct current. The Marquette Gas and Electric Company are also now supplying gas with a big gas plant.

The first real movie theater opened in May of 1907. It was called "The Grand Family Theater", and ran an ad in the paper. Films will be shown for an hour, and be continuous. Prices will be 10 cents and 5 cents.. A second theater opened the next week in the Voelker Building. It was the Majestic Theater, and it will change films twice a week. The Grand Theater then said it was going to change its films three times a week. In June they showed movies of the World Series. After school began, a movie on Yellowstone Park was shown at the Ishpeming First Street High School Auditorium for 10 cents and a quarter.

The Lake Superior Mine notified the city of more caving ground, and the city has decided to run the main pipeline west from Salisbury to Winthrop Junction and then back to Ishpeming west of the Lake Superior Mine and Washington and Greenwood Streets..

The State of California sent a railroad car to Ishpeming (and many other towns) to recruit people to come to California. It was all about farms and produce, but also had a large "shark" to bring in the public.

The Section 16 Mine has installed an electric haulage system in its levels so that drifts can go further from the shaft. The Gately's Store has a 10-win baseball team this year, and all of the team is under 15 years of age.

A big July 4 was planned in town this year with a fireworks "eruption" of 30 minutes, a big parade, special trains to bring people in, and stores open all day. Prizes were given to stores with the best mercantile and auto displays. The week after the July 4th celebration, the Sons of St. George had a big gathering in town and used some of the structures left by the previous celebration. There was also Cornish wrestling, a parade, and sports. Mr. Ziehr of the Copper Country won the wrestling tournament.

Drinking was always a problem and three Marquette girls were arrested for drinking at a bar. Mr. Newett hinted also that the server should have been arrested. In the ads, a house is for sale at 172 W. Superior Street. The city plans to make the walk from town to the cemetery all concrete.

The circus coming this year is the Noris and Rowe and handbills are up all over town. It was a sad day in that the parade downtown didn't happen until noon, 30 people had quit in Marquette and 12 more here. The show was excellent, but few were there. It had even greater problems with an accident in Trenary a few days later. Seven cars of the train went into a ditch. Seven horses were killed. Wagons sank into the sand up to hubs when unloaded. They had no parade in Manistique and only one 5:00 performance. The train then left at 1:00 a.m. for the Soo.

The Ishpeming Schools opened. Mr. Leonard Flaa was a new manual training teacher, and he stayed and taught until 1958, teaching for 50 years. The Salisbury school has eight teachers and the high school, 18. A new truancy law states that all children 7-16 must be in school.

Women are working at some of the mines, doing surface jobs. Women, of course, are working by performing acting and singing roles at the Ishpeming Theater. In September, Isabel Irving had the leading role in "The Girl Who Has Everything."

Train travel is still heavily advertised, and one can go from Ishpeming to the west coast for $40. The Post-Office mail volume in October of 1907 was 27,715 pieces handled in one week. The Post Office postmaster tells us that 2004's weekly average is 99,472.

A lot of homes that were not hooked up to sewers now are being hooked up in 1907. Some did not get hooked up until the 1950's. The first mention is made of Halloween in the paper. Mr. Newett notes there was little damage, with windows being marked with soap, and wires across sidewalks at six inches. There were no arrests. Six girls are now handling 600 telephones in the upstairs of the Miner's Bank. And here's a "what's new" ad: "Secrets of Sexine Pills for Men." More people are writing checks instead of using cash. They can be used as receipts, as well, notes the newspaper.

The 1877 Presbyterian Church has been totally remodeled and has been rededicated. A tragic death took place at the Salisbury Mine when a bad timber let go. Mr. William Johnson, new to

the U.S., ran from the dangerous looking area, but forgot his candle. When he went to retrieve it, he was killed by a cave-in. Mr. Newett also noted during the deer season that 50 men in U.P., Wisconsin, and Minnesota died this year. A fire in the A Shaft of the Barnum Mine pump house under ground resulted in the deaths of two mules.

A note appeared in the paper in December that Big Louis Moilanen of Calumet has returned after a year of touring with the Forpaugh and Sells Circus. He is 8 foot, 5 inches in height and enjoyed the work. In the December 21 Christmas issue, the history of the poem, "A Visit from St. Nicholas" was printed in the Iron Ore, and the year ended.

1908

It looks like 1908 will be a good year in Ishpeming. Mr. Newett tells us that currency is again plentiful, that checks are being dropped from use, and that the mines are paying their payrolls again with gold coin. Mines look good, also, and it is thought that the North Lake area of town might have some new mines. The Roman Catholic Church tells us that there are 93,022 members in the Upper Peninsula of Michigan. Even the temperatures in January have been good. It has been 50 degrees and there is no snow. Icemen have to put snow on the roads to make deliveries with their sleds. Even taxpayers were happy when the City of Ishpeming announced on February 1 that they had overcharged all taxpayers, and that $20,000 would be returned to them. Travel is going further distances, and in May a large party of Ishpeming people are sailing for Europe from Quebec. In September a note is made that Fred Eggan and his wife, the hardware store people, have just returned from Europe after a trip of three months.

One can tell how large the fight will be for women to gain the right to vote when Mr. Newett prints in the paper regarding women, "that they can still play bridge, after which time they have little time left for politics." Mr. Newett also tells us that there is an epidemic in town. Four men committed suicide by hanging recently. Another tried to turn his stoves "gas" on, but a neighbor smelled the fumes, and "rescued" him from ending his life. The bride had chosen a different fellow.

The Ishpeming Library now has 6,000 volumes taken out (borrowed) monthly. Many of the theatrical groups coming to entertain seem to be casts of younger women, with their photos often in the newspaper. The Ishpeming Record made a nasty comment about a group of Chorus Girls, and Mr. Newett received a nice letter from one of them saying she enjoyed his review of their show. Many girls also came with the show "Red Feather." Mr. F. Braastad also wrote a letter to the Iron Ore, stating that he would like to see Mr. Keese for Mayor. He also invited the city merchants and employees to have a large picnic at his summer resort on the west end of Teal Lake in July. Horse-drawn busses will be used

Four men were seen loitering around town and upon inquiry they said they were attending the Firemen's Convention in Marquette shortly. The police here sent them there real fast, and the Marquette police are eyeing them up to keep an eye on them during the convention.

With a lot of movie competition, the Majestic Theater on the Saturday of April 11 is awarding some lucky person, the new stuffed animal named after Pres. Roosevelt, a "Teddy Bear." In late May the Grand Movie Theater closed and its owner left town with his movie machine, but left light fixtures and 150 cheap opera chairs behind. The owner of the piano he was renting

came and claimed it. Shortly thereafter, two men from the Soo lined the projection room with asbestos in case the film caught on fire. Admission would be only a nickel for both adults and children. The Majestic Theater seemed to be doing very well, and in December of 1908 was showing a movie film on Canada.

In May a study showed what is still being preached, but had a long time to take effect, and that is that studies in 1908 showed the danger of smoke in the lungs. Baseball is so popular that the high school will have a team for each grade. The Ishpeming Hospital started a program of a "visiting nurse" for mothers and their children of men who worked in the sponsoring mines. This program, also I believe lasted into the 1940's, but am not sure if this was the same lady who also visited all the schools.

Ishpeming has a new brokerage house in the Jenks block and operated by D. T. Morgan and Co. The Iron Ore still has its front page usually devoted to copper and gold mines in the western United States. The present pastor of the Division Street M. E. Church used his pulpit on May 17 to preach against high school dances. The entire sermon was published in the paper.

This important event also took place in May of 1908: Mr. C. L. Phelps was recruited as the Principal of the Ishpeming High School from Aurora, Illinois, and was a graduate of Dartmouth College. His salary would be $1,500 a year. (Teachers' salaries would be $400 to $600 a year.) Mr. Phelps was well liked in Ishpeming, and after he left to go to Calumet in 1910, he was recruited back, to become the Superintendent of the town's schools here. The present Junior High School was named after him.

Mr. Trebilcock is in the concrete business, but the term cement is still being used for sidewalks being built all around town. He has 14 men working in three different groups. High school graduates are increasing and in 1908 there are 54 of them. There was an arrest at Lake Sally by the city watchman, Joe Smith, when a man at the lake decided to bathe. The new Steel Web Picket Fences are now popular and being put in many front yards. Some homes still have them.

Mr. Mather came to town in July and invited 40 old mine employees to his cottage in the Cleveland Location and gave them all a souvenir. The Negaunee Home Bakery opened up a store in Ishpeming at Main and Pearl in the Pascoe Block. A new restaurant is opening up on South Main Street. Gas stoves for the ladies' kitchens are getting nice ads in the newspaper. At Union Park, the City officials play the Businessmen in a friendly game of baseball. The business men won, 13 to 7.

Entertainment for 1908 involved Professor Albert Smith who came to the Ishpeming Theater and was an escape artist. While here, he was also locked up in the city jail with his clothes locked in a separate cell, and he came out dressed. And in spite of movies, stage shows are still very popular. The economy must be quite good as there are also many more ads in the newspaper, and many full-page ones.

Mine deaths were down to 2.93 per thousand workers last year. There were only 16 deaths, with 5,362 employed. Two years ago, deaths were almost doubled with 5.49 deaths per thousand workers. Railroad safety has also been improved, and new steel passenger cars are replacing the wooden ones.

At the Mines, the CCI is going to develop a new mine at North Lake, just north and west of town, and is building both a large boarding house and a shaft. The compressed air to run the mine will be piped all the way from the Barnum Mine's

Cliffs Shafts in a six-inch iron pipe, 18,000 feet long and in "a perfectly straight line." (January 29, 1910)

In November, as now, Deer Hunting Season arrived. Mr. Newett this year notes that women are deer hunting, and they should be not be mistaken for a "dear." He spent several columns about men telling their deer-hunting stories which were very entertaining. A 260 pound, dressed deer was killed this year. There was confiscation of three tons of illegal deer hides from the U. P. in Green Bay. Mr. Newett also noted that Michigan had the highest number of deaths from deer hunting.

Mr. E. A. Johnson built a house on High Street, just east of the Swedish Baptist Church. This church on Third Street was torn down in 2004. The Electric Railroad Line had an open house and showed off some new cars. Mr. Newett wrote a long article about them.

Christmas ads and toy ads were greater and bigger than ever, and there are now some pictures of what St. Ni colas (Sant ni claus) looks like.

1909

There is a bobsled run down High Street from on top of Strawberry Hill down on to Lake Bancroft. The Lake Bancroft Skating Rink is also getting ready to open for business. In the motion picture business, more non-fiction films are being made and some films on Sweden, Russia, and Egypt, and an auto race in France, and even the film of the 1909 Ishpeming Ski Tournament were now being shown. The theaters seem to open and close periodically and change hands often. In May, the Bijou had a movie film fire, but the Fire Department saved the building. 100 people escaped. The Majestic Theater placed a note in the paper that they have passed the fire codes.

The city had a meeting to commemorate the 100th year of Abe Lincoln's birth. A new Lincoln Coin Club for coin collectors was begun, and a series of articles on Pres. Lincoln was begun in the Iron Ore. Mr. Outhwaite had met Mr. Lincoln when alive, and also saw his body in Cleveland. Also noted was that the Outhwaites have a summer home south of Ishpeming at Island Lake.

Gately's recent ad in the paper noted that for $1.00 down, you can buy anything in the store. The Leininger's Store on Main Street is putting in a cement block basement for storage purposes. The Ishpeming Library has ordered its Glass Floor as an interior improvement. This floor was seen in the film, "Anatomy of a Murder", and is still present.

While many people were thinking that iron ore would soon run out, Mr. George Maas of the Maas mine submitted a report to the Iron Ore, saying that there is enough iron ore in Marquette County to give 30,000 miners a thousand years of work. Because of two large mine paydays this year on Washington's Birthday, the stores are going to stay open on the ski tournament day.

At the theater, a popular play from Minnesota, called "Yon Yonson" is showing. It is about a lumber camp. It obviously was about a Swede. The great actress Lillian Russell also appeared at the Ishpeming Theater in May in "Wildfire." For those who like to cross-country ski, there was a six-mile tournament. For those who like to travel, the fare has been reduced from town to Seattle to $32.50. It is only $7.50 for a round-trip to Detroit. The New YMCA was completed and dedicated with a large ceremony. In the

fall of 1909, classes to those who needed help with English, Algebra, Chemistry, and electricity, were held. Courses were $6.00 each.

Many of us got our shoes from Mr. Eman on Cleveland Avenue. It was in this year of 1909 that his father started the shoe store, which is listed as being in back of the Bijou Theater in the Voelker Block. The Eman Shoe store in the 1950's was a store or two east.

Ishpeming residents heard a loud explosion once again, and this time it was at the Pluto Powder Plant at the Winthrop Location (National Mine). Several buildings there disappeared, but not one injury or death.

The biggest news for 1909 came in May, when it was announced by the Cleveland Cliffs Iron Company that they are beginning a Pension Program for all men who have worked for 25 years for CCI. It will also serve widows and orphans. The money will be about 26.5 percent of a years of service and wages.

The first note is made, that with 3,911 school age children now in town, the city needs some playgrounds on vacant lots. Graduations in June totaled 66. One student was sent to the Lansing School for Boys for truancy. The town is getting so old, now, noted Mr. Newett, that there will be this year, a Scandinavian Old Settler's Reunion, including a parade.

Up to this time in history, when there was a mine death funeral, the mine would stop work for the day. A new suggestion will be to take a half-day for the funeral only, but that the money saved by the mine for the other half of the day worked would be used to help the widow.

Concrete was used in September to improve Main Street over the several railroad tracks. Two new laws also went into effect. Up to now, cocaine was legal, but now will be on a list of prohibitive drugs. Cigarettes will be illegal for those under age 21.

CCI is now putting up steel towers for its many electric lines from its power plants to go to their mines. Steam power at their mines will be soon eliminated, as well as the smoke stacks and their dirty emissions.

The Bijou Theater has stopped showing films and is instead featuring Vaudeville acts which has resulted in "full houses." Stores are getting so caught up in Christmas Advertising that the first ad showed up in the November 6 edition of the Iron Ore, saying, "Time to decide on a Christmas gift." A Victrola phonograph is advertised for the first time, with a price of $125.00. Skud's store advertised that it would have Santa in its window next week. Mr. Sellwood's store had a large picture of Santa in its ad, and he had a beard, but a different style of hat. Mr. Braastad put in such a big ad that it ran side-ways on two pages. For two weeks the newspaper is 12 pages, rather than 8. Christmas was really getting commercialized.

The newspaper heard from former residents from time to time, and in December, word comes from Mr. Frank Mills, a former mayor of Ishpeming, that he is now living in Colorado and is enjoying fruit farming. A Negaunee man, Frank Condello, had a wonderful Christmas present. He was found alive in the Negaunee Mine after being buried for seven days.

1910

The Bijou Theater has dropped vaudeville because they say they are sent third rate entertainers, or worse. Just two weeks before this, Mr. Newett, had given them a positive feedback for two twelve-year-old actors in "His Pal." We are also made aware that there is a third theater in town, in the Kennedy Building on Main Street. It is a five-cent theater.

In January of 1909, a large new piece of logging equipment arrived by rail. It was a locomotive on tracks, to be used in the woods to haul out timber. It was a big attraction.

Times are quite good in Ishpeming in 1910, but some people still are relying on the county to supply them with free wood. Mr. Newett printed the names of those who are getting it. The city also decided that it could no longer give the Ishpeming school system free water, as too much was being wasted. The good news in the paper was that the mine wages at all mines would go up 10% on April 1. An ad in the Iron Ore in May from Oshkosh, Wisconsin offered employment to 5,000 men.

Some high school boys, after school, are going to a local bar where they are being served. So said one of the local clergymen in a recent sermon, and of course it was then printed in the paper. In April several saloon owners were arrested, and fined $125 each.. Everyone is excited about a new free entertainment coming in April; it is Halley's Comet.

The first aluminum pots to be advertised are part of a campaign at Gately-Wiggens in town. They are also giving away free aluminum souvenirs. For the first time, asphalt is mentioned as a road covering, although at this time the city has a new rock crusher and will be content with gravel roads.

More and more discussion around the country is about "wets" and "drys", that is, prohibition. The state Supreme Court has told Marquette County that they must take a vote to change any laws about alcohol. People are invited to town to speak for those opposing alcohol. In the

April vote, the "drys" do well, but the "wets" win. There is an effect, however, and the city council for the year denied four saloon licenses, approving only 35. The Ishpeming Ski Club held a Ghost Party and all came in sheets and pillow cases and danced all night until the end when they revealed who they were.

There are still quite a few wolves in the area, and the U. S. government plans to send in a band of men to start hunting and trapping them to improve the deer herds.

Stock selling for the past few years has gained a bad reputation. In addition, stocks have been selling at quite low prices. Several people in town put their money together for a western investment when the receiver of the funds disappeared with the money. In town a woman swindler, Jennie Moore, used high-pressure talk to local people to sell shares of stock in the Canadian Shakespeare Gold Mine. Mr. Newett printed the details of her swindling. She left for Marinette where she threw herself in front of a C&NW train and was killed.

A business block at 213-215 East Division is for sale along with hotel furniture, so it must have been a hotel. The Bijou is still going and has decided to give a free give-away each night. Natural gas is now being found and is being used in some places of the USA. It will not arrive in Ishpeming until the 1970's. But bottled gas will replace city gas, whose days are numbered. Still another new invention is the typewriter, which is becoming more common. A Detroit firm is selling used ones in town for $15.00 to $35.00.

An Ishpeming teacher living at the Elizabeth Johnson House went for a walk by the Lake Superior Mine, on a bank on the north side. It gave way, sending her 80 feet down into the open pit. The mine sounded the alarm and she was found alive and taken to the hospital.

If you have a photo with the name of Mr. Nelson on it, it may be from before May of 1910, because on that date Photographer Nelson moved to Iron Mountain.

Cliff's Shafts made some changes with a new steel trestle between A and B shafts, and one cable only to be used to balance the cars to and from the shafts. Ore had been coming up in cages and now will come up in skips.

Ezra Meeker, who traveled the Oregon Trail as a young man, repeated the trip in 1906 and now the federal government is providing $25,000 to mark it for generations to come.

A slick Fakir showed up at the city square in June of 1910, selling soap and pens for a dollar and then gave the dollar back. He then sells a whole bunch and leaves quickly not returning the dollars. Where he sold them was the only thing that was "square." A "seedy" circus also came to town in August and Mr. Newett had gotten word from Missoula, Montana, and Duluth, that the horses looked bad, and the costumes as well. He found a better word: "rotten." A third group, the Cosmopolitan Carnival Company was turned down for a street permit by both Ishpeming and Negaunee after the Iron Mountain newspaper reported that it was not a good show. Business in Ishpeming was against it also as much money would leave the area. One good show did come in September at the Cleveland Park. It had a "Model City" on display, possibly as city of the future, and many boarded the streetcars to go and see it. Their business was 25% better than expected.

Trebilcock Brothers continue to put in concrete curbing. This summer it is Wabash and west of Lake on Division Street.

What about airplanes? Isn't there anything abut airplanes? In June 25, 1910, we have the first word about airplanes. An airplane went from New York to Philadelphia and back in three hours and twenty-nine minutes. It made additional stops during the trip.

Competition still exists in the theater business and now the Bijou has an orchestra three nights a week and a quartet on the other three. No movies are allowed on Sunday yet. One man got arrested late in the year for showing a movie within two miles of the Ishpeming City limits on Sunday. A new town item is that there was another new theater by the name of Lyric. It seated 300, and the lobby ceiling has 150 incandescent lights and a well-lit sign board outside, has five 18-inch fans and a three piece orchestra. At the Ishpeming Theater, dramas are getting more risqué. The year before this, there were a group of girls appearing in bathing suits, and in this year, a show went on with people in pajamas and in nightgowns. There didn't seem to be any complaints, however.

There had been new suggestions for steel in the past few years. One was for railroad ties, but that didn't work out. Now the consideration is for legs and caps in mine drifts. They were used at the Mather B Mine in the 1950's, so some inventions take a long time to take effect. The Section 16 mine had a wooden shaft house, and it was taken down by sawing the timbers part way, and hooking it up to a steam engine. The shaft will be improved with a steel housing, and one level will eventually tie in with the Lake Superior Mine to the north.

There is a Marquette County Fair each year, but nothing much in the newspaper. Someone complained that horses (racing?) seem to be more important than agriculture, and Mr.

Newett said as this was a dry summer, agriculture will be affected again.

In September, schools began, and this year Ishpeming has a total of 85 teachers. All of them were listed by schools. Another report on Mine deaths showed 29 or 4.43 per 1000 workers. 6,546 men were employed. Only five deaths were in Ishpeming City limits with one at the Salisbury, two at the Cleveland Lake, and two at the Section 16. The Section 16 also had a cave in on the west end of the Lake Angeline Pit, 20 feet wide and 50 feet long. The newly built public road was not affected.

The Tuberculosis Hospital, to be named Morgan Heights, will be built on what was then, the main road to Marquette. That was a new item. The oldest item is that the old Ishpeming Cemetery was still a disgrace on the north end of Strawberry Hill.

Sports fans: The newspaper for the first time tells us about the World Series, and that the Chicago Cubs and Philadelphia Athletics are the two teams for 1910. The YMCA is working towards 1000 members in its program. The building has a huge gymnasium with a running track up above it. There was no bear hunting season this year and that has caused some gripes, said Mr. Newett.

For the first time, the newspaper has a section of national and world news. Getting Modern! If news is coming in nationally, money is going out nationally. People are also sending more money out of town by buying from mail order houses. "Thousands of dollars of Ishpeming money is being sent," said the newspaper.

Food prices are as follows: Butter is thirty-five cents a pound; catsup is three bottles for a quarter, sugar is a dollar for 20 pounds and flour is seven dollars a barrel.

There was some worry on the part of Mr. Newett regarding the last ten-year census. Evidently, for the first time, the population of Ishpeming went down by 807 people. "Seems like an error in Washington," he said, and figured out on paper that we had 4,370 births and only 1,920 deaths. Marquette still only had 11,503 people, while Ishpeming has 12,448.

THE REPUBLIC IRON CO.—Situated at Republic, Mich. Chas. Hickox, Pres., Cleveland, Ohio; W. D. Rees, Sec. and Treas., Cleveland; Geo. Wilson, Agent, Republic: Peter Pascoe, Supt., Republic.

RIVERSIDE IRON CO.

REPUBLIC LAND AND MINING CO.—J. R. Devereaux, Pres.; D. H. Merritt, Secy.

ESCANABA RIVER IRON & LAND CO.—J. B. Maas, Pres. and Gen'l Mgr., of Negaunee; Jos. Cornish, Supt. In the S.W. ¼ of N.E. ¼ of Sec. 18, 45,-25. J. R. Wood, Superintendent, Appleton, Wis.

SAMPSON MINE.—Is near the Humboldt railway station, in the northerly hillside which extends to the west. Richard A. Parker, Agent and Superintendent. Sec. 1, 47-29.

THE SALISBURY MINE.— One of the mines belonging to the Iron Cliffs Co. The property is in S. ¼ S.W. ¼ of Sec. 15, 47-27. Alexander Maitland, Negaunee, General Manager.

EAST NEW YORK IRON COMPANY.—Located W. ¼ S. W. ¼ Sec. 2, 47-27, 80 acres. S. K. Wambold, Appleton, Wis. President; W. H. Johnston, Ishpeming, Mich., Vice President; C. R. Ely, Ishpeming, Mich., Secretary; M. J. Luther, Streator, Ill., Treasurer; Joseph Selwood, Duluth, Minn., Gen'l Mngr.; J. Parke Channing, Ishpeming, Mich., Agent; C. S. Broughton, Ispeming, Mich., Clerk. Capital 60,000 shares at $25 par value, $1,500,000. Shipments for 1890, 36,430 tons of Hematite.

IRON VALLEY MINING CO.—Orlando F. Barnes of Lansing, Pres.; J. M. Finn, Sec. and Treas. N.E of S.W. Sec. 2, 47-27. Hard Hematite and Blue Hematite.

U. S. GRANT MINE.—NE¼ Sec. 5, 47-26. Anthony Broad, Pres.; Wm. F. Anderson, General Manager; Josiah Broad, Superintendent.

WHEAT MINING CO.—Alex McGary, President; Wm. Proat, Agent and General Manager.

ABOVE IS LIST FOUR OF FIVE 1891 LISTS OF AREA IRON ORE MINES.

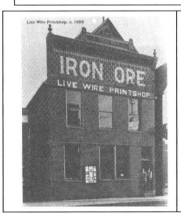

Live Wire Printshop, c. 1898

HERE IS A PHOTO OF THE IRON ORE'S FINAL HOME ON WEST DIVISION STREET. "LIVE WIRE PRINTSHOP" WAS THE GENERAL PRINTING PLANT. MR. NEWETT WAS THE OWNER AND EDITOR.
PHOTO FROM THE OCTOBER, 1982, CALENDAR OF FRIENDS OF THE ISHPEMING CARNEGIE LIBRARY.

Chapter 21:
Automobiles and the Roads

In early 1906 there was the crossing of the United States by automobile, and an article was in the Iron Ore. Another indication in 1906 that the automobile is becoming more popular was an article that rubber plantations are needed for auto tires.

Local cars are such big news, that on April 7, 1906, we are told that Mr. Arvid Braastad has a new Racine-Pierce, Mr. Simon Wahlman has a new Cadillac, and the Bosh Brewing Co. in Ishpeming has a new Franklin. Franklin cars had an ad in the paper every week for years. In May, the ad told of how the car goes 95 miles on two gallons of gasoline. Another ad was a Cadillac for sale. It was a 1905. Great speeds were now being attained by automobiles, said an article in June of 1906. In July, a local person drove from Ishpeming to Champion in 39 minutes. Later in the year, two boys were killed, but not locally, and were traveling a mile-a-minute.

We don't know who suggested it, but someone thought of the idea of getting a car for the fire chief to get to a fire quickly and prepare for equipment. The city of Negaunee made a nice completion of the highway from Ishpeming. Ishpeming was building many new streets as the Braastads' opened up new lots for sale in the north part of the city. With so many cars, the county was also concerned about its roads, and so the high hill over the rock bluff just east of the old Morgan Furnace would be improved. The county will also build its first concrete bridge in the vicinity. It is hard for us to believe what roads must have been up to this time period.

In 1907 there was a nice report from area men who attended the Chicago Auto Show (February 9, 1907). There was also a new ad in the newspaper for a Reo auto for $1,250.00 A picture of a Reo in another ad gave a price of only $675 for a run-about. It was a 20 horsepower with two cylinders and are made in Lansing. . The car ads for Franklins seem to be fewer now. Maybe people are enjoying heat by purchasing cars with "radiators." Horses were still abundant, and two black delivery horses on Main Street went wild, hitting two telephone poles and then running all the way home to their barn in Negaunee. Still in February of 1908, Mr. Nelson sold several Franklins in one week and sent out an order for more. They arrived in town on May 9th.

Rules for driving did not exist from the first. Even before laws were made, however, Mr. Newett preached on several occasions that autos should "stay to the right". He asked auto drivers to give horses plenty of room, and if a horse looks jittery, to pull over and stop.

Gasoline is being spelled gasolene at this time, and one can see in reading the old newspapers, that spellings do change, irregardless of what is printed in the dictionaries. In June we read of the first arrests of automobile drivers. Three people were arrested for "fast driving of an auto" over 15 miles per hour. Mr. Newett soon wrote that cars are not going to go away. In August of 1908, one of the town's blacksmiths went out of business. By the end of the year, Mr. H. F. Heyn at Division and Main sold out his harness and saddlery business in the Mitchell Building. On the other hand, the owner of the Franklin and Buick garage quit his job with the Grand Union to sell his cars full-time in early January of 1909.

Longer travel trips are being enjoyed by autos, and in late summer of 1908, Charles Kirkpatrick made a trip from Escanaba to Ishpeming with his Stanley Steamer. The road was "heavy" in some spots, he reported. Ads for the Franklin used local people in news type of ads. A good one in January of 1909 told of how a local doctor used his Franklin without worry in twenty-degree-below weather.

In 1908, the first USA automobile statistics are printed. An estimated 150,000 autos are now on the road, and last year 52,000 cars were manufactured and sold.

With the amount of increasing autos, the Copper Country, in 1909, asked for a road down to the Ishpeming area. The problem is the large swamp and rough area in the Baraga area at the west end of Keweenaw Bay. Ishpeming is working on a new and better road north from town to the Negaunee Mines by Teal Lake.

The first notice of a truck being bought for company use was in April of 1909 when a lumber company here bought a two-ton "Rapid" truck. A few weeks later the paper reported that it was operating well. The listing of new people in town who have purchased autos is getting to fill a column or two. Races continued to show the best cars, and one in June of 1909 went from Seattle to New York and was won by a Ford. This may have increased the local sale of Fords, and Mr. Newett by 1911 wrote an editorial in his paper telling people of the "risks" of buying a cheap auto. Perhaps he was trying to help out his non-Ford car dealer friends.

One can imagine the effect of autos on electric street cars. To help the street railway, autos used for hire are now being charged $50 a year, as street cars are. A license also became a local requirement and in October the Pioneer Motor Co. of Marquette decided to stop its taxis between there and Ishpeming.

In September, an ad for a Buick Runabout was shown, with a $1,000 price, and in December of 1909 the first ad for an Oakland auto was printed. Note was made that it is half the price of a Franklin. There were probably other ads for cars as well, but they may be been in Ishpeming's three other weekly papers at this time, the Ishpeming Record, and the Peninsular Record, plus a Swedish paper. People were also reading the Marquette Daily Mining Journal.

People are getting real comfortable with their autos, so much, that a Mr. Bronson had his Reo shipped to Florida for his family to use during the winter months. He will join them in the spring. In a January 1910 ad, we find that Mr. Nelson is also selling White Steamers, Zimmerman's and 2 De Luxes. In 1911, Packards were being sold and at the end of that year, an Overland Car Dealership began.

Road improvement continued and in the spring of 1901, work is being done on the road to Iron Mountain at Witch Lake. Complaints appear in the paper as well about the roads from time to time. In May a complaint was about the road from Champion into town. By June of 1901, work is being done on the road between Dexter and Clarksburg. Many townships are working on their roads.

In Ishpeming, in August of 1910, the city first experimented with asphalt oil. 65 barrels went on and was called "road oil." Negaunee was so impressed, that they started doing it also. The word "tar" is used the next month when the city square and part of Pine Street was tarred. The tar was brushed into the street and then light sand put over the top. It will replace the crude petroleum products used previously, reported Mr. Newett.

Road travel became possible to Iron Mountain only in August of 1910 when a steel bridge was built over the Michigamme River where it crossed, south of Republic. Part of the road is no longer in use because changes made by the Republic open pit mine. Within a few weeks, three autos made the trip over the Iron Mountain Road to the Menominee Iron Range. They went there in 3 hours and 58 minutes and back in 3 hours and 35 minutes. The trip back, they noted, included driving 1.5 miles on an incorrect road. Another report told of auto travel to Munising. At this time the road went through Chatham. In 1911 the auto trip to Munising went via Green Garden, Carlshend, Rumley, Chatham, and AuTrain.

Auto tires were the largest problem on a car. In 1910, when cars went fast, the tires wanted to hoop, or go oblong on the rims. This was quite a problem when they came off. There were a lot of highway problems, also, and in the fall of 1910, local auto owners got together to discuss organizing "to affect: roads, courtesy, legislation, and regulations."

In spite of the growth of auto traffic, manufacturing companies must have overproduced and the newspaper announced in October that many 1909 cars were still unsold and were being offered at very low prices.

We note that no one is traveling west of Champion by auto. Roads in that direction are bad. In November, Covington is seeking land to make a 12 mile road towards Ishpeming to Nestoria, west of Michigamme. This would allow a road at least from Ontonagon to Ishpeming. Mr. Newett wrote "No road presently exists that a team could utilize." It is difficult to believe that with all the new and wonderful inventions aiding life at home, that it was so difficult, other than by train, to go anywhere else.

One road that Mr. Newett mentions often is the problem west of Champion. There was a road that is still on the north side of US-41 and which followed the old 1890 Iron Range and Huron Bay Railroad grade up the Peshekee River, and then crossed on a rickety bridge. In March of 1911, Mr. Newett preaches that a "good bridge is badly needed across the Peshekee River. The road through this area was up and down a great deal. Maybe it was easy for horses, but it was difficult for 20- horsepower autos full of people. The McCormick Estate personnel used the road to Michigamme at this time, rather than to Champion. The new Peshekee concrete bridge was built in 1914, and is still there between the present bridge and the railroad bridge. The road also had a new route, avoiding the hill, by following the railroad track from Van Riper Park to the river and going along the shoreline of Lake Michigamme.

The coming of auto tires with air in them led to at least one group of boys throwing tacks on the road to disable cars. So far no one had been caught. It was a rather serious crime, seeing that tires failed so easily without that tragedy.

For the first five months of 1911, Mr. Nelson sold 17 new cars. New auto inventions were being developed as well. Not all of them came to be. The Westinghouse Brake Company invented an air spring to make autos drive smoothly, and eliminate the need for air in tires, saying that all a wheel would need is a rubber band around it. Another failure was the idea of a car starter that worked by pushing a button and would work by compressed air. Eventually it did work by pushing a button, but the work was done by electricity.

For the first time, Ishpeming and Negaunee worked at oiling the road between the two cities. Mr. Newett was also pushing for an improved Teal Lake Road between the two cities as there were fewer railroad crossings for autos. The county improved the road between Republic and Witch Lake in August of 1911.

In August of 1911, there is this, which we have been taking for granted: "Drivers of autos should have to take some sort of examination". Mr. Newett said there were way too many accidents. Some of the accidents are simply because autos have lights, but carriages and buggies, and wagons do not. Even bicycles are required to have lights on at night, noted Mr. Newett.

Several Ishpeming men went to the January 1912, Detroit Auto Show. Those interested in this area may find a list of all the current auto companies and the names of automobiles in the January 6, 1912, Iron Ore.

In the same month of January, note is made that the new Marquette County Highway is very nice to Marquette, except for a very sharp curve abut two miles east of Morgan Hill (By the old Morgan Heights Sanitarium which was also built in 1912.) which was very bad. In the coming months there were many accidents, and finally the County Road Engineer, K. I. Sawyer, built up the edge of the dead-man's curve, and banked it, which was something new. And then to alleviate the problem further, a centerline was placed on the road to keep cars from colliding with each other. This is believed to be the oldest centerline in the nation. The sharp corner is no longer part of the regular road, but can be seen to the left, or north, on the present road going to Marquette.

By the winter of 1912, Mr. Nelson and his car company of Franklins and other autos was doing so well, that he is wintering in Arizona. We also note that in this year, the first mention is made of a six-cylinder auto, and it is also a Franklin. The 1913 Franklins sold for $2,900.

In the summer of 1913, the L'Anse to Ishpeming road began to get some attention, and the route west of Ishpeming is discussed, as to whether it should go into Diorite, or south of it. Note is made in September that a quarter-mile past Diorite are two large mud holes and wagons often need to be pulled out. Mr. Newett notes that in all of the past road building, a lot of low-iron mine rock was used for road fill, and that it could have been sold now to steel mills..

In 1913, the first auto tax appears. Automobiles will be taxed by the amount of horsepower they have, at 50 cents per horsepower. 40 hp will be $20. The following year, this tax was declared unconstitutional. There was excitement from an announcement that the Chicago Motor Club Reliability Run will come through town. The county has hired its first motor cop to patrol the road. An auto ordinance has passed that drivers must drive on the right side of the road. This caused a problem for the Franklin Auto Company, as most of its cars have the steering wheel on the right side. Thus only one auto was produced the next year, their car with the left-side steering wheel.

The National Auto Association had been formed by 1913, and in 1914 the first local Auto Club was formed. They decided to start putting up road signs. Also in 1914, two Chalmers cars were seen on city streets. So many people are buying gasoline that prices fell from 17 cents to 12 cents a gallon.

The county in 1914 began road construction from the Baron Mine in Humboldt to Champion, and at Covington, men are building three miles of road necessary to connect Baraga to Ishpeming.

Mr. Newett writes that the newest complaint he is hearing is that more and more people seem to be driving their autos without using their mufflers to save gasoline. The State of Michigan soon after this made auto mufflers a requirement, and the auto companies announced that new cars would no longer have a muffler "cut-out" option.

Trucks still do not have a lot of power in 1915. The city of Crystal Falls bought a new fire truck, only to find out that it can't get up the Main Street hill of that town. Mr. Newett noted in April that all vehicles will now need $3.00 license plates. Also, for the first time, auto road maps of the U.P. roads are for sale by Mr. Eason in town.

In the spring of 1915, new roads are planned at the Humboldt Barron Mine, and west of Champion from Dishno Creek to Michigamme. That road will run closer to the lake and save two railroad crossings.

Speeding is still a problem. Some arrests were made on Third Street for people going 40 mph. A Ford employee caused a serious accident when taking a newly received car for a joy ride. To make speeding legal, Chicago built a large speedway for Auto Derby Racing. The first winner, announced on July 3, 1915, went 97.6 miles per hour.

This special statistic appeared in the September 4, 1915, issue of the Iron Ore: Two million cars are now registered in the U.S.A. 113,386 are registered in Michigan. In 1914, 626,000 cars were manufactured in the U.S. And in 1915 there is also an announcement that H. O. Young has brought the first Auto "Sedan" to Ishpeming. It has a permanent roof. It was a sight to behold, no doubt. Now cars could have heaters to warm the occupants, all except the Franklin, which was air-cooled.

Accidents continue, and in October of 1915, there was a serious accident between a motorcycle and a horse and wagon. The cycle was on the wrong side of the road, but the wagon had no lights on at all. There was one death.

In December, a used car ad appears for a Pullman, with electric start and electric gear shift. In 1916, a new product for auto fuel was invented, called Benzol. It was to replace gasoline. Franklins ran well on it said the paper.

More road headway is noted when the county in 1916 put out advertisements for someone to install guardrails on roads. Autos going 50 will be stopped for speeding. Note is made that there are now three roads going to Negaunee, the Teal Lake, the Old Jackson, and Jackson Street. Ishpeming will be asphalting their end of the road this year.

The dead-man's curve, east of Morgan Heights, with its center line, will be removed in 1916. Roadwork this summer included improvement of the road to L'Anse by way of Nestoria to Herman. And here was an exciting announcement, a note that that a state highway would be built from Big Bay to L'Anse via Skanee. On the 1933 road map this was shown as M-35, but not finished through the Huron Mountain Club. It never was.

People were still purchasing Franklin cars in 1917, and 30 are on order. Many citizens are now buying Cadillac and Overland autos. The State reports that the number of Marquette County driver's licenses now totals 731, plus 69 for motorcycles, and still others for chauffeur's in 1917.

An important new 1917 road has been built to join the east end of Division Street (at the Cleveland Mine) with Bluff Street (The Jackson Road) at the Cleveland School, by going through the valley. Deadman's curve by Morgan Heights has not yet been solved, except that Mr. Sawyer is going to bank up the outside edge of the curve.

In the summer of 1917, there were auto races in Marquette, with $2,000 in prizes. Fraud was claimed as there seemed to be a pre-determined winner. Quite a few cars are also being stolen and rewards are being offered. The Soo is arresting inebriated drivers, and Mr. Newett says he would like to see that happen locally. Nelson's garage reported that one of its new Franklins arrived, and was not quite so new. The conclusion is that some tramps had lived in it for some time as it traveled to Ishpeming by rail.

Are the roads improving? A local man, driving his Hudson, drove from Ishpeming to Iron Mountain in two hours, average 26 miles per hour. His gas mileage was 14 miles per gallon. The Ishpeming-Negaunee road was redone with an extension of the Jackson Road so that travel can now be made to Palmer without going to Iron Street. Negaunee's paving was done in early 1917, and Ishpeming, in September, is completing paving with "Tarvia."

The road from L'Anse to Baraga in 1918 is being aided by the state, and a steel bridge is being built in the large swamp. (This bridge can still be seen.) More and more are traveling the roads. A study on a rainy July 4th, 1918, showed that an average of 108 vehicles per hour passed the check point on the Mqt.-Ish. Road.

The city of Ishpeming in 1918 bought a new Packard truck for watering the streets and for hauling. Mr. Nelson has to go right to New York and drive the newly ordered Franklins to town as no railroad transportation is available. A week or so later he drove a Franklin to Colorado, and made it there, a total of 1,633 miles, in only six and a half days from Ishpeming. There is still a problem, also, of muffler cut-outs, and Marshal Trevarrow will be arresting people.

Road work continued in 1919, and the March 1, 1919, Iron Ore, had a full front page article on the current local roads being built in the area. The reader is invited to study it further in detail at the Ishpeming Carnegie Library. One of the great problems yet is that roads, believe it or not, are not numbered in any way.

An interesting note in the June 14, 1919 newspaper has to do with the closing of the Negaunee-Marquette highway for rebuilding. This must have been the Morgan Heights road. The article notes that the "old" Neg.-Marq. Road will be used, and that a mile of highway will be built at Eagle Mills to connect the two roads.

A major announcement in the fall was that the State of Michigan will start providing highway signs to help tourists.. A road number will be put on each sign and they will be at all crossroads and every half mile on telephone poles if possible. Counties will do the work. In the future signs will also be put up for bad curves and bad driving areas.

The paper also reported that many local cars continue to be stolen, including a new Ford on Division Street that week

Mr. Newett went to an auction for a farm in Michigamme a few years before 1919 and found dozens of wagons present. In September the same farm was auctioned again and he counted 175 cars and only four wagons.

It was reported that Henry Ford cannot build enough cars. In October, a group of Ford men were in the area, looking to buy some iron ore mines to supply ore for their blast furnace in Dearborn. They were able to do so. One of the new mines would be the Imperial in Michigamme, and the Blueberry, just west of the Barnes-Hecker.

According to the January 17, 1920, Iron Ore, a road is being planned from the Dead River to Skanee, and a note that concrete abutments will be put in at the edges of the Dead River for the new bridge to Skanee. Perhaps this road is to replace the planned road from Big Bay when passage through the Huron Mountain Club was not possible. The new road will go from Negaunee to Skanee.

The city replaced its five-year-old Ford with a new Dodge, and also purchased two trucks, and then bought a third 1.5 ton for garbage, ashes, and gravel use. Flannigan Bros. of Marquette has purchased three large 18-passenger cars for a bus service to Ishpeming. A newspaper article notes that there is worry that there will not be enough gasoline in the world to fuel all the cars. Maybe, for the same reason, the latest 1920 Franklin ad says that the car now gets 20 miles per gallon, as well as will go 12,500 miles on a set of tires.

Henry Ford invested in the U. P at this time, with a saw-wood plant near L'Anse in Pequaming, and a large "Woody Plant" at Iron Mountain, hiring 2,500 people to make the wonderful wood sides on their more expensive models.

And last of all, in 1920, is the arrival of the first State of Michigan Auto Tourist Book of Highways. It has all of the automobile routes and shows, says Mr. Newett, even area roads, such as the Cliff's Drive.

HERE IS THE 1933 ROUTE OF MICHIGAN 35 HIGHWAY THROUGH THE HURON MOUNTAINS. THIS IS A SECOND PLAN, LEAVING FROM NEGAUNEE AT THE MID-WAY LOCATION. THE ORIGINAL ROUTE WAS TO BE FROM BIG BAY, WHICH ONE CAN SEE IS NOT SO ON THIS MAP. NEITHER VERSION EVER CAME TO BE, AND A NICE, DEVELOPED, ROAD NEVER CAME TO BE.

THIS MAP IS FROM THE "OFFICIAL PAVED ROAD AND COMMERCIAL SURVEY OF THE UNITED STATES," 1932.

BELOW IS A AD FOR THE TARVIA ROAD SURFACE COVERING FROM A 1910 COLLIER'S MAGAZINE.

VOLUNTEER IRON CO.—Geo. Alger, President; Alfred Kidder, Agt.; Capt. Thos. Walters, Superintendent.

PITTSBURG & LAKE SUPERIOR MINING CO.—Joseph Kirkpatrick, President and General Manager, Palmer, Mich.

NEW YORK IRON CO.—Sec. 2, 47-27-W. L. McCloskey, Pres.; Aug. Voiling, Supt. Red Specular Ore.

BESSIE MINING CO.—N½ Sec. 1, 47-29. Ed. Lobb, Pres.; G. B. Lobb, Supt. and General Manager. Limonite.

GERTRUDE MINING CO.—Sec. 1, 47-29. Wm. Pelmear, Pres.; Jos. King, Supt. Limonite.

REPUBLIC MINE.—Sec. 6, T. R. Pres., Sam'l P. Healey, Cleveland, O.; Wm. D. Rees, Gen'l Mngr., Cleveland; David Morgan, Agt.; Peter Pascoe, Supt.

RIVERSIDE IRON CO —James O. StClair, Pres. and Gen'l Mngr.; E. G. StClair, Sec. and Treas. Sec. 3, T. R.

FITCH IRON CO.—Jas. Pickands, Pres., of Cleveland, O.; H. G. Dalton, of Cleveland, Treas.; Jno. F. Armstrong, Supt. Sec. 24, 47-28.

SAGINAW MINE.—Lee Peck, Gen'l Mngr and Supt. Sec. 12, 47-27.

LOWTHIAN MINE.—Sec. 21, 47-27. C. H. Hall, General Manager; Jno. Trebilcock, Mining Captain.

CLEVELAND HEMATITE MINE.—Sec. 2, 47-27. F. P. Mills, General Manager; S. L. Mather, Pres.

EAST JACKSON MINE.—Sec. 6, 47-26. J. S. Foley, Supt. and General Manager.

ROLLING MILL IRON CO.—Sec. 7, 47-26. Luther Beecher, of Detroit, Pres.; Geo. Beecher, Supt. and General Manager.

EAST BUFFALO MINE.—SE¼ Sec. 5, 47-26. Ed. Lobb, Pres. and General Manager.

ABOVE IS LIST 5 OF FIVE LISTS OF MINES

BELOW IS THE FAMOUS ISHPEMING THEATER. GOING INTO BANKRUPTCY SOON AFTER IT WAS BUILT, IT WAS PURCHASED FROM THE BANK BY MR; BUTLER WHO THEN OWNED TWO THEATERS. THIS THEATER WAS USED FOR STAGE SHOWS, WRESTLING TOURNAMENTS, AND MOVIES. THE WINDOWS ARE THOSE OF AN APARTMENT UNDER THE BALCONY. THE BUILDING WAS TORN DOWN IN THE LAST FORTY YEARS. AND WAS ON CLEVELAND AVENUE, NEXT TO MR. BRAASTAD'S LARGE STORE.

PHOTO CREDIT: THE MINING JOURNAL

Chapter 22:

1911 Through 1915

1911

Trebilcock Brothers began 1911 with 5,000 cement blocks on hand. There are many houses still standing that are made of these blocks, including the former Trebilcock home on Third Street, next to where the former green house was. The new North Lake Mine Shaft was also being built of concrete. The new Post Office at Bank and Second Street, where it still is will be built, and a Jaedecke Building as well. One small building addition that is still very visible at the corner of Division and Main was built in 1911. It is in the corner of city hall, and had a door to a public bathroom which the town needed. Two Rudledge brothers, who have worked in the Detroit Packard factory, are returning here and will open a Packard Auto company.

The city is now operating two sidewalk plows, but they must be pulled by horses. To supply our mines with equipment made locally, the Lake Shore Engine Works will soon be manufacturing in Marquette. At the February Ski Tournament, Mr. Mather came once again to award the medals, and hopefully watched the dog races in the morning. To provide a service and make extra money, several churches and the Nelson House are offering meals for 50 cents, especially for those who arrive before lunch on the special excursion trains. The street car conductor had a close call when he looked out the side of the car and his head hit a pole and he fell out and the street car continued without him. Boys at the First M. E. Church (Division Street) have formed an official Boy Scout Troop.

The 1911 fire report for 1910 showed 24 alarms and a need for more fire hydrants. At the Ishpeming Theater, 50 young people entertained with their talents. Two of the movie house owners paid fines of $22.50 for showing movies on Sunday. We find that Sam Apostle began his business in Ishpeming during this year, making candy using molds. Rev. Allen of the Presbyterian Church celebrated his 15th year here. Mr. Conibear of the Salisbury Location, and the CCI mines, returned to town at this time and became the State Mine Inspector. The author was lucky to have him on his paper route in the 1950's.

The most deaths in the year were from a large explosion once again at the Pluto Powder plant in National Mine, three miles south of town. Ten men died in the February blast. The YMCA, in order to raise budget funds, had a national person come in to run a fund raising program. Names of large givers to the YMCA were published in the paper, and in eight days, $22,858. was raised. The greatest group of contributors were workers at the Salisbury Mine. The YMCA members also started a new practice of raising money for the next several years with an annual "Circus" held at the YMCA gym. This first year it was already very good and it became a popular event, all performed by local people.

For those who study guns, an ad was in the paper in February for the Steven's visible loading repeating rifle. A man wanted out west was arrested here, and police from Montana's Silver Bow County arrived to pick him up.

We have some shipping records for 1910. There was a total of 4,238,000 tons of ore shipped. The Cleveland Cliff's Iron Company shipped 46% of that total. The Negaunee Mines are now also going strong, with the Negaunee Mine sending out 349,000 tons. The CCI is also paying out $150,000. during this spring in the moving of the two Negaunee cemeteries. Many homes in East Negaunee will also be moved. Lots of unmarked graves are being found. Probably many were single men killed in the mines, with all their families in the old country.

Wrestling is a common sport with professionals coming in and competing with local men at the Ishpeming Theater. A good comedy also appeared there in March, entitled, "Miss Nobody from Starland." The Lyric Theater has a new combination schedule with Vaudeville again, with talented individuals and teams appearing, and then also showing movies each night.

Ishpeming had a nice honor when the newest Jones and Laughlin iron ore carrier was named after Captain Walters of the Lake Angeline Mine. Ships need to be larger and so a new lock at the Sault will be built and will be 80 feet wide and 1,350 feet long and 25.5 deep.

The Parochial School is going to be built at Front and Pine, and the American Mine, west of town, will be the first mine to have its men eat lunch underground by allowing them to work only 10 hours rather than the 11 they will get paid for.

A new fad for women arrived at Skud's Store in the form of Harem skirts. The author has no idea of what they are or if they are still around with a different name. Ads for Singer Sewing Machines are also seen for the first time. New homes continue to be built. Baby carriages are coming into style with all the new sidewalks and paved roads, but they are called, believe it, or not, "go carts." The CCI is laying out several blocks for homes on Empire and Michigan Streets, to Oak, and notes that the swamp will be "covered" At Braastad's there was an ad for new 2.25 horsepower air-cooled gasoline engines for $46. delivered. That would eliminate a lot of steam engines in many industries as well as farms..

From time to time there are fires at local mines, but in May of 1911 there was a larger one with seven deaths at the Hartford along Teal Lake. Smoke even came up in the Cambria shaft. Both shafts were sealed to snuff out the fire. This fire started an entire new campaign for safety in the mines, and a need was seen for oxygen helmets for rescuers. The Ironwood Mine had sent some and they were invaluable. The Hartford shaft fire repairs were begun when the mine was reopened in June.

The hospitals are busy with 37 births in April and 29 births in March. Surprisingly, even with some children born at home, most are born at the hospital to miners' wives. There were 30 deaths in the same two months. Ishpeming is having a recount as it believes there are more residents than got counted in the last census. The newspaper also believed that 1911 would set a new record for the tonnage of iron ore shipped to the steel mills.

For some reason with the coming of autos, more horse and buggy accidents are in the newspaper. One at the top of the Burt Office Hill (Lake Superior Mine Office) resulted when a carriage with three people went into the electric railroad rail groove and it startled the horses, who immediately turned and headed for home, throwing out the riders and driver.

The city now has also a Big Brother organization. Whether it is the same as today's Big Brothers, is not known. There is also a campaign going on in the U.S. government to reduce first class postage from two cents to one cent.

Circuses will be coming here again. Mr. Newett personally said that the Yankee Robinson was not recommended. He had received word that a lot of crooks were a part of it. It came, but after leaving, its $12,000 large elephant died, as well as one of the leading persons in the show. The other two circuses were the W. H. Coultior and the Sun Brothers. A large, 17-railroad car Patterson Street Fair would also entertain at Union Park. It evidently was a carnival ride company, and had 20 of them, but also had free acts and an animal exhibition of lions, tigers, and trained elephants. Another group, the Barkoot Street Fair wants to operate in town, but businesses feels that it takes away more money than it brings in for them. It, too, went to Union Park and had a very good reception from the public. Still another show appeared; the Campbell's Big Consolidated Railroad Shows came, with 400 people, 200 horses, city of white tents, and a street parade. It came on a Saturday, and on the previous Wednesday, the Skerbeck Circus came and had very low attendance because of the "big show" a few days later.

Airplane flying is getting more popular and in the first six months over 28 U. S. flyers had died. At the Hancock July 4th celebration, there was a race between a car and an aeroplane. There were several popular boat cruises on the Great Lakes, especially for newly-weds.

Believe it or not, the postage for first class letters, which had been two cents, was reduced to a penny a letter. Read that sentence again if you want! Most of us thought that the penny postcard was a good deal.

Two Ishpeming inventions took place this year and both inventors were workers at the Salisbury Mine. They were following in the footsteps of Captain Buzzo who was inventing new drills. One employee invented a bell system for raising and lowering cages and skips in the shafts and the other man was building a recording device to show how much ore was being taken from which levels and so on. The bell system caught on and became universal in most mines. The other invention was worked on for several more years and tried in some mines.

September arrived, and it was announced that President Taft would visit Marquette. Ishpeming residents hoped they might get him to come there, but it was not to be. Mr. Newett printed his speech anyway in the Iron Ore. President Taft was also the first President to have a Presidential automobile.

One puzzling item took place when the city told the Electric Street Railway that they would have to remove their poles on Main Street as they were unsightly. This was done, with no explanation of how the street car wire would now be held. Perhaps the cross wires were fastened to buildings as the street was getting quite full of store buildings, although the Gately-Wiggens and Butler Theater next door have not yet been built. In November the project was completed, and Mr. Newett noted that the Main Street looked a lot wider.

This year, "Uncle Tom's Cabin" appeared again, and the famous cast included bloodhounds. Another new movie theater opened up at Thanksgiving time, called the Royal and it was at Main and Cleveland. At the Salisbury Church, Rev. Keast and his wife arrive. In later years, Rev. Keast passed away and his wife returned to pastor the church about 1950, and did a fine job in every way, including a Sunday school enrolling about 80 children. A concrete sidewalk was put in from South Angeline Street and Callow's Store to the Church and Salisbury School. Note was made by the city that the old one is rotten and is being "stolen," no doubt for use this coming winter.

Ishpeming people were already burning hard-wood clippings in their stoves in 1911. They were the remains of hardwood flooring being made by the Consolidated Fuel and Lumber Company in Negaunee. Hardwood flooring was the new thing in new homes.

The new Fire Hall will be built and it will be on Lake Street at the Superior Lumber site. The cost will be about $30,000.. A great deal of discussion over many months took place. The old Fire Hall was at Bank and First. It was sold, but when the new owner failed to make needed improvements, it was condemned and torn down within a few years.

Is there any crime going on? Yes, there is. Myers store has been robbed at least twice, and several arrests have been made for illegal hunting. There have been bar knifings from time to time. One man was cut up with a razor blade several times during a card game. Three youth also robbed Cromwell's Bakery of $21. on West Division Street. In December, the Circuit Court docket in Marquette listed 29 criminal cases, including four murders.

In non-crime deaths, five were killed the first week of the 1911 hunting season. By November 18, 15 had been killed in the U. P. The season then ran from October 15 to November 30. There were so many deer hunters that came to the U. P. to hunt, that trains were running late with all the baggage. One Ishpeming woman was shot at mistakenly as a deer, and the man who shot her settled with her for $100.

There were 32 mine deaths in the previous year, and 39 mines are producing on the Marquette Iron Range with 6,385 men working. (Some of these of course were women.) An interesting note is that in spite of the good

economy, quite a few Finns and Italians have returned to their homeland.

The CCI is building the Carp River Dam on Deer Lake's east end and is using the new product of concrete. A six-foot pipe will carry the water for six miles to the power station Power lines will then go to the Maas Mine, Pioneer Furnace, Dexter, North Lake and CCI Gwinn area mines. A concrete dam is also being built at Silver Lake. Wahlman and Trebilcock are the builders. The weather was still nice in November. In the Copper Country, the Calumet and Hecla Company shaft no. 4 is now down 8,100 feet at a 38 degree angle. 5,280 vertical feet is a mile down)

Something new to the author was made known in November of 1911 when it was announced that a bear cub was added to the "Zoo" at Cleveland Park. It is the only mention ever made by Mr. Newett of the zoo. And where was Cleveland Park?

An interesting thing happens in town now and then: A group of medical doctors arrive regularly in Ishpeming and ask for those with serious disorders to come and be seen. They travel around, like a Rochester Clinic, and are always present for just a day, this time at the Urban Hotel. It is called the United Doctors' Institute and they wish to see the most serious medical cases. Mr. Newett never makes any comment about it and thus it must have been quite legitimate.

The Knights of Kaleva have now bought the Donohoe building at Division and Pine, now the Globe Printing. Some rooms will be added to the hall upstairs for Kaleva meetings.

A sad note is that with the onrush of automobiles and better roads, the Electric Street Railway in town has gone into receivership.

Also a sad note is that liquor licenses in town now number 41, and in Negaunee, 33. A few months later, the State ordered Ishpeming to eliminate six licenses.

A good note to end the year on is that the State of Michigan is considering compensation for injured workers, to be paid for by companies. We note also that a Mr. Edward Hickey, who has worked for the Oliver Company since 1864, will retire with a pension on January 1, 1912.

1912

We note that Braastads still has an east part of the third floor of the store which was unused, and it will now be used for business. They also bought a Reo 1.5 ton truck for the store, a second purchase of a truck. In May of 1912, Julius Braastad took over the large store.

A fire occurred at the Miner's Bank, and the Negaunee State Bank, the same night when an electrical storm passed through town. Both banks also have the telephone companies upstairs, and so phones are working poorly in both towns.

An event happened at the Ishpeming Theater when Mr. Ed Butler decided to end all vaudeville and show only films, with Tuesday night being amateur film night. We have no idea of what this was about. He does continue to hold some wrestling tournaments, however.

The price of butter is high, and oleo margarine is being legalized as a substitute. In March, the farmers organize to start a Farmers' Market in town, but "Local Merchants do not favor the plan." Some stores are selling small Victor record players for $10.

On April 20, there was the announcement of the sinking of the Titanic in the Iron Ore. Note

was made that 1000 were saved because of Marconi's wireless telegraph invention. An investigation is taking place, however, on the valuation of sex in saving those who survived.

Professional baseball exists again this summer in town, and a catcher was hired from Massachusetts, and others were imported also. A first exhibition game was held with Marquette.

1912 was also the year that Ishpeming started to replace its arc lights with the nice five-globe clustered, incandescent lights. 72 will cover Main and Front Streets downtown. In addition, every intersection of town will have a single 100-watt light, or a total of 157 lights installed. Main Street is also getting concrete gutters.

Whether autos are having an influence on summer or not, Mr. Butler closed the Ishpeming Theater for a few months A large 30-double length railroad car "Show" came to town, with rides and its own lighting plant. The Ringling Brothers also came again, and advertised a train one mile long. On August 15, the second appearance of Bill Cody's road show, now titled the "Combined Buffalo Bill's Wild West and Pawnee Bill's Far East Shows" came to town.

A historical death took place, when one of the men who built the "Plank Road" for the earliest iron ore shipments to Marquette died in July. He was Mr. Frank Zoberlein, the town's oldest resident. The Plank Road was soon replaced by a railroad built by Mr. Ely that could haul 1,200 tons daily.

More and more electricity is also being made and the Salisbury Mine closed for several weeks as the steam plant was removed, as well as the large Cornish pump down on the 18th level. Each will now be run by an electric motor. Mr. Maas invented a new item to tell the angle that a diamond drill is going down, as they never go completely straight down. It will be easier to tell exactly where the ore is that is found. More on mine safety is also being realized when Mr. Conibear informed Mr. Newett that a new Safety Car is being built and will travel among the U. P. mines and teach miners about safety and rescues. This was a very successful venture. Mines are very short of employees and the Cambria Mine asks for 200 men in the Iron Ore.. The Negaunee Mine was seeking 100 men. Ore is being imported to the U.S. as not enough is being mined. In Minnesota there is talk about having to import Negroes to work in their mines. During 1911, there were 42 mine accidents, with 15 being fatal.

Cows are soon to be tested for tuberculosis, with Marquette and Munising already doing this. Another change is that Post Offices will now be closed on Sundays and no services will be offered. Parcel post for packages is also a new service that will be offered. Gasoline is now 12 cents a gallon, having gone up three cents recently. Mr. Newett reminds citizens that the new 9:00 p.m. siren curfew for children is not a joke.

It is now September, and Mr. Newett reports that there were several auto accidents in the past week, with three being on the road to Marquette. One driver will go to trial for hitting two boys on their bikes. The Ishpeming City Band during the early summer did a concert in Escanaba and will also be playing at the Escanaba State Fair. The Urban House just north of Sellwoods has been moved back on its lot on Main Street and will have a new front put on. It later became the Anderson Hotel and was next to the Carnegie Library. Several other stores this fall were modernized with new fronts..

A big election for the ladies is coming up, with a vote on Women's right to vote. Only the ladies can't vote on it. It will not pass this year. A Negaunee man built an airplane and hoped to fly from Teal Lake to Houghton. A propeller broke before take-off. The First M. E. Church in Ishpeming received a nice used pipe organ from the Negaunee Presbyterian Church.

In October, John Phillip Sousa's band appeared at the Ishpeming Theater for a cost of 25 cents to $1.00. The Ishpeming Library was presented with a 15-volume set of "The Science of Railroads." The library custodian has been vested with police powers to arrest children making noise on the library steps. Mr. Newett was not too happy in October when he found that President Roosevelt was suing him for $10,000 in damages because the Iron Ore said he was drinking and getting drunk while in the county.

The President later won, but Mr. Newett only had to pay six cents. Mr. Newett was Republican, however, and when the election got close, he printed the Republican Ballot in the paper, but not the Democratic one. Also in October, the Singer Sewing Machine store informed the public that the sewing machine was now able to be purchased with an electric motor, and that 125 machines were on order.

The new Fire Hall on Lake Street is being completed, and the bell moved. The Deer Lake dam is also complete and the lake is being flooded behind it. People are driving on the new road. The Ishpeming Theater's latest theatrical is "The Girl Who Dared." In order to advance the town, a group of prominent Ishpeming men have decided to form a new group, the Ishpeming Advancement Association. .

In December, 17 U. P. men were killed during deer hunting season. Braastads, after having a giant ten-cent sale, opened its Toyland and has a large half-page ad in Mr. Newett's paper.

There are many, many other Christmas ads as work and money are plentiful. The new ad for Franklin autos notes that they will have automatic starters and electric lights. On December 21, Braastads announced that it is going out of the clothing business, but expanding their grocery sections, in Ishpeming, and in Negaunee.

The year of 1912 closes with weather so warm that it has not been possible to build the outdoor ice rink yet. A Mr. Laitinen was arrested for carrying a loaded revolver, the C&NW has ordered 1000 steel cars to carry iron ore, and the Cliffs Shafts (New Barnum) is now drifting 1000 feet underground under the Nelson House, and The Braastad store, to the former Moro Mine on Bluff Street in the Cleveland Location area and taking ore on the 12th level.. One or two Moro shafts can still be seen in 2005.

1913

Diorite is building its own jail and a large hall for the community. A January ski tournament in Minnesota is still paying money to winners. The Ishpeming tournament does not give money and the jumping is still yearly on Washington's Birthday with dog races for the kids in the morning. Jumps up to 160 feet were expected here. An Ironwood skier, Mr. Hendrickson, came down the hill twice and did a fine somersault each time. Attendance was excellent. Special ski rates were given by the LS&I RR. After the tournament, however, there was a serious accident at Republic when the CM&St.P RR crashed at the station and a conductor was killed. There were nine coaches of people returning home from Ishpeming.

Ishpeming will see a change in the road to Marquette, as land is badly caving in just east of Negaunee. The cemeteries will be moved, the

DSS&A has already moved at a cost of $750,000, and the road to Marquette will now leave from the Baldwin Kiln Road north by the Maas mine. Sand is already seeping down into the mine and several men died in one disaster. CCI has purchased the property from the Oliver Company.

Those interested in old cars will note that the March 1, 1913 Iron Ore had a picture of a "Michigan 40" auto on sale. Mr. Tillson, the druggist, died suddenly, but an Ishpeming girl, Ida Mae Hopkins, who left town, has made good and now has the name of Virginia Evans and has a leading role with the Comic Opera Company. The editor of the Ishpeming Swedish newspaper, the Superior Posten, Mr. Andrew Lind is touring Florida, including Kissammee. Evidently Mr. Newett is interested in reading the report of his tour. Mr. Newett also ran an ad for Castle Brew Beer, "in the brown bottle," made in the former castle in west Marquette. Another interesting advertisement every week is that, in spite of many, many autos and trucks now being sold locally, there is now an ad every week for Studebaker wagons.

A cast of New York Players are at the local theater performing "Trail of the Lonesome Pine." This was also made into a Laurel and Hardy sound movie, available yet today. A local pastor, Rev. Rutledge, is heading up a new force against alcohol and has been elected the chairman of the Anti-Saloon League.

The reader will remember the price of some of the copper stocks earlier in this book. The Quincy stocks are now selling for $1.50 a share, and the Calumet and Hecla for $10.00. Quite a large drop! A new deer law is also in effect. A hunter can kill two deer, but one must be a buck. Although the winter started off very slow, it is now April 19, and there is so much snow that the road to Negaunee has not yet been plowed for auto use. The Ishpeming Theater is not doing well financially, owes money to the Miner's Bank, and is looking for a buyer. Mr. Newett suggests that the city purchase it. Instead, in May, the Bank itself bought it. People are hoping it will remain an "Opera House." In July, Mr. Butler bought the building, and soon installed two electric motion picture machines so that there would be no pauses between reels. In October he brought Howes Travel Festival Show of Motion Pictures to his new theater.

In June, the LS&I began passenger service twice a week to North Lake. 48 graduated from the Ishpeming High School. There was another tragic death when Mrs. Robert Morris drank carbolic acid following the death of her two children. . For the children and young of heart, the Sun Bros. large Tent Show is coming on July 15, with Animals, aerial artists, and a good band.

A gigantic July 4th celebration is planned for town. The banks are closing for three days. The Iron Ore will be printed three days ahead of the usual Saturday, so the men can be off. It was to be a "Homecoming Event" as well. One man made a balloon ascension and then jumped out and parachuted down. Over 700 people returned to visit.

In Negaunee, the road to Marquette has been moved to the Maas Mine from the Negaunee Mine and Main Street by the CCI, and the completely abandoned property will be caved-in. Mr. Newett, in his paper, also notes that Glendale, Montana, once a large mining town, now is in ruins. The Copper Country area of the U. P. is also hurting with a strike. 1000 men left the area. Things are very good in Ishpeming, and a new "Hook and Ladder Truck" arrived for the Fire Department. There is no mention of a motor, and it no doubt was still pulled by horses.

In mining, "Portable electric mine lamps are being studied for use." Large Electric Shovels are now also being manufactured, but steam shovels are still in use here. An interesting figure is the total number of iron ore miners in the Upper Peninsula of Michigan: 15,939. For Marquette County, there are 3,895 men working. There were 233 serious injuries, and 16 deaths, with most being underground in the past year. 36 mines are operating in the county. Mines here are so busy that there is a worry that there will not be wood available to purchase for stoves this winter. There is plenty of timber, but all are too busy to do cutting or selling.

In sports, the Ishpeming Football team was excellent for a while in 1913. They beat Negaunee 64-0, and Marquette 31-0, but then plaed Sault Ste. Marie and lost, 98 to nothing. In November, they also got beat by Menominee, 55-0.

As cold weather set in, an ad in November appeared in the paper for "Wintering in Florida." For those staying in town, the Braastad store is offering "S & H Green Stamps" for use toward gifts. You get one stamp for ever dime spent in his store. He is also going to have a 5-piece orchestra playing from time to time for Christmas shoppers, and Santa will appear. For the shoppers in 1913, one can buy Marigold oleomargarine in quarter-pound sticks.

This is not Ishpeming news as such, but a group of students at the Houghton School of Mines are dropping balls down a deep Quincy Mine shaft and finding that the rotation of the earth prevents them from ever reaching the bottom.

For the children, Mr. Mather, in his yearly tradition, gave prizes for children who had the best gardens during the summer. Adults got prizes for the best kept premises on CCI property.

The year ended on a sad note for the entire U.P., when 70 people, mostly children, died at Red Jacket (now Calumet) when someone at a gathering on a second floor of a building shouted "Fire."

1914

January gives us some statistics for 1913. There were 322 births, and 131 deaths. The Fire Department responded to 16 alarms, and requested more hydrants. Twenty-two men died in county mines here. The Ishpeming Advancement Association suggests a city playground on the north half of the old Main Street area cemetery. They also are suggesting a new Hotel and an improved Cliff's Drive, and also that a milk inspector be hired. It is announced that the present Post Office will be built at Bank and Second Streets. The entrance is said to face Bank Street, however. The paper notes that Mr. Braastad owns all the land in the area and will move the roller rink building currently where the Post Office will be, a bit south on the other side of the street.

A new law requires companies to pay employees twice a month, so local stores will now stay open two nights a week on pay-day weeks. The February Skee Tournament reports that Sigrid Hansen, a professional rank jumper won with 289 points. Henry Hall, of Ishpeming, had the longest jump, going 137 feet. The State of Michigan announces that all fishermen this year will be required for the first time, to get a license, and not just non-residents. But, Stop the Press! In May, the paper notes that local fishermen will not need a fishing license.

Mr. Joseph Sellwood, the Ishpeming businessman died and his will was published. He left $674,500 to his family. The "will" went to court where it was decided that the wife deserved a greater share of the money. On a separate note, some of our readers are acquainted with the former 900 foot walking-suspension bridge on the east end of Deer Lake at the Dam area. It was built in 1914.

Gately-Wiggens built the store on Main Street at Pearl that still stands, next to Mr. Butler's Theater. The Theater was built in 1914 as well, and was made to seat 750 and had a stage.. It will also have a fountain in the lobby. Gately's will be two stories, with windows at the top floor as well, and will replace two wooden "shacks" which will be torn down. One of the shacks was the "Old Loth" building that was built in 1869 and was the first building in the "swamp." One store left town. It was Grinnel's Music Store. They will continue to operate in Marquette.

In April, Mr. Newett expressed his anger in his paper when the Lake Angeline Mine discharged several old men with no pension plan and hired younger men. He told how these men spent their lives working for this mine and stated that it was a "cold-blooded proceeding."

The students at the Houghton School of Mines made the news again in Ishpeming, by coming to town and performing a "Comic Opera" at the Ishpeming Theater. They continue to be famous for similar productions from time to time, but more so because it was an all men school.

People can now buy Government Bonds by purchasing stamps to fill books at the town post office. These continued at least through World War II, and were popular with school children.

This summer, the improved roads are being oiled to hold down the dust. The Advancement Association is seeking to get ornamental lights on Division Street. A five pound, two ounce trout was taken from Teal Lake. On Memorial Day, all bells rang for five minutes and flags flew at half-mast until noon. Mr. Trebilcock's concrete work is doing so well that he has 72 men on the payroll.

The biggest news of the summer, in fact, of the year, was the announcement that the Lake Angeline Mine would close on December 1. It is currently mining under Terrace Hill, to the south. A great many mines are also laying off men in groups of about 30 up to 160 men. CCI cut wages by ten percent.

The second biggest news was that Mr. Fred Braastad is going to sell his big building on Cleveland Avenue, and his business, and is going to retire. He says he will not be leaving town. In fact, in October he purchased the Baptist Church at Third and High to make into two floors and two apartments. The building is 32 x 60 with a good rock foundation. Other stores in the summer of 1914 are closing on Wednesday afternoons, but will be open on Wednesday nights.

A big group in Ishpeming, the Sons of St. George held a large gathering in town during July, with contests, and free vaudeville entertainment. Even more excitement was generated at the fair-grounds with aeroplane, auto, and motor cycle races. Many are excited about seeing the aeroplane. Motorcycles are becoming popular and a club has now been formed. Entertainment at the local Lyric movie theater is showing the #6 in the series "Perils of Pauline."

1914, of course, also had big world headlines, and Mr. Newett's Iron Ore paper announced that war had been declared by the Kaiser of Germany. Even the New York Stock Exchange closed.

The Ishpeming Advancement group brought the Chautauqua group to the Union Fair grounds in August, but the meetings were not well attended by the public. The tents were then brought to town but too much was going on. The group continued to come for several summers.

The new Miner's National Bank is being completed with the arrival of the new Vault door, weighing 15.5 tons. The Simon's Block at Main and Division is remodeling and eight upstairs rooms will now have electricity. A new store in the Donohoe Block at Division and Pine will be the Ishpeming Furniture and Hardware.

It is now Christmas time and Carpenter Cook donated 200 pounds of candy for use by Santa at the Ishpeming Municipal Tree. The City Band and the Choral Society will provide music.

As the year of 1914 ends, the Miner's National Bank reminds people to start their new "Christmas Clubs", and it is noted by Mr. Newett that the amount of ore shipped from the Marquette Range this past year was less than 1913.

1915

January tells us that the Trebilcock Brothers will be cutting 8,000 cords of ice this year over a period of six weeks. Mud Lake will provide refrigeration ice. At the movies, it will now cost a nickel for admission. Pine Street from the top of Strawberry Hill has been made into a bobsled run, with the help of the fire department.. (Pine Street ran across the tracks at this time to Front Street, next to the Carpenter Cook Building, now gone). Mr. Gavato's Candy Kitchen store was closed by creditors, but Peter Apostle of Marquette bought the Candy Kitchen stock for $600. He owns the building.

Miners' safety lamps are now in greater use and are being manufactured in the U.S. rather than being imported from Germany. In February, both Ishpeming and Negaunee decide to hire some of the unemployed, so that men might work, rather than have to accept charity. One boy recently was riding in front of a railroad engine to Escanaba to find work when he nearly froze, fell off, and died. Ishpeming will pass a sewer bond and hire men to install sewers.

The Paris Fashion Store of Marquette is going to open a new store in the Anderson Building. Ishpeming is thinking of changing the clocks for the coming summer, the electric street car company says it will create problems as it runs to two cities. The famous Sunquist Orange Company ran an ad in the paper and listed eight local Groceries and their addresses for the readers. At Braastads Amusement Hall, the "World's Fastest Walker" will be a coming attraction and will walk one mile before a person of "the little wheels" can skate for two miles.

There is little about the war, and nothing seems to be affected in Ishpeming by it. In the May 1, 1915, issue of the Iron Ore there is a note about German Submarine Warfare. The May 15 issue notes the sinking of the Lusitania, not only carrying passengers, but "secret" war material from the U.S. A new Curtis war-plane will be built that holds three people and flies high. Immigration was down to only 48,000, and many, including local Italians have returned home to help fight in the war. The mines are also having a hard time to fine mules for underground hauling. Most have gone for use in the war, and only 12 were found in all of Chicago.

Several men retired from CCI mines and began to receive their "pensions." Another 34 CCI miners received their high school diplomas!

Stores this summer will close Thursday afternoons and be open on Thursday nights. The Miners Bank will be open on Wednesday nights.

A new marble industry is underway near the former Ropes Gold Mine. Cutting of blocks began in May, and equipment is soon to arrive. When the first blocks were cut, they were hauled to the railroad on wagons and sent out to be polished. The public waited anxiously for the results. They were acceptable. In November they hauled a ten-ton block of rough marble to Marquette. The new name of the company is the Verde Marble Company.

Another new industry for the U.S. will be the farm tractor. Henry Ford announced he is working on such a machine to pull a plow. Mr. Elson, of Ishpeming, has built his new pop bottling plant at the Barnum Location. It is "one of the U. P.'s best." Also, the first five and dime store came to town in the Voelker building at Cleveland and Main. The Woolworth store stayed in town into the 1960's or 70's, and many of us shopped and worked there, including my wife. Mr. Penglase is building a two story building on the north side of the Butler Theater. In the early 50's it was the National Food Store, and then became an addition for the J. J. Newberry five and dime.

A long 20-year pastorate by Rev. Allen of the Ishpeming Presbyterian church came to an end in July when he and his wife returned to their home in Kentucky. Mine Statistics showed only nine deaths on the Marquette Range, and out of 115 existing mines, only 32 were operating in 1914.

We know that the Pittsburg and Lake Angeline has closed. In August of 1915, they announce that they will sell all of their property. In a bidding process by only two companies, being secret bidders, the Cleveland Cliffs Iron Co, won the bidding and bought the mine for only $27,000. It included 60 dwellings and all of the mine buildings.. Most of the machinery had been removed, and many of the homes had been sold, with Paul Zulkey purchasing the large former Mine Captains' Home on Angeline Street. Within a few months, the CCI had found a rich amount of iron ore on the east end of the hill to the south, in an area that became called, "Sleepy Hollow." The ore was so close to surface that it was mined by a Trebilcock concern, rather than by miners. The CCI moved, or tore down, 30 homes from the east end of the mine where the new ore was. That just about ended Angeline Street as a street of homes..

For some time, Ishpeming had been talking about installing an incinerator in which to burn items. In August a trip was made to see the one in Iron Mountain, and it was agreed to build one, but a larger one. In November, water and sewer were brought to the site, located in south Barnum Location at the end of Johnson Street, and construction began. The new "Double Incinerator" was open for public viewing before Christmas. It will burn all the garbage in a 27 x 40 foot brick building. A total of 12 tons a day can be handled. A test of a large dead horse was put in and it burned up in one hour and there was no smell.

The State of Michigan began paying a bounty on rats in 1915, and in August, many boys brought in 173 of them and received a nickel for each. In September, the county fair came, and Mr. Newett told his readers to attend, but not expect much. "It is not a Panama Exposition."

Another tragic death was averted when Mr. John Tremethic was saved from hanging. He told of how his garden had frozen out with the two late frosts this year, and he didn't know how he was going to feed his family.

Sidewalks and curbs were put in on North and High between Oak and Pine. But people are not so much walking now, as driving, and the weekly paper social column is of people traveling far and near by rail and auto.

A man from Chicago appeared before the Advancement Committee regarding bringing a Sewing company to the area. This was, of course, the beginning of the large Gossard factory at the Braastad building, and also in Negaunee, and Gwinn.

An Ishpeming native, Dick Harding, is building the new Dixie Highway from the South U.S. to the Detroit Area. Roads in the U. P. are still not too good, and a 175 mile trip from town to Bessemer proved to be a "nightmare." Another nightmare was caused by three boys who broke into the Ishpeming Golf House and did great destruction. All received a lecture from the judge. The Meen Brother's Creamery which became Northern Dairy is also getting ready to open at about this time. Details are in the Cow chapter.

Mr. Newett was interested in oddities, and here is one from Huxley, Nevada where a diamond drill found a bed of petrified clams at 1700 feet and Redwood timbers at 1900 feet down. It might be a good project of someone to investigate.

By the end of the year, the Butler Picture House opened, showing a Mary Pickford film of five reels and 1.5 hours long. An orchestra will play. The projection room is protected from those attending with a steel and concrete fire-proof area.

Chapter 23:
The Wildlife and Not So Wildlife

In this section we shall cover Horses, Dogs, Wolves, Deer, Fish, Lynx, Bears, Geese, Fisher, Partridge, and Flies, and in that order.

HORSES

The first news about horses was that they were used in racing at the Ishpeming Driving Park which seemed to be located in the north Third Street area. A purse of $100.00 was given to the winner. Ten years later, the fine, large Union Park between Ishpeming and Negaunee was completed and races were there. They were so popular that horse owners in Oshkosh, Wisconsin, were hoping to eventually attend. In a race in 1892 offered ten purses, with a total of $1,375 to be awarded.

It was in 1892 that a headline read that there were two runaways. Today one thinks of some teen-agers, but the story was about horses. And from then on, there were many of them. Here is part of the November 16, 1892, report: "A team belonging to Gil Hodgkins made a lively spurt from Read's Lumber Yard on Tuesday. They went without a driver and kept straight ahead till reaching Pine Street where a part of the sled was left. The team continued to Bank Street and back to Pearl, where they noticed the door of Losselyong's was open and started in. They went foul of a telegraph pole and stopped.

In 1902 a runway team of a grocer ran away without the driver, and coming down Pine Street into town met a horse team pulling a wagon with a lighting pole strapped on. One of the runaways ran directly onto the pole and was

impaled on it. The horse had to be killed with a blow to the head with an ax. "The horse was a fine one and a severe loss to the owner," said Mr. Newett, and added, "The driver, who arrived quickly after the accident, was all broke up, crying like a child, when he saw what had resulted."

Horses were brought to town to sell, as were the cows. The Pioneer Livery in Marquette hosted a load of Logging Horses, weighing 1600 to 1900 pounds each. These, of course, were primarily for heavy industry and farm work.

Another accident in 1918 resulted when a wagon tongue became disconnected and ran faster than the horses, striking them. Being startled, they immediately began to run frantically. The driver pulled on the reins, but one broke, and the other one, pulling strongly told the horse team to turn, which they dutifully followed, right into a large store window of the former Franklin Garage. The men were badly cut with some broken bones.

In the case of some runaways, people tried to grab the reins of the team and stop them. A Mr. Dobbs was able to do this in 1903, when all others were running away from the wild team, and even a small boy was knocked down but not injured.

On two occasions, Mr. Newett was concerned about the health of horses not being cared for. In 1889 he wrote: "There is someone driving a white horse in this city that ought to be arrested for cruelty to animals. The beast has a hind leg that is three times the size of an ordinary one, and this he is forced to drag painfully after him while he pulls heavy loads. The authorities should prevent the owner from torturing the poor animal." The other story is found in the June 13, 1914, issue of the Iron Ore. There is a milk dealer in this city by the name of George

Stokoe, who drives a horse that is so lame that the poor animal is barely able to hobble along, and the driver is continually laying a long black whip on the beast's hide to get a little more speed out of him. It is a pure case of cruelty to an animal and the owner deserves to be arrested and shown no clemency."

Of course, Mr. Newett might have also put himself in the shoes of both of these men who were trying to make a go in life.

DOGS

If Mr. Newett thought that cows ran the town, he must have thought that dogs ran a close second. In 1881 he noted about the danger of dog biting to pedestrians, and states, "we desire to say that it would be a charitable act to kill about 300 of the poor brutes, who are half-starved, half dead with work, and objects of relentless, brutish abuse." By 1885, Newett's editorial stated that there are "about 500 dogs that need killing." He tells of how Dr. McKenzie had four dogs attack his horse team, taking hold of the legs of the horses..

In 1887, someone took it upon themselves to poison 30 dogs. We all know how dogs would attack those of us riding bicycles. So it was then, and Mr. Newett suggested an attachment of bikes to hold a shot-gun.

Finally in 1903, dog tags began to be required, and the pound-master went from house to house to check each animal. All found not licensed will be shot said the Ishpeming officers. By 1905, 179 dog tags had been issued. Tags were only one dollar.

In 1905, a Mr. Ed Moilin was brought into court for shooting the dog of Mrs. Johnson of West Ishpeming. Mr. Newett wrote it all up, stating that Ed "should have been liberally rewarded

for his act instead of being fined" for killing the "vicious dog." The pound master tried with a net to begin picking up dogs, but the net did not work. In one week, instead, he shot twenty of them. Owners are now keeping them locked up at home.

The good side of dogs is that they were a boy's best friend if taken care of, and Mr. Newett fully agreed with dogs of this nature. He faithfully, year after year, publicized the winter "Dog Derbies". They seem to have begun in January, and often were held for two weeks in a row. They started in 1914 began at Braastad's store and ended at Main Street, going down Cleveland. All winners got nice prizes, and it brought people to the business district. In 1915, Audubon Jenkins was the third place winner. Many of you may have known him for his fine Boy Scout work. The races were of many types, and some had 25 dogs in them. It was humorous to watch the people trying to keep the dogs at bay until the signal to go.

One year, Mr. Newett noted that extra dog racing entertainment was provided by a local judge when he fell down while going across the racetrack which was on steep Strawberry Hill of Main Street that year. The race date eventually got moved to the morning of the ski tournament, held on Washington's Birthday, and stayed there for many years.

WOLVES

When the Lake Superior Mine opened in 1857, Captain G. D. Johnston took charge and stayed in charge until 1875. He eventually ended up in Cripple Creek, Colorado, where he died. He once told a story of how he got up late at night in the boarding house he had built at the mine. From the second floor he looked out and "plainly saw and heard the wolves talking over the loose lumber below." This is from the obituary of the July 28, 1891, Iron Ore.

In 1904, Marquette County began to pay a bounty on wolves. Bounties were seventeen dollars for adults down to seven dollars for whelps under 3 months old. This not only allowed farmers to protect their livestock, but brought many hunters from out of the area to earn some money. A story printed in the Iron Ore in February of 1907 told about some "green horns" from Indiana who came with their own designed device from which to hunt. It was a sled with a sheet iron cover, punctured with holes to serve as ports. They would push and pull this sled into wolf country and have the wolves smell them and prepare for attack, at which time they would get inside their contraption and begin shooting. For two weeks they pushed and pulled their fort over rough roads in the woods, the snows being deep, and hills abundant. No wolves were seen nor heard, noted Mr. Newett, as it was winter, and the animals were all inside, and the wolves not near any farms. They soon went back to Indiana, and left their straw bedding, kerosene, and sheet iron home behind.

Local men are having a difficult time trying to kill the wolves as well. They avoid traps, and are difficult to poison. However, they have learned a lesson from a man in Baraga. He has a live female wolf tied up outside his cabin door, and she invites her friends from some distance with her music. His results have been quite good.

Four Ishpeming fellows, Henry Beigler, Victor Trays, Leo and George Voelker, Jr., came across a family of wolves in the woods. The two adults did not escape death from the gun fire, but left behind, seven young ones. The men brought them all home, where they will raise them for the larger bounty of $117. Mr. Newett heard

that the State of Michigan might begin to offer bounties on wolves of $100 each, and thought the result might be that people would begin to raise them for a regular income. The State did give bounties soon after that, and by 1913, $27 was given for each wolf killed. Michigan paid out $6,000 in bounties in 1912. Even the Federal Government wanted to get into the picture, and in 1910 this headline appeared in the paper: "Uncle Sam Preparing to Wage a War of Extermination Against the Pests." At least one Federal person was sent to the U. P. to study the situation of extermination.

From 1913 to 1920, only one other wolf story appeared in the paper. It was a man who hit two on the road which went through Herman from Michigamme to L'Anse. Of course, we went back to pick them up and it was a profitable trip. The wolves about disappeared as the governments seemed to desire, only to return in the twenty-first century as old farmlands are re-bought, re-developed, and renewed by people seeking some space in which to live once again.

THE DEER

There are so many deer stories told in Mr. Newett's paper that they deserve a book of their own. We can't begin to tell them here. In the year-by-year sections we have tried to include the changes in laws, and statistics from time to time about deer and the deer season. We do tell you that illegal deer hunting was very rampant. People were found with dozens of deer pelts from out of season. In 1914 it became illegal to have dogs loose in the woods during hunting season. Also in 1914, the April 4 edition, the paper told the arrest of James Twedale, who was found with 15 "fresh deer heads in his possession." In these same years, the number of deer killed during deer season was quite low compared to previous years.

The fines for killing deer were quite high in comparison with daily wages being paid. Two local men were arrested back in 1887 after bragging about killing a doe in June, and fined $50.00 each. Mine pay at that time was generally less than two or three dollars a day. Yet it didn't seem to be any deterrent through the years..

In the summer of 1905 we find this note: "The deer license for residents has been increased from 75 cents to $1.50, thus giving the game warden's department $15,000 from that source of revenue, instead of $5,000. The number of deer which any one person can take is reduced from three to two. Non-residents may ship one deer out of the state. Shooting deer while they are in the water is prohibited."

FISH

In the early days about 1880, fish were poorly regulated and there seemed to be no limit what-so-ever, including trout. Even worse, it seems that fish can be sold legally on a commercial basis.

July 23, 1881: "Large catches of speckled trout are being made by some of our citizens. Seventy-two pounds were taken from a little stream, about four and a half miles from this city, in two hours, by three fishermen Saturday last. The stream was not, up to that time, supposed to contain fish."

July 30, 1881: "A man with forty pounds of speckled trout was in the city last Tuesday and sold them for the neat sum of ten dollars. And there are those who pretend to say that the streams are all fished dry."

Some people got their fish an easy way, by setting off dynamite. This was illegal, and Mr.

Newett sought to find the guilty parties. The year was 1892. Some trout, taken in a legal way were quite large. Three were taken in Whale Lake (now unknown?) that totaled almost nine pounds and the largest measured 19.5 inches.

As Lake Angeline was being drained for mining in 1892, one fish weighing six pounds, and another weighing 4 pounds were caught in the flume. We do not know what kind of fish they were, however. We do know that trout were being planted in streams near town by 1894 with this note on April 28: "The young trout for planting in the streams of this vicinity arrived Thursday." The hatchery at this time was at Sault Ste. Marie. By 1900, the plantings are more detailed. 57,000 trout were planted on April 21, 1900. "The Ishpeming Sportsmen's Association deserves much credit for the trouble and expense they have been to in stocking the streams of this section......In three years the trout will attain a length of from twelve to fifteen inches." It was also noted that in July some bass would be planted. In 1906, the Iron Ore noted that 80,000 brook trout had been planted locally. In 1907 there was a new fishing law. No trout could be caught after August 15.

One humorous item happened in April of 1910, when Game Warden Hogan noted that a railroad car with a consignment of 1,200 pounds of fish was enroute from Baraga to Chicago. Believing this to be all illegal shipment, he procured all the necessary paperwork for a stoppage of the train in Green Bay, at which time, the particular railroad car was returned by another train to Iron Mountain where Mr. Hogan met it, and opened it up. Rather than becoming the famous man he hoped for, he discovered he had made an error. It was not trout, or pike he found inside, but suckers, which was a legal shipment. He did four things. He re-iced the fish, repacked them, sent them on their way after paying the shipping charges from Green Bay to Iron Mountain, and then tried to keep the entire story a secret.

In 1895, this article appeared on how to get worms with which to fish. Many have tried it since, and it works: "Drive the stick four or five inches into the ground with a stone, and then begin to twist it with a rotary motion. Every few minutes hit the top a rap and drive it further down into the ground, and keep on twisting. In five minutes the worms will begin crawling out of their holes, and all you have to do is to pick them up and put them in your can."

Lynx, Bears, Geese, Fisher, Partridge, and Rats

We only have a sentence or two on each of these, but they are worth mentioning in this history book.

In 1887 a hunter captured a lynx alive and put him on exhibition at the "Castle Garden" in Ishpeming. The paper noted that it is greatly respected by all who have seen it.

In all the years of the Iron Ore that I have read, I remember only this one article about a bear. Either they were rare, or never bothered the public. On October 13, 1906, however, a story was reported by Arnold Grip who was hunting birds up by the Dead River, when two bears spotted him and charged with large growls. "Arnold, who had only a light 16-gauge shot gun, concluded camp was the place for him, and immediately started. He says he thinks if some one could have held a stop watch on him that the quarter-mile record would have been reduced by several seconds. He looked back several times and the bears were close behind,

they continuing after him until close to camp." That night he did not think the camp needed neither wood from the woodshed nor water from the well. He also noted the bears were very large.

In the pumping out of Lake Angeline, a Howell pump was used, and one day at the place where the water was discharged into the flume, a large goose came out. Authorities decided that the goose must have been sucked in and gone through the pump. Thus they retried the experiment. "It required several seconds for the suction to gain possession of him, but it finally did and he disappeared below the surface and entered the pipe. After his disappearance it was over a minute before he was ejected from the big 22-inch discharge. During this time he was being carried around within the big centrifugal pump the buckets of which probably propelled him at a far more rapid speed than he had ever before attained, but he finally emerged from his temporary confinement, and was shot into the launder.....He was out of breath and had lost the use of his muscles, but in a few minutes he revived, arose and waddled back to the rest of his flock and is now enjoying his former good health."

This short note on April 28, 1900, about a fisher: "Game warden Case Downing visited the Dead River section Wednesday. He found a trapper with a fine fisher, but the trapper was within the open season, the closed beginning the first of May."

On several occasions there are new laws for partridge hunting. Several times it was to say there would be no hunting season for them that particular year. This was true in 1919. "Under the present state law the Game Commissioner can declare a closed season on fish or game in any section where the supervisors vote to keep the season closed, and Commissioner Baird voiced the sentiment of most of the sportsmen when he decided to ask that there be no hunting of partridge in 1919."

In 1914 the state began to pay bounties on rats. . Here is a story of how Garnet Cundy received $1.30 from City Recorder R. H. Olds: "He claims that he has a cat that can beat all of the other cats in the city catching rats, and he hopes to earn considerable money through her efforts. The rats are taken by Janitor William Whate to Needham Bros. laundry, where they are burned."

FLIES. YES, FLIES

We have saved the best until last, the small fly. A contest for children was thought up by Mr. Braastad at his store and published in the Iron Ore on April 27, 1912: "F. Braastad and company are going to encourage fly-swatting in this city and they have announced that they will give $100.00 in prizes to the four children of Ishpeming who kill the greatest number of flys between now and the first of October. The first prize will be $50, the second will be $25, the third $15, and the fourth $10. Every Monday morning the contestants must bring their kill to the store, where the flys will be counted." The article noted that flys can be killed in any manner. (Note original spelling of flies.)

Well, how did the contest go? Here is the October report: "The contest created a great deal of interest among the children of the city and a large number participated in the fly campaign. Several million flies were murdered and Mr. Braastad stated that he was pleased with the results." Details of the article showed that Marie Russell of 600 S. Pine Street was the winner, with 29 ounces of the disease spreaders. Second Prize went to Thomas Bennett, Jr. at 316 West Ridge Street who had over 22 ounces. John Snow at 401 N. Second Street was third,

and Esther Mullgren of 40 North Bluff Street won the $10.00.

Mr. Newett added that "Mr. Braastad deserves a great deal of credit for conducting such a contest and it is certain that a lot of good will result from the good work inaugurated by him."

HERE IS A PHOTO OF THE CHIDREN'S DOG RACES ON THE MORNING OF THE SKI TOURNAMENT, ON FEBRUARY 22, 1907. THEY ARE COMING DOWN STRAWBERRY HILL. THE ISHPEMING CARNEGIE LIBRARY IS ABOUT HALF-WAY UP ON THE LEFT AND COMING DOWN IS THEN THE URBAN HOUSE HOTEL, AND THE LARGE TILLSON DRUG STORE. THE PHOTO COMES TO US AS PRINTED IN COLLIER'S MAGAZINE. MR. WILL BRADLEY WAS THE ART EDITOR AND NO DOUBT WAS HELPING OUT HIS OLD "HOME TOWN."

HERE IS THE IMPORTANT INVENTION OF THE WHEEL WITH THE DIAL, SO THAT THE HOISTING ENGINEER CAN TELL WHERE THE CAGE OR SKIP IS IN THE SHAFT. THE LARGE DRUMS ARE THE HOISTS WITH CABLE ON THEM.

FROM THE 1913 IRON MIING AND AGRICULTURE U.P. OF MICHIGAN SOUVENIR EDITION OF THE MINING JOURNAL.

Chapter 24:
The Special News Items
From 1916 to 1920

1916

We are in the final five years of our <u>Early History of an Old Mining Town</u>. Things will be still moving ahead with great "gusto."

The first 1916 issue of the <u>Iron Ore</u> on January 1 tells us that the CCI Company will be getting electricity from the Dead River north of Negaunee. The CCI and other mines will also be using a new "mucking machine" which scoops up ore in a drift or stope after a blast and throws it over itself into a car behind. Such cars were used through the last underground mines of the 1970's.

Entertainment will be at its finest when Actor Forbes-Robertson of England will be in Ishpeming for his final United States Performance this year. The Butler Theater plans to show "Birth of a Nation." When it came, however, it was shown at the large Ishpeming Theater. In June a play was advertised with a photo of 15 pretty girls, which no doubt brought customers. Discussions around town included what pictures the new calendars have on them, to the half-page advertisement that the "Upper Peninsula of Michigan Should Be a Separate State."

In February, the miners again were given a raise in pay, plus it was expected that the CCI stock dividend would be large. The CCI is also operating this year, 18 ore boats, four more having been added. The Cleveland Cliffs Iron Company is also naming its new mine between Junction and Lake Angeline, the Holmes (The middle name of the CCI vice-president). A 11 x

15 foot shaft is now underway. Ore will be at a shallow depth noted the newspaper. The CCI "Happy Hollow" mine on the far east end of the Lake Angeline mine is producing 69% deep "blue" soft iron ore. It is being taken out with a steam shovel, right from where it lay, and will be used to enrich other ore. It is on the hill south of the East End Mine. The remains of foundations of the small homes remain near-by, and that were moved to remove this rich surface ore. Work also continues at the Iron Mountain Lake (now Lake Ogden) in deciding where to put the shaft. A new road has been put into the area from Hill Street. 50 men are now working and buildings are going up.

A large article is printed regarding the American Mine in Boston Location. On February 19, 1916, the paper reported that a drift 140 feet under a swamp, west of the shaft was allowed to drain the swamp. Water came flowing in, but carried sand and mud which plugged the drift to a large extent.

The 1916 ski tournament simply read "No records broken, but no bones either." Note was also made that the Athen's Mine in Negaunee will bottom at 2600 feet. The Butler Theater is having attendance problems. It will now be open only on Wednesdays and Saturdays, afternoon and evening, and on days when the Ishpeming Theater is not showing films (Both are owned by Mr. Butler). The city, to end weight problems of deliveries, has installed a scale behind the city hall.

Mr. Mather came to town and made some promotions. The famous Charles Stakel had to leave Ishpeming and go to Republic. He had been in charge of the Negaunee Mine shaft concreting work. Note is also made that miners currently working in shafts are making more than $5.00 for an eight hour a day.

The city, now incinerating its garbage, has asked residents to keep garbage as dry as possible, and to not put ashes in the garbage. The newest crime is that a "fire-bug" is starting fires, with three in one night. After ten fires, a $20.00 reward was offered. After one additional fire, in June the culprit was caught by the state fire marshal and he was Arthur "Jumbo" Peterson of Maurice Street. He always lit them on the way home from the bar. Mr. Newett noted that he always burned buildings that should have been torn down anyway.

Gately-Wiggens purchased the old DSS&A Railway station on Bluff Street as a warehouse. The 1915 library report showed that 93,380 books were withdrawn. J. T. Nichols committed suicide and left a note for his wife about his ill health. A young girl and an assistant doctor announced that they were married two months ago and began to live together.

By May, iron ore shipping was going full speed from the winter stock-piles, and a record 43,000 tons was shipped from the LS&I dock in one week. People are buying auto tires, and the Goodrich Tire company ran a full page ad for its tires for both cars and bicycles. On June 15, schools closed for the summer. It was also proposed that the "Dixie Highway" run from Miami to the Keweenaw Peninsula of Michigan. (U. S.-41 did this, but did not go the Detroit route.)

There is continuous weekly news of the Verde Marble Company. New machines arrive north of Ishpeming. In July they shipped 5 large 5,000 pound blocks to Omaha, Nebraska. Note is made that a railroad is needed to the quarry.

By June, the Holmes shaft is already down 475 feet and the hoist will be installed with ten foot drums for cable. The large "Sullivan" hoist from the Queen Mine in Negaunee has been moved to the Section 16 mine in Ishpeming. Safety in the mines continues to improve and the CCI announced that with 3000 men working in Michigan, Minnesota, and Canada, there has not been a death since last October. That record was broken when Alex Rajala died at the CCI Lake Mine on the fifth level in September, 1916. Three or four more men died in December when their shaft bucket, hanging under the skip, let go and went to the bottom.

The County Fair was to have an aviator as an attraction this year, using his plane to race automobiles, but Charles Niles was killed at Oshkosh in July. Attendance may be quite good anyway and young boys are busy selling tickets. The one who sells the most will be given his own pony. Hardly any carnivals or circuses came this year as the railroads were all too busy to handle such traffic. Somehow, the Howes London Show came with two fine performances and the usual morning parade down-town. A Carnival came as well on two separate 35-railroad car sections. It was Parker's Greatest Shows with three riding devices and great side-shows. It covered several downtown Streets. They had a large night Mardi Gras light parade.

Not much about the war, except that the Oliver Mining Company will give all soldiers their old jobs back upon return. Young boys are joining the National Guard noted the paper. In November there is the first note of an Ishpeming death in WWI. Mr. Edward Lind, was fighting after signing up with Canadian Forces and was on the front in France.

Downtown, the Oddfellows Ahmeek Lodge will remodel at Pearl and Main, where it still is. The Chautauqua will be returning again, and have a magician to draw people. The Butler Theater will close to encourage attendance as well. In actuality, it never reopened for some weeks and it was announced by Mr. Newett on September

9th, that after having been closed this summer, it will now begin to show films on Saturdays. By November non-film entertainment is also to be presented at the Butler.

A Negaunee cave-in made the Ishpeming news in September when a hole 75 feet wide by 150 feet long occurred. It was noted that the area was known to be dangerous and had been fenced off. Other land was building up, and such it was in West Ishpeming, where 90 lots were designed on new streets and sold for $88 to $178 each. The housing lots, being so short in the area, were all sold by 3:00 of the first day. Sellers said they could have sold 50 more.

It was noted in October of 1916, that Mr. Maitland has closed the Volunteer Mine in the Cascade Range of Palmer as "All ore is gone." Probably one of Mr. Newett's most humorous entries, but he didn't know it. It became part of the enormous Empire Mine, currently still operating. Mine statistics showed 13 deaths for the previous year, with 3,332 miners and 1,578 people working at mines on the surface.

The wet-or-dry vote for prohibition is up for a national vote in a few weeks. Liquor dealers and others are busy in the campaign. Mr. Newett says "If State is dry, it will be worth it."

Houses sold so well at West Ishpeming that another group called the Cloverdale Tracts (46 of them) are for sale for $1.00 a week payments, with free auto rides to the area, which is located close to Deer Lake and Teal Lake Roads on east side of the road and south of the cemetery. One gets there by going north on Third Street to Teal Lake Road. (The author has no idea where these lots were.)

After stripping the dirt land of the far eastern area of the Lake Angeline Mine, the rich, soft, iron ore is now being mined simply with a steam shovel. Quite a few homes had to be moved from Angeline Street on the north side of Terrace Hill. Some were sold and moved and those left were brought to North Lake by the CCI. Former residents told of how they could see this beautiful blue ore in their basements.

At Christmastime, the Miner's Bank sent out $26,000 in Christmas Club money, and the Iron Ore is filled with very nice Christmas ads. Someone is selling 4-8 week-old pigs for $3.00 to $5.00 each. The Salvation Army showed a movie matinee where a child can attend a movie by bringing two potatoes to the theater. The Carnegie library is ordering two copies of several popular magazines, so one can be lent out.

The saddest item is that Prohibition did not pass this year, and so a long list of people paid $500 each for liquor licenses.

1917

The first issue of the 1917 Iron Ore informs us that the CCI will be building a club house for its workers in North Lake, near the school. The next issue of the paper has a nice article about Saffron, and notes that the Upper Peninsula buys the most of it in the USA. Also noted was the death of a man many had come to see at his Ishpeming Shows, Buffalo "Wild Bill" Cody.

There has been a ski tournament every year, but now it will be enlarged to a several-day event. No mines will work for the two day Carnival. The Iron Ore had a nice ad for the event, and a queen was chosen. After the carnival and tournament, the professional skiers met and organized the National Ski Association and decided against giving "cash prizes" in the future. In March, Henry Hall of Ishpeming jumped 203 feet at Steamboat Springs, Colorado, for a new world's ski-jumping record.

In Mining, the Section 16 mine was connected with a drift at the 1000 foot level to the new Holmes mine. The opening would act as a fresh air passage, and a safety escape. At the Cliffs Shafts, the Lake Shore Works in Marquette has built a small Halby's Steam shovel, and it will be used underground in some of the large stopes. At the Verde Marble Quarry, three large blocks of marble, one weighing nine tons was carried by Trebilcock Bros. to the C&NW for shipping. Progress is being made on a railroad into the Quarry.

A great many companies are cutting ice blocks, including the railways, for their box cars, which are otherwise not refrigerated. So much freight is coming to town by train, that there are serious traffic jams at intersections. Mr. Braastad is selling generators by Delco, for use in homes for $275. They will light 40 lights or run small motors. The Elks are building new meeting rooms in the new Penglase Building. The Advancement Committee is pushing for a new hotel for Ishpeming as many are staying in Negaunee and Marquette. The J. C. Penney store will be coming to Ishpeming and have its new store in the Penglase Building next to the Butler Theater.. It will be added to the 125 current stores. Newspaper advertisements now feature Easter ads, complete with bunnies and lilies.

The CCI and Oliver companies will raise wages on May 1 by 10%. Others are expected to follow. City laborers are now getting $2.75 a day. The city of Ishpeming will be purchasing a ten-ton road roller that runs on gasoline. The number of high school graduates this year will be 73. "The Birth of a Nation" was so popular it will return again to the Ishpeming Theater.

The headlines on April 7 read: CONGRESS DECLARES WAR ON GERMANY. Two weeks later, there was a large down-town parade of 1500 people, and a program at the Ishpeming Theater, even though all could not get in. People are encouraged to plant gardens this summer and to ration their own food. The unused part of the golf course will be planted as well. People are encouraged to raise chickens. Liberty bonds will be sold and people will earn interest. 110 people sign up to be a unit of the Red Cross. Conscription will begin for men between ages of 21 and 30. The Mining Journal claims that many Ishpeming men did not register.

Another bit of unsettling news came in the June 9, 1917, issue of the paper: FREDERICK BRAASTAD DIES. Mr. Newett noted that the town never had a better father, and that he was great in his "charity".

The Finnish had long endured the attitudes of others that they did not believe in democracy. Now, the Swedish are enduring similar attitudes when the Superior Posten Swedish Newspaper published here spoke up in support of Germany in the war.

In June, the decision was made to build the current Ishpeming Hospital. In July, the Michigan Verde Marble Company found it would have to build its own spur from the C&NW track. Girls are now learning how to swim, and are requesting the use of the YMCA pool to learn and practice.

In August there was the sad story of an accidental death of a little girl by a neighbor boy, when a pitchfork landed in her head. She was the oldest of three children, and the mother was a widow. Last winter their barn caught fire and they lost their only cow. The girl's name was Elsie Aho from West Superior Street.

Henry Ford was gaining some enemies when it was felt that he didn't want his son Edsel to serve in the war. He never did go. Even the stage shows are now about the war. A cast of 50 came to the local theater to do "My Soldier Girl." Citizens are questioning whether German should still be taught in our public schools.

Another new mine is announced to be west of the North Lake Mine, and east of the Chase. It will have a 1,100 deep shaft and eventually will be called the Barnes-Hecker Mine. Another mining venture closed when the Jackson Iron Company was dissolved. Mr. Newett notes that the old forge can still be seen and that there is a monument there, and notes that its blooms were carried to the mouth of the Carp by 6-horse teams for 10 miles. The CCI was the last owner.

Mines are still booming, and those laid off quickly find work. The yearly mine report shows that 5,569 men were employed underground and on surface and that there were 15 Marquette county deaths. Mr. W. H. Johnson, a local Mine Captain, will retire to a home in Florida with an orange grove. He is 70 years old and was a former Ishpeming Mayor.

About October 10 there were several killing frosts and an inch of snow. Potatoes increased to $1.00 a bushel. One third of the year's local crop was frozen in the ground. U.S. postage is going up to 3 cents for a letter, and two for a postcard. A new concrete sidewalk will be built from Callow's Store to the Salisbury School. Braastads store is being remodeled, and the east stairway will be removed so that a large meat refrigerator can be installed. A loading dock door in back of the building will be sealed up.

Miner's Bank Christmas club checks sent out this year total $32,000. It was Christmas, and there was a stage-coach hold-up on the road to the American Mine near Clarksburg. It had $2,000. in currency for cashing checks. The stage driver was luckily just shot in the cheek and an x-ray found the bullet which was removed. Henry Holstein arrested and the money was recovered.

The Merchants had a very good Christmas this year.

1918

In 1918, the second oldest Marquette County Mine, the Lake Superior Iron Company is still in business, operating the Section 16 mine. Mr. Newett notes that this old company has now mined out, and shipped, 17 million tons of ore. The CCI has a flag flying with 150 stars on it, each with an employee's name who is currently fighting in the war. Men in a Negaunee CCI mine found a drill bit, 1,285 feet underground where it had broken off. It was at 45 degrees, which explained why the surface linkage broke.

The railroads are shortening their routes. The CM&St.P stopped going to the Copper Country and will now stop in Champion. Those going to the Keweenaw Peninsula will transfer to a Copper Range train in Channing. The C&NW may end its run to the Copper Country also, but that is not yet finalized. The city will save on fuel for the war by shutting the town's lights off on Thursday and Sunday nights. U. P. residents are being encouraged to raise more cattle and pigs. Only one or two street cars per hour are operating between the two cities to save coal. People can now only buy sugar in two-pound lots. Children at schools are not buying War Stamps, and the CCI will give several stamps free to help each book. The Franklin Auto Company will now be manufacturing engines for the Rolls Royce Company in England. Although there was a report on the Washington's Birthday dog races, there was nothing about a skee tournament. Too many men are probably serving in the war. For the children, there was a contest to collect tin-foil. It was declared a success. Soon after this, the Wrigley Gum company quit using tin-foil.

One soldier wrote a note home which ended up in the paper, saying not to send cheap Woolworth toothbrushes "as they fall apart." People are encouraged to send books to the men in uniform. The Carnegie Library has already gathered 500 of them. Everyone is working, and in order to keep enough employees, the Oliver Company in April gave a 15% raise. U.S. Steel did the same. It was announced in May that a total of 223 Marquette County men were in the present war call-up. 97 of these left from Ishpeming on the C&NW evening train on Saturday, May 25. Mr. Newett noted that there should have been a parade for the men, just as Negaunee had.

In March the CCI removed the last pillars between the Maas and the Negaunee Mine, and the surface land was "brought down." At the Verde Marble Quarry, the contractor putting in the railway quit, and a second company was hired. A 65 foot timber of large size was delivered from Oregon for a new derrick. It has no knots. The U. S. Government is planning to spend lots of money on improved American Roads.

Wrestling was still very popular, but Mr. Butler had to cancel two matches at his Ishpeming Theater because he found out about some "arrangements." Others gathered on the street with the steep hill between the Episcopal Church and the Nelson House to see a contest of trucks. Only one made it up. Movies are still popular, but many are against Sunday showings. Mr. Newett took the following stand, saying that it seemed to him that many who were against Sunday movies had never seen a film, and those against Sunday movies are against all movies.

A Mr. George Badger died at the Cliffs Shafts when a cage door opened and he fell 450 feet. It was noted that Badger Hill, in the south of Frenchtown was named after his grandfather. As the war worsens, the government set a new rule, that all men, married and single, up to the age of forty, will now be eligible to serve.

Dams are being built on the Dead River, and it is decided that one more yet can be built. A total of 30 million kilowatts a year can be manufactured free. The McClure has three miles of tube from its dam to the power plant.

Dr. Mudge, an Ishpeming boy, has returned as a medical doctor, and Dr. Main, an Ishpeming dentist has installed an x-ray machine. Mr. John Millimaki has come to town after graduating from college and will be a veterinarian. The Braastads have platted land and put in roads just north of the cemetery, and will begin selling shortly through the Cody Land Company. Lots sold from $37. to $127. each, and for a dollar down and a dollar a week. No interest and no taxes the first year was also in the contracts.

The Barnes-Hecker Mine Shaft is going down by June of 1918, and it is noted that they had a lot of water problems at the start. The shaft will go down 1000 feet, and the headframe for the shaft house will be moved from the Chase mine nearby. Air pressure will be sent from the North Lake Mine. Note is made that a nice dry is completed and a Main Street has been built for the community.

For the past few years there has been an ongoing argument as to what should be done with $35,000 in funds saved by miners at the former Lake Angeline Mine. In June of 1918, the Michigan Supreme Court decided that all living men and relatives of men should receive their rightful share. It was a sad end as almost everyone will get almost nothing. Many men said that with the total, the employees could have bought the mine and its newly-found blue ore, rather than the CCI, and they could all be rich.

In the summer of 1918, the cities of Ishpeming and Negaunee got together and made a beach at Cedar Lake on the Cliff Drive, including a bath house. People are buying wood for the winter and are paying $15 a cord. Several large slabs of Verde Marble have been delivered to the new Ishpeming Hospital and people are coming to look at them. They were used in the lobby. The first week of July brought a killing frost, and many have to replant their potatoes. Mr. Newett started to print letters from the "front" from his son "Billie." He soon was in a hospital from inhaling the dreaded mustard gas, but continued to write.

Michigan must have been declared a "dry" state about this time as there are warnings about not making too much personal liquor, and Negaunee is finding so much illegal alcohol that they are asking Ishpeming for needed storage area. The Hotel Scott in Hancock closed as there was no alcohol, and lots of whiskey is reported in the Ontonagon area. In Ishpeming, Mr. Newett notes that, overall, "drunks are now scarce", and people who formerly went to bars need somewhere to go.

And here is our first report of a concrete road. The Keweenaw Peninsula "boasts" of a mile of concrete road, and Mr. Newett reports that is it "very nice" on July 20, 1918. Mr. Newett also puts in a "dig" once in a while yet about the

Fords, regarding Edsel's not serving in the war. He notes in August that a Ford Party was attended by the Dodge's and the dodgers.

The road from Morgan Heights was tarred or "taried" to Marquette. The Cleveland Location road to Negaunee is now tarred and also the road west of Ishpeming. Many are traveling now to Champion Beach on Sundays. However, in August the Government began asking people not to drive on Sundays. It also asked citizens not to take photos of anything that might aid the enemy if they got into the wrong hands.

There was more poor news about the Barnes-Hecker. On August 24, the newspaper reported that the sinking of the shaft is going slowly and that the ground has been troublesome. The shaft is at 350 feet, and has required much concrete work..

Over a dozen youngsters from the Division Street area have been arrested for shoplifting in stores. Parents will have to pay or the boys will be sent to reform school. There was also a bad fire in town this summer, originally caused by sparks from a steam engine, but then spread into the peat bog underground and could not be put out.. There was much deep smoke in town, and it burned until reaching a ditch dug around the area.

The draft is enlarged more. Now, all between ages 16 and 46 are eligible to be called to war. 32 men will leave from Ishpeming and the west end of the county in August. In September, the fourth Liberty Loan Drive began and Mqt. County will try to raise $395,000 with bonds. They do it, and surpass it with a total effort of $510,000. The CCI reported that 3,357 of their employees averaged bond purchases of $100.00 each. The Iron Ore Companies are asking that miners here be exempt from serving in the war, as men would rather serve, than work. Many girls are starting to work in the labor force in general. Most iron mines are working yet, but shipping stopped early so that boats can be used for the war. Several have been sent on the Atlantic Ocean. Note is made in October of 1918 that trammers who push the ore cars are now the big wage earners in the mines, making up to $12.00 a day. Most miners are making only about five or six dollars a day.

The new hospital is getting ready to open and there is a fine Iron Ore article about all the three floors, and wash area, and food preparation area. The hospital also purchased a Winston 6 ambulance. No open house was held as there was "influenza" of some type in existence in the fall of 1918. The epidemic was quite serious as Ishpeming schools closed at this time as well. It is our first note about "flu."

The Verde Marble Quarry announced on Thanksgiving that their railroad was complete and they had shipped out marble using their new engine. Announced also was that a fine concrete sidewalk will be built on Jackson Street from Negaunee to Ishpeming. It was so warm in November, that strawberries were blooming a second time, and lilacs were budding as well.

The largest headlines, set in big type, came on November 16, 1918, when it was announced that "GERMANY SURRENDERS----WAR IS OVER." Mr. Newett notes that not a single area boy was killed in the war, but some died of illness and disease. His own son recovered well. The Governor asked churches to open in spite of the flu, and have special services. Mines are asking for mining men to be released first. Mr. Newett also tells his readers not to cash in their Liberty Bonds, but to keep them as an interest paying investment.

Winter sports still included a High Street bobsled run to Lake Bancroft, crossing Pine and Oak. The Section 16 mine and Holmes are having some water problems as the swamp between them is draining into the drifts, but it is planned, and the water will be pumped out from the shafts. Crime included the stealing of car tires which are still hard to purchase. Many people marked their names inside the tires for identity. The Government has released hard coal for consumer use again. It was a fine Christmas Day, and the year 1918 came to an end.

1919

Believe it, or not, so much timber has been used to make charcoal for the past 50 years, and so much has been used underground in mines that the year began with an article concerning the scarcity of timber in the Upper Peninsula of Michigan. The flu has subsided. 500 people were bobsledding down High Street onto Lake Bancroft on New Year's Day. The street is continually iced, and there is talk of a rope tow to get people back to the top. The state of Wisconsin is working with the U. P. on tying roads together between the two states.

The local telephone company wants to charge for out-of-town calls. Mr. Newett notes that no one has ever been charged before. Henry Ford will start paying employees $6.00 a day. The five-cluster electric lights downtown are so popular that merchants are asking to have them on more streets. And a national news item is that the popular and former President, Teddy Roosevelt died of a blood clot on the brain.

The war is over and in Detroit, 25,000 men are now out of work as government war contracts end. The CCI is making so much electricity, that it is selling it also to the Michigan Gas and

Electric Company.   Dr. Van Riper visited Ishpeming on January 25, 1919, to take a break after treating 1000 flu cases in the Champion area. He reported to Mr. Newett that he only lost two people who were past saving when he found them.

Local liquor people are pushing for a national amendment for a light wine and beer. The state of Michigan is trying to do more publicity about venereal disease, and tells parents to inform their children about it. It is estimated that 1 in 10 are afflicted with it. Braastad's store will be giving up its dry goods part of the business, and hope for someone to purchase it. A month later Braastads announced the closing of their grocery business as well.   The furniture business, they noted, will continue for now. Women's skirts are so tight this spring that the street cars are getting held up by women trying to get on and off the steps of the cars.

This was the year when women received the right to vote, and in February, Ishpeming registered 1,576 ladies.   Women are also now getting letters, hoping to influence their voting.

In March, more information comes to us concerning the Barnes-Hecker. The shaft is down to the second level, but still slowing because of the wet ground. The powder blasts in the bottom of the shaft have to be small to prevent damage to the concrete work above. Less than eight years later, on the date of November 3, 1926, a large piece of land in the south east direction will come into the mine at 600 feet down on the first level after a blast, and kill a total of 51 men, the worst disaster on the Marquette Range.

In April there was one of the biggest traffic jams that ever took place on Main Street. A notice in the newspaper a week earlier announced that Ishpeming girls would display new clothes in the windows of Gately's Store. They noted that it was for women, but men could come. Well, everyone came! They wanted to see the pretty live girls in the windows. Soon the police were summoned to control the traffic as the cars and wagons were so numerous. Mr. Newett printed the names of the eight young ladies who participated in the show, and noted that they were "easy to look at."

The newspaper listed some old open pits and noted that three of them are west of Third and north of Empire.   At the Cliffs Shafts there will be a big change in looks. Thus far, the shaft-houses A & B did not look as they do now. They were only metal buildings built up in the air. Now, the paper notes that Concrete Shaft Houses will be built over the present iron ones that are covered with corrugated steel. It also notes that there will be no interruption of mine work while the concrete is being poured. Details of the work and how it was done was in the July 26 edition of the paper.

Prohibition passed a second vote in the year 1919, and many local men are being arrested for defying the law. However, cases of drunkenness were only 18, down 98 from the previous year before prohibition. In June, two men died from poorly made illegal liquor and taking Hoffman Drops.

The Library gave its annual report in the news, and noted that 900 books had been purchased, and 414 discarded as "worn out."   A total of 94,047 items were signed out, and the library had been closed for two months during the year. The old fire hall has been purchased by Louis Boyd for $8.00 and he must fix it up or tear it down. It ended up getting torn down just a few months later.   And there is good news for letter writers.   Would you believe that first class postage in 1919 went down from three cents to only two cents, and that postcards can now be mailed for only a penny, versus two cents previously.

A new invention to put on one's floors is Congoleum, which was also called linoleum. They will lay flat and have a rug imprint on them. The surface will be hard and shiny. On June 22, John Phillip Sousa's Band will play at the Ishpeming Theater. In July a carnival came, and the soldiers now home can attend and get everything free. A caretaker has been stationed at Cedar Lake Swimming area at a cost of $117 a month.

The East End Lake Angeline Mine is still finding good ore near the surface and it is noted that "D" shaft is in use, and men are using part of the engine house as a dry. The mining is at the east end of the dry lake bottom. The Happy Hollow area of the Angeline Mine was being mined at the surface by Trebilcock Bros, and they are hauling the ore to the railroad track with teams.

The carnival came to town and so did Pinkerton Detectives, who arrested a carnival man who operated the Athletic tent. He had swindled $30,000. from people in Oklahoma. Louis and Isadore Dubinsky of Negaunee also came to Ishpeming and will open a store of clothing and furnishings in the Heinemon Building on Main Street.

Mr. Newett finds more about Edsel Ford regarding avoiding the war. He now reports that Edsel is telling people he wanted to go. Mr. Newett also reports that there are 78 graduates this year and he prints their names on p. 7 of the August 2, 1919 Iron Ore. It is also reported on that date that farmers are bringing in potatoes from their fields already. It must have been a nice summer. . The Lyric Theater has reopened on Main Street. The Verde Marble Company

has purchased a plant in Marquette to cut and polish its marble.

Mine deaths for the previous year were 16. Twenty-eight mines were in operation and employees numbered 3,265 underground, and 1,783 on surface. Night classes are being held for all people who wish to learn English. A new Road Makers' Magazine is listing some of the new main trunk lines in the U. P., and their new numbers.

In November, a Lions' Club is formed. People are now buying farm tractors. And one final article appears about Edsel Ford and his possible kidnapping: "Anyone interested in kidnapping Edsel Ford will need lots of luck. Even the Government couldn't get him out of the Ford Company. And who would pay $200,000 to get him back?"

People are causing abuses of their telephones. Calls will now be limited to five minutes, and no one is to spend time "listening in" to others conversations, or just "visiting on the phone." Oh, remember those party lines?

The paper has big ads for the Ishpeming Theater, but none for the Butler. The news notes that salary for Methodist pastors is going up to $1,500 a year from the $1,111 currently. Mr. Nelson will build a new garage on Division Street between Main and Pine.

A Chiropractor has located in Ishpeming, and will provide his services in the Ishpeming Theater rooms under the balcony and above the first floor.

As 1919 draws to a close, we find that 2,132,000 tons of iron were shipped from Marquette, and 5,097,000 tons from Escanaba. Coal is still very short as there had been a large national coal strike. The C&NW ended the day train in

Escanaba from Chicago, but continued to run the night train to our area. The DSS&A is only going to go to Nestoria to Duluth three times a week.

Live Entertainment is still very popular at the Ishpeming Theater and in December a troupe of 60 appeared in "Going Up." The show had played for 500 nights in New York, and seats sold for 75 cents to $2.00. Show time was at 8:45 every night.

In one of the Christmas editions of the paper, the history of St. Nicholas and his birth in Russia was given. The concrete head frames of the Cliffs Shafts were completed and brass plates put on them. And Mr. John P. Outhwaite died at 75. He is buried in the Ishpeming Cemetery on the north side of Olive St.

1920

Things are very, very, good as we begin this final year of our book. The January 3 paper notes that the 15 U. P. counties only had two bankruptcies in the past year, and Mr. Newett tells the public that they are selling their linotype machine in order to buy a new fancier one for $3,500. In 1919 there were 241 births and 181 deaths recorded. Thirty men became U.S. Citizens. Two men, one from Marquette, and a "Dr" Leonburger from Ishpeming have been arrested for being chiropractors without licenses.

In February, plans were announced that the new concrete covered shafts of the Cliffs Shafts will be coated with a finely ground ore. We don't believe this ever took place. What did take place in town was that the flu came back. And what also happened was that the CCI raised wages once again by ten percent. Ishpeming teachers received an increase of pay as well, by $10.00 more a month. Naturally, by April, hair

cuts went up also, from 40 cents to 50 cents. In May potatoes were selling for $5.00 a bushel.

There was, once again, a ski tournament. And in addition to dog races, children are now getting ponies, so there was also a pony race. It is March now, and the car ferry to the Lower Peninsula is back in operation. It will cost $6.00 to cross with your car. And local stock is being sold in a new wooden toy factory called the Marion Toy Company. It is moving from Ohio to Ishpeming. It is located at Third Street behind the Consolidated Lumber Company by the railroad. A 40 foot addition has been built for the company.

But the large news was this. The Braastad store will completely close and be replaced by a large corset factory of the H. W. Gossard Company. Start up was within a couple of weeks, and the company, in training sewers, noted that they expected much wasted material for a few weeks. However, in training, paper will be used rather than woven cloth. 500 will be hired, and employment might reach 2000 stated the newspaper. Trainers and managers poured into town and ads were in the paper searching for rooms to rent. Families are also moving to town, hoping to find work at the new factory. The Gossard opened on April 19, 1920, and by the 24th, had a shipment of brassieres going to Chicago.

In mining, there are evidently records set and broken that often never get published for the public. However, the Oliver Company noted that the Holmes Mine now holds the record for the fastest drifting when an 8 foot by 8 foot tunnel, 484 feet long was completed with only 432 man-hours of work. Another interesting fact was that it was announced that there is iron ore on the south side of Lake Sally, and that a shaft was sunk, but then left idle. That is the same area of the Tilden Mine, today, and the south side of the lake has a huge waste rock pile.

Another interesting ad was for an Apollo Player Piano. The ad notes that it is not mechanical and there is no pumping of any pedals. Very Interesting! The sportsmen are in favor of a "no deer season" in 1920, but we don't know if this ever took place. The Standard Oil Company is busy building additional gasoline facilities, but has not been able to keep up with the demand, and so is currently limiting each vehicle to only five gallons per purchase. The town is considering some traffic controls so that pedestrians can get across the streets.

Not to be beaten, the Barnes-Hecker mine reset the record for drifting when they went 511 feet in 474 man-hours. Another record was set when a steamer carried a record 13,025 tons of iron ore from Marquette to the Sault Ste. Marie, Canada, steel mill. It took 283 railroad cars to fill the boat by the LS&I..

Ishpeming is selling "Booster Buttons." They say, "Boost for Ishpeming." Someone will win a 1920 Ford. The Quaal and Quaal Store opened on Cleveland where the current St. Vincent DePaul parking lot is now. Business men are getting together and making credit ratings of their customers regarding charging for goods.

There has been a national coal strike and it was touch and go for the Ishpeming-Negaunee Gas plant. In June, however, two cars of coal showed up and were put to use, obtaining the gas from it. There is still also the problem of illegal liquor. There were quite a few local arrests when an intoxicated lady was arrested and started to name names. Police found out also the existence of a "house of ill-repute."

The circus this year was the Yankee Robinson. As usual, there was a 10:30 parade and shows at 1:00 and 7:00. The A. G. Barnes Circus was turned down by the city for a license, as well as several other traveling groups, after the city of Marquette ran into problems with Yankee Robinson..

In July the big attraction was a County Pageant on the South West Bowl of Teal Lake, where the entrance is to the current Teal Lake Estates. A new road from Teal Lake Drive, north of the Nelson Mine was built. So many autos were expected that the highway was made one-way. In from Negaunee, and out to Ishpeming. It was a huge success, with 20,000 people and 3,300 autos in attendance. It was in a field with the lake in the background as people sat up on the hill to the south. The presentation involved hundreds and lasted for three hours. Mr. Newett noted that it was a beautiful natural amphitheater and it was the "First County Pageant in the history of the U.S."

This, my friends, I am sorry to say, brings this volume to a close. Thank you for your time, and patience, and for any comments you may have.

THIS COUNTY PAGEANT TOOK PLACE IN THE AREA JUST WEST OF THE LONG, DOWN-HILL ROAD ENTERING TEAL LAKE ESTATES ON SHORELINE DRIVE. NOTE THE TWO PILES OF LOOSE ROCK AT THE BACK OF THE LAKE, JUST RIGHT OF CENTER.(SEE ARROW) THEY CAN STILL BE SEEN FROM THE SHORELINE DRIVE ROAD.

CREDIT TO THE NEGAUNEE HISTORICAL MUSEUM AND THE D. MURK FAMILY..

Biography of Robert D. Dobson

Robert "Bob" Dobson is 81years old, and has had a varied career. In his high school years, he was a printer at the Globe Printing Company in Ishpeming. After he and Ethel Jean (Saari) were married in 1961, they graduated from Northern Michigan University and taught school in Skandia and in Gwinn. They then moved to Ohio where Bob graduated from Seminary after three more years and they served two churches near Van Wert, Ohio, losing one in a tornado.

As pastor and wife, they served at Michigan Technological University in Houghton, as associate pastor in Marquette, in Taylor, and then in Menominee, Michigan. In 1992 he received a second master's degree and taught courses for the Menominee, Michigan, School System, and Lakeland College, and for NWTC in Marinette, Wisconsin. Ethel was the Title I teacher in Menominee Public Schools and both retired from teaching in 2000. In 2003, they returned to Negaunee to live, and Bob began to research and write local history books.

He has now published eleven books and a CD of newspaper notes from both the Ishpeming Iron Ore, and the Negaunee Iron Herald newspapers (over 1,700 pages) and the notes were used for writing his local history books. The notes are searchable, and can used by adults and students alike in doing their own historical local research.

My thanks to the many people who have enjoyed the books and have a collection of each one of them. At age 81 now, Ethel and I will still spend our time selling, and mailing, but not writing any further. It has been a wonderful 20-year post retirement enjoyment. I still find time to sit down and enjoy reading my own books.

If you have never had a chance to read one of my books, an introduction to what they are all about can be found on the back cover. Shalom.

Here is a photo of the Dobson Family. Our son Eric, and wife, Laurie on the left, and son Dale, and wife, Karen on the right. Mrs. Ethel Dobson and Mr Robert Dobson are at the center.

Our Newest Marquette County, Michigan Book:

Two Wagon Roads, a Plank Railway,

Mr. Ely's Rail Road, and the Dead Man's Curve

(ALSO KNOWN AS "THE DOBSON ROAD BOOK")

Other Dobson History Books:

Ishpeming Area:

The Early History of a Mining Town

The Second History of Ishpeming, Michigan

It was an Underground Mine: The Salisbury Mine

Two Biographies: Mr. J. Maurice Finn, Will Bradley

Growing up in the Salisbury Location

Negaunee Area:

The City Built at the Shiny Mountain

The History of Negaunee, Michigan, Part Two

We are Going to the 1845 Jackson Mine

Other Marquette County Non-Fiction Research

A History You AUTO Know

The Railroad That Never Ran (The IR&HB)

BOOKS CAN BE FOUND IN LOCAL STORES, MUSEUMS, AND ON AMAZON AND EBAY.

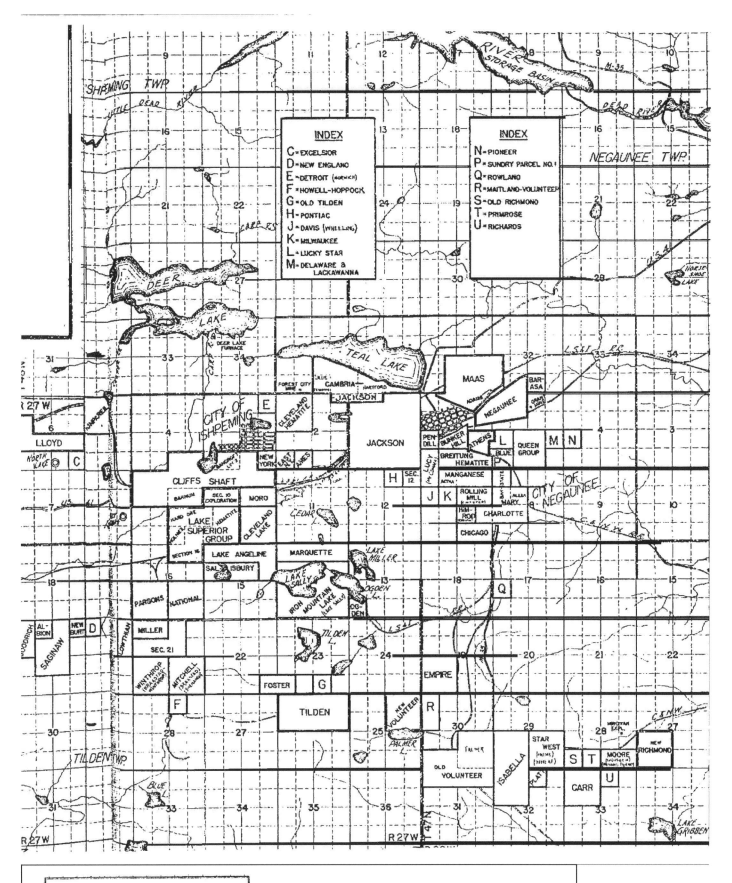

INDEX

C = EXCELSIOR
D = NEW ENGLAND
E = DETROIT (NORWICH)
F = HOWELL-HOPPOCK
G = OLD TILDEN
H = PONTIAC
J = DAVIS (WHEELING)
K = MILWAUKEE
L = LUCKY STAR
M = DELAWARE & LACKAWANNA

INDEX

N = PIONEER
P = SUNDRY PARCEL NO. 1
Q = ROWLAND
R = MAITLAND-VOLUNTEER
S = OLD RICHMOND
T = PRIMROSE
U = RICHARDS

LAKE SUPERIOR IRON ORE ASSOCIATION
MAP OF THE
EASTERN PORTION OF
MARQUETTE IRON RANGE
SHOWING LOCATION OF
MINING PROPERTY

DRAWN BY

SCALE
ONE MILE

DATE
OCT. 1937.

Note that not all mines are shown because of name changes, and property changes up to 1920. Mines closed and often reopened with new names by new owners.

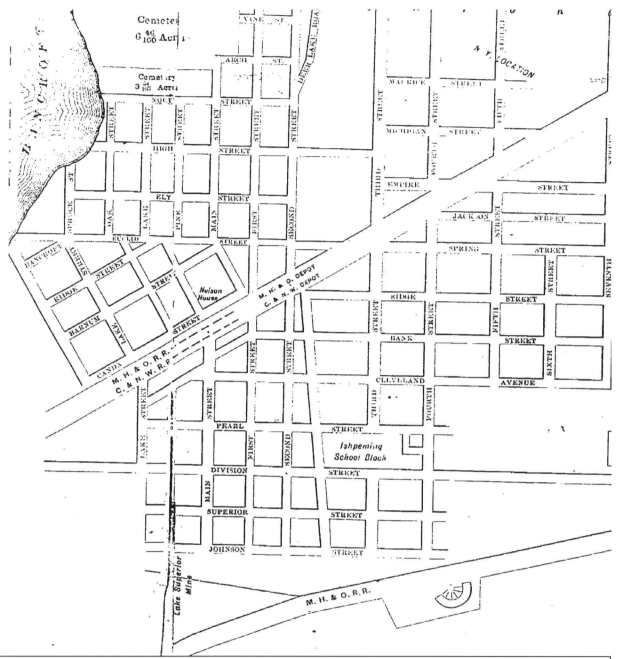

Here is the earliest City map we could find. It is from the Ishpeming City Directory of 1886. Note is made that Main Street is the division of east and west streets and that Cleveland is the division for north and south streets. Note that the Protestant and Roman Catholic Cemeteries are up to the edge of Lake Bancroft and from the Ishpeming playgrounds south up to North Street and east to Main Street,. Also note the strange street (but not named) that goes on an angle north and south between Second and Third Streets. Bluff Street developed along the MH&O grade from east to west, and part of the sharp turn around the steam engine round-house still exists on Bluff Street. Another interesting note is that there was a mine and large drift in the former pit in front of the Pioneer Bluff Apartments. It is marked "Lake Superior Mine." Details of these notes are in the text. You will note a lot of other changes from today's city map, including some of the street names.